The Uses of Phobia
Essays on Literature and Film

DAVID TROTTER

This edition first published 2010
© 2010 Blackwell Publishing

Blackwell publishing was acquired by John Wiley & Sons in February 2007. Blackwell's publishing program has been merged with Wiley's global Scientific, Technical, and Medical business to form Wiley-Blackwell.

Registered Office
John Wiley & Sons Ltd, The Atrium, Southern Gate, Chichester, West Sussex, PO19 8SQ, United Kingdom

Editorial Offices
350 Main Street, Malden, MA 02148-5020, USA
9600 Garsington Road, Oxford, OX4 2DQ, UK
The Atrium, Southern Gate, Chichester, West Sussex, PO19 8SQ, UK

For details of our global editorial offices, for customer services, and for information about how to apply for permission to reuse the copyright material in this book please see our website at www.wiley.com/wiley-blackwell.

The right of David Trotter to be identified as the author of this work has been asserted in accordance with the Copyright, Designs and Patents Act 1988.

Wiley also publishes its books in a variety of electronic formats. Some content that appears in print may not be available in electronic books.

Designations used by companies to distinguish their products are often claimed as trademarks. All brand names and product names used in this book are trade names, service marks, trademarks or registered   trademarks of their respective owners. The publisher is not associated with any product or vendor mentioned in this book. This publication is designed to provide accurate and authoritative information in regard to the subject matter covered. It is sold on the understanding that the publisher is not engaged in rendering professional services. If professional advice or other expert assistance is required, the services of a competent professional should be sought.

Library of Congress Cataloging-in-Publication Data

Trotter, David, 1951-
 The uses of phobia : essays on literature and film / David Trotter.
    p. cm. – (Critical quarterly)
 Includes bibliographical references.
 ISBN 978-1-4443-3384-8 (alk. paper)
 1. English fiction–History and criticism. 2. Motion pictures–History and criticism. 3. Phobias in literature. 4. Phobias in motion pictures. 5. Psychic trauma in literature. 6. Psychic trauma in motion pictures. I. Title.

 PR830.P455T76 2010
 820.9′353–dc22

                                    2010009591

A catalogue record for this title is available form the British Library.

Set in 10 on 12 pt Palatino
by Macmillan India
Printed and bound in Singapore
by Fabulous Printers Pte Ltd

For Colin MacCabe

Contents

Acknowledgements

I am grateful to publishers and editors for permission to reprint, with revisions, the following essays:

'Household Clearances in Victorian Fiction', *19: Interdisciplinary Studies in the Long Nineteenth Century*, 6, 2008.

'The Invention of Agoraphobia', *Victorian Literature and Culture*, 32, 2004, 463–74.

'Naturalism's Phobic Picturesque', *Critical Quarterly*, 51, 2009, 33–58.

'Some Brothels: Nineteenth-Century Philanthropy and the Poetics of Space', *Critical Quarterly*, 44, 2002, 25–32.

'Modernist *Toilette*', *Moveable Type*, 5, 2009.

'The British Novel and the War', in Vincent Sherry, ed., *The Cambridge Companion to the Literature of the First World War* (Cambridge: Cambridge University Press, 2005), 34–56.

'Ford against Joyce and Lewis', in Andrzej Gasiorek and Daniel Moore, eds., *Ford Madox Ford: Literary Networks and Cultural Transformations* (Amsterdam: Rodopi, 2008), 131–50.

'Hitchcock's Modernism', *Modernist Cultures*, 5.1, 2010.

'Phoning', in Matthew Beaumont and Greg Dart, eds., *Restless Cities* (London: Verso, 2010).

'Lynne Ramsay's *Ratcatcher*: Towards a Theory of Haptic Narrative', *Paragraph: A Journal of Modern Critical Theory*, 31, 2008, 138–58.

Introduction

The aim of the essays brought together in this book is to investigate phobia, not as a pathological condition but as a robust and versatile moral, political, and aesthetic resource. Strong feelings of aversion, of one kind or another, have vividly informed the literature and film of the last century and a half. Some of these feelings have been designed to overwhelm us as they explode off page and screen: to drive us to horror, shame, or embarrassment. The value of phobia, by contrast, lies in its inability or reluctance to overwhelm. Phobia, however intense, can always be managed to some degree – even when it cannot be wholly understood. It constitutes, as Adam Phillips has observed, an 'unconscious estrangement technique'. 'To be petrified by a pigeon is a way of making it new.'[1] What follows is a series of descriptions in essay-form of some of the uses to which writers and film-makers have consciously put that unconscious estrangement technique. In putting it to use, they have been able to say and show things they could not otherwise have said and shown. Phobia is never all there is to be said and shown. But it's a subtle and provocative something, full of consequence, which we ignore, if not exactly at our peril, then at the loss of a great deal of pleasure and instruction.

Phobia harks back faintly to Phobos, ancient god of fear, panic, and flight. In Greek myth, Phobos was one of four children produced by the union of Ares, god of war, and Aphrodite. He features in Hesiod and Homer as his father's companion in battle.[2] He is the dangerous supplement to the war-god's uncontrollable blood-lust: both its consequence, as terror struck in the enemy, and that which becomes manifest should it ever be found lacking. Modern phobias, by contrast, are by no means restricted to the battlefield. They are the opposite of martial. Modern phobia gets absolutely everywhere.

The irrational dreads I shall discuss in these essays arise out of provocative ordinary circumstance: the sight of moles on a woman's skin, the touch of a chewed quid of tobacco, the stench of urine in a phone-booth. If and when they do make themselves felt on the battlefield, their function, as we shall see in Chapter 6, is to alleviate rather than intensify the panic which would otherwise result in headlong flight.

As far as I'm aware, the earliest full description of a range of phobias was that provided, with tongue partly in cheek, by Benjamin Rush, signatory to the Declaration of Independence as well as a professor of medicine. Writing in the *Columbian Magazine* in November 1786, Rush defined phobia as 'a fear of an imaginary evil, or an undue fear of a real one'. In his view, the stimulus to fear and aversion could equally be an object – cats, rats, insects, ghosts, doctors, dirt, bad smells, thunder, and rum ('a very *rare* distemper') – or, more abstractly, a condition: solitude, powerlessness, want. Whatever its origin, phobia made, and still makes, good copy. Rush had some stories to tell, especially about women afflicted with an excessive aversion to dirt, one of whom he once saw 'fall down upon her knees, with a house-cloth in her hand, and wipe away such of the liquid parts of the food as fell upon the floor from a company of gentlemen that dined in her house, muttering, at the same time, the most terrible complaints, in low Dutch, of the beastly manners of her guests.'[3] Rush's brisk, genial survey is not all that far, in substance and tone, from the self-help books which began to appear on the market two centuries later.[4] Phobia now, like phobia then, is 'an anxiety disorder characterized by an overwhelming fear or dread of certain objects, animals, events, or situations' – and apparently the 'most commonly diagnosed mental disorder in Western psychiatric medicine'.[5] Phobia has always been an ordinary affliction. On 31 October 1801, Coleridge wrote to Humphry Davy to say that he was coming to London shortly, and that, given his 'perfect phobia of Inns and Coffee-houses', he would be very grateful for the offer of a bed.[6] Modern phobia underwhelms even as it overwhelms.

Benjamin Rush's list includes anxieties provoked both by too much of something (cat, rat, insect, or glass of rum) and by too little (company, power, wealth). Current psychiatric theory distinguishes between specific phobia, where the problem is possession by a particular object, animal, or event; and agoraphobia and social phobia, where the problem is dispossession of the capacity to comprehend and adapt to a particular environment. Phobia is a disorder of proximity and exposure alike: of presence, and of absence. According to the psychoanalyst John Bowlby, the only 'true' phobia is specific phobia; while all the rest constitute forms of separation anxiety. 'In the case of a phobic person,' Bowlby argued, 'what is most feared is the *presence* of some situation that other people find much less frightening but that he either takes great pains to *avoid* or else urgently *withdraws from*.' In agoraphobia and social phobia, by contrast, what is most feared is 'the *absence or loss* of an attachment figure, or some other secure base,' which the phobic person would normally '*move towards*'.[7] I won't in these essays make any such distinction between true and false phobias. But the terms Bowlby proposes for a clinical understanding of phobia seem to me the ones most likely to help us to grasp its cultural significance. I like his sense of movement across terrain, of approach and withdrawal.

Like Bowlby, and like Bowlby's near contemporary Michael Balint, I favour an understanding of phobia which places the emphasis less on its supposed instinctual sources than on its constitution and development as a (peculiar) way of perceiving and relating to the world.[8] Phobia, I want to say, is an affliction of being (of too much or too little being). I want to say it at a time when ontology, or the theory of being, has been widely dismissed as the last desperate trick of a Western metaphysic finally confronting its own implausibility. Like Ian Hacking, I feel no commitment to the project of a theory of being like that developed by philosophers up to and including Martin Heidegger. Like Hacking, I nonetheless think that it is convenient sometimes to speak in general terms about 'what there is', about the ways in which objects of all kinds come into existence.[9] Phobia is an ontological disease. It might even be ontology's dis-ease with itself. It provokes us to ask whether ontology, underwhelming even as it overwhelms, might not after all have its uses, as a moral, political, and aesthetic resource.

Not a great deal has changed since 1786 in the general understanding of phobia as a persistent, irrational fear of something which in itself poses little or no danger. However, the more detailed understanding of the pattern in phobia – a period of anxiety and stress, in some cases involving sharp panic attacks, which usually gives rise to superstitious avoidance behaviour – is a product of the taxonomic fury of the last three decades of the nineteenth century. In Chapter 2, I describe how that detailed understanding – that invention of categories – came about. My emphasis there is on literature's investment in psychiatric detail. I claim that George Eliot knew all she needed to know about recent developments in psychiatry when writing *Daniel Deronda* (1876). Gwendolen Harleth, in that novel, suffers from what could perfectly well have been described at the time as agoraphobia. Eliot's interest in diseases of presence and absence, not simply as an affliction in young middle-class women, but as a form of knowledge to which even the men most sympathetic to their plight are incapable of doing justice, dates back to her portrayal of Esther Lyon, in *Felix Holt the Radical* (1866). Phobia serves as a moral and political resource to Esther and Gwendolen, in their struggles against patriarchy; and as a moral, political, and aesthetic resource to Eliot, in describing them. In Chapter 4, I argue that this aesthetic resource shaped a distinctive moral and political feminism in writing of various kinds by women from the 1860s through to the 1920s and beyond.

To the extent that our understanding of phobia derives from the taxonomic strategies of a late-nineteenth-century medical bureaucracy, the phobic subject must count among the array of 'made-up' persons whose invention has long preoccupied social and cultural historians. The existence from at least the 1780s of the outline of an agreed definition of the syndrome suggests that we should not place too great an emphasis on the taxonomic fury of the 1870s and afterwards. Even so, a question remains, about the phobic subject and about her or his particular, and therefore diagnostic, connection to what we might want to call modernity. Is being phobic a way to be modern?

The answers I propose to that question in the essays that follow could be said to develop the concept of 'dynamic nominalism' put forward by Ian Hacking, in an argument largely but not exclusively concerned with the invention of multiple personality disorder as an idea and a clinical phenomenon in or around 1875. The claim of dynamic nominalism is that in some cases a category and the people in it 'emerge' in the same place at the same time, as though in complicity. According to Hacking, it was not possible to suffer from multiple personality disorder before 1875. What we do deliberately depends upon our ability to describe to ourselves what it is possible for us to do. If new modes of description appear, 'new possibilities for action come into being in consequence.' According to this argument, the description of a disease encourages people who would not otherwise have done so to discover in themselves, and act upon, its symptoms. Hacking claims, for example, that during the nineteenth century 'systems of reporting' created in Europe and in the United States an 'entire ethos of suicide'.[10] A proposition these essays develop is that the very much fuller descriptions of phobia available from around 1870 onwards, in literature and cinema as well as in the psychiatric journals, created new possibilities for action, including aesthetic action.

It would be wrong, furthermore, simply to oppose nature and culture, behaviour and label. The systems of reporting on suicide, phobia, and much else besides took shape at the same time as and not altogether independently of the fashioning through further endless industrial (or techno-scientific) revolution of a veritable 'second nature': an all-encompassing urban environment made over above all by electrification, to which human consciousness had somehow to be adapt itself. Did this second nature generate new aversive behaviours? From the outset, agoraphobia has been regarded by some commentators as an entirely proportionate response to the escalating dangers of modern life. In 1889, in an angry critique of modern urban planning, the Viennese architect Camillo Sitte put the outbreak of an epidemic of agoraphobia down to the emptiness and vast extent of the spaces carved out by modern thoroughfares such as the Ringstrasse. Sitte lamented the decay or destruction of ancient town centres which had held panic at bay by irregularity, curvature, and the balance of masses.[11] More recently, a connection has been made between the first accounts of agoraphobia and the widely influential analyses of modern alienation undertaken by Georg Simmel, Siegfried Kracauer, and Walter Benjamin.[12]

I think that there is something to such claims, if pursued at the appropriate level of historical specificity. Phobia arose, in the clinical literature, at the moment of a sharpening of the distinction between public and private experience, through the kinds of town-planning Sitte objected to, and in many other ways. It could be understood historically as the symptom of an ineradicable permeability. The new urban public spaces might have been cleared for surveillance and control; but privacy left its traces within them, in matter apparent only to phobia. In Chapter 9, I examine the feelings of anxiety and disgust long associated with the urban phone-booth, an institution whose rise and fall coincides with the second industrial revolution, and which will not survive for a great deal longer in the digital era. Calling from a phone-booth and engaging the services of a prostitute are both ways to be private in public. As a consequence, the urban phone-booth (like the brothel) has often been imagined as a place not just of (tele)communication, but of nausea. Nausea, note, and not shock. For Walter Benjamin, the telephone shocked, in a modern way, because it rang peremptorily and without warning in the depths of the bourgeois home, turning it inside out.[13] The Romantic view, formulated initially by Blake, Wordsworth, Baudelaire, and others, and still amply evident in urban theory from Benjamin and Simmel to Michel de Certeau, is that urban experience is defined by bewilderment, shock, and resistance to shock. My enquiry into the often repellent but rarely shocking urban phone-booth suggests otherwise.

The outline of an opposing thesis must at this point be apparent. The 'modern subject', according to Mark Seltzer, 'has become inseparable from the categories of shock and trauma.'[14] Paul Lerner and Mark Micale argue that, having 'transcended' its origins in nineteenth-century clinical medicine, trauma now serves as a metaphor for the 'struggles and challenges' of contemporary life, 'a touchstone in a society seemingly obsessed with suffering and victimization'. This expansion in the concept's scope might itself be understood, they conclude, as 'constitutive of "modernity"'.[15] Roger Luckhurst's highly informative genealogy of trauma theory describes two major phases in its evolution: emergence, in the discourses of law, psychiatry, and industrialized warfare, in the period from around 1870 to the Second World War; and reformulation as a politics of identity, from the 1960s onwards, with a new emphasis on survivor syndromes of one kind or another. Trauma theory, Luckhurst argues, was an 'effect' of the rise of a technological and statistical culture designed to create, distribute, and assess shocks to the human system.[16] For all these scholars, trauma in some sense constitutes modern subjectivity.

Trauma theory dwarfs phobia theory, in terms both of its command over popular and institutional discourse, and of its attractiveness as a topic of scholarly investigation and debate. Kirby Farrell is frank enough to acknowledge that the appeal of trauma as clinical syndrome and trope lies in its absoluteness. At bottom, she notes, a 'heroic disaster' is 'preferable to a lonely, messy, vegetative death in a nursing home'.[17] 'Psychiatry knows traumatophile types,' Benjamin claimed. 'Baudelaire made it his business to parry the shocks, no matter where they might come from, with his spiritual and his physical self.'[18] Trauma theory certainly knows traumatophile types. The 'survivor-position', as Luckhurst remarks in a discussion of the studies of Hiroshima survivors and Vietnam veterans undertaken by Robert Jay Lifton in the 1960s and 1970s, has taken on a 'kind of glamour'. For Lifton and others, the survivor is a prophet or visionary, Baudelaire *redivivus*. Furthermore, Luckhurst adds, trauma 'passes from analysand to analyst and, through advocacy and activism, becomes a privileged site for identity.'[19] That phobia has no heroes makes it all the more likely, in my view, to prove productive as a focus of investigation into the vicissitudes of modern life. I can't provide a genealogy of phobia theory with anything like the heft of the genealogies of trauma theory provided by Luckhurst and others. But I will where appropriate offer alternative diagnoses. It was, for example, by means of the concept of hysteria that trauma theory gained a foothold in psychiatric discourse in the 1870s;[20] and the general preference for symptomatologies featuring abrupt bodily seizure has led, among many other things, to Gwendolen Harleth's classification as an hysteric. To me, her problem, and in a sense also her solution, lies in agoraphobia. One incentive to write about Alfred Hitchcock, in Chapter 8, was that his films have so often been discussed, mistakenly in my view, in terms of trauma.

Where cultural production is concerned, phobia theory could be said to offer an alternative to two primary emphases in trauma theory: its orientation towards the past, and towards the unrepresentable. Trauma inhabits the past. 'Hysterics,' Freud concluded, 'suffer mainly from reminiscences.'[21] An event can only be understood as traumatic *after* it has happened. Since the traumatic event is not experienced as it occurs, Cathy Caruth observes, it becomes 'fully evident' only 'in connection with another place, and in another time'.[22] The reason why that event can never be known as it occurs is that it breaks into consciousness from outside, surviving as a bit of the real lodged in the symbolic order (in memory, in representation) but unassimilable to it: a 'symptom of history', Caruth says.[23] Essential to the definitions of trauma which gradually took shape during the final decades of the nineteenth century was the idea of a memory 'embedded in the neurophysiology of pain and fear rather than in words and images'.[24] As Luckhurst demonstrates at length, the cultural outcome of trauma theory's dominance in professional and popular discourse since the 1960s has been an obsession, in literature, film, and other media, with unrepresentable pastness.[25]

Phobia proposes a different way of thinking. Although the disorder may have an origin in past events, and even in some cases in buried trauma, treatment usually takes the form of drugs or cognitive-behavioural therapy, rather than exhumation through psychoanalysis. Phobia may once have shocked deeply, but that is almost always the thing about it least worth enquiring into. Some fascinating experimental studies of the experience of phobics have indicated that phobia may well be a disorder of visual perception in which particular aspects of the environment provoke or sustain aversive response.[26] Psychoanalytic theory itself has acknowledged that some sufferers keep the symptom intact as a way to negotiate the present rather than disavow the past. Such symptoms can be seen as 'conflictual, imperfect, and distorted attempts to achieve something which is necessary in psychic life.' Their intactness constitutes an achievement, an idiosyncracy, a 'personal motif'.[27] The phobia sufferer does not need to be told to get over it. Getting over it, with difficulty, is in the nature as much of the disease as of the cure. These essays concern the ways in which literature and film have set out to stay in the present, morally, politically, and aesthetically: no easy matter, where representation is concerned. It is for this reason, for example, that I ask in Chapter 10, in relation to Lynne Ramsay's *Ratcatcher* (1999), whether there might not be a 'haptic' narrative, a story which sticks to us as we stick with it.

Furthermore, the phobic object or scene is never unrepresentable. Far from remaining unconscious, phobia is informed throughout by a person's perceptions and beliefs about the environment, and about the nature and scope of the phobic stimulus; and it has as its context other people's perceptions and beliefs.[28] In that respect above all others, phobia theory differs markedly, in its bearing upon cultural production, from trauma theory. In the 1990s, deconstruction morphed into traumatology. The concept of trauma now occupies the place in critical theory once occupied – when deconstruction was – by the concept of aporia, or irresolvable paradox. It presides over the same quasi-theological preoccupation with a symbolic order in meltdown: with folds, fissures, and gaps in the human stimulus-shield; with those moments when our capacity to make meaning and value out of experience fails us, and we come to in a 'beyond' conceived, if not (for the most part) as divine grace, then as the purest of negativities. The hunt for the textual stigmata which stand in for such openings onto the beyond goes on. In so far as the essays assembled here have an implicit polemical aim, it is to secularize the attention criticism has quite rightly paid, and will continue to pay, to those moments when our capacity to make meaning and value out of experience fails us. They focus explicitly on potential meltdown of one kind or another, from the enforced sale of household goods through serial killing, terrorist atrocity, and plague to suicidal depression, taking in along the way a full range of minor scrapes and setbacks. They aim to demonstrate that the representation of phobic feeling in literature and film has made it possible to know ontologically what meltdown is. The phobic object's great advantage is that it constitutes the most *im*pure of negativities. The pigeon that terrifies remains a pigeon for all that, even to the person terrified by it, let alone everyone else.

Of course, some events overwhelm. Some events can only ever be represented as impossible to represent. The argument I put forward here is not that all events can be represented, but that the representable is as well worth representing – and as provocative in the representation – as the unrepresentable. Phobic literature and film represent the representable. In doing so, they find it convenient to speak in general terms about 'what there is' and about the ways in which objects of all kinds come into existence. They deliberately reduce the meaning and value we attribute to what there is to a minimum or degree zero which doesn't quite amount to nothing at all (to purely nothing). There is pleasure and instruction to be derived from imagining – every now and then – what the world might look like if we were to stop having ideas about it. Trauma's aesthetic principle could only ever be the sublime. Phobia's, I argue in Chapter 3, is the picturesque: that principle distinguished from the beautiful, in eighteenth-century aesthetic theory, by its ruggedness and its irregularity, and from the sublime by the fact that it did not provoke awe. The phobic picturesque has informed some of the most compelling representations of ordinary experience from Dickens and Thackeray through Katherine Mansfield and Ford Madox Ford to Buchi Emecheta, from Jean Renoir through Akiro Kurosawa and Martin Scorsese to Lynne Ramsay. The phobic picturesque is by no means all there is to modern literature and film. But there has been rather more of it about than one might think.

In considering the psychopathologies of everyday modern life, we need not, and should not, restrict ourselves to evidence provided by the history of psychiatric classification. Hacking's dynamic nominalism can help us to conceive a spectrum of made-up persons whose special talent or obligation is to live and feel one or other of the psychopathologies of everyday modern life. At one extreme stands the person under treatment, whose syndrome or pattern of behaviour (call it trauma, phobia, or multiple personality disorder) has been orchestrated by experts. At the other stands the person who has undertaken, as the occasion demands, to perform in a describable manner. This is a person whose behaviour as a whole may well defy the most plausible description we can offer of a part of it. Hacking's example is the Parisian *garçon de café* who, in Jean-Paul Sartre's memorable account, plays at being a waiter in order to be a waiter. The class of waiters, Hacking concludes, although not at all hard to label, enjoys an existence autonomous of the act of labeling.[29] To put it crudely, the person under treatment, unlike the *garçon de café*, is never off-duty.

One reason for thinking that phobia might prove a more productive focus for the investigation of modernity than trauma or multiple personality is that those who suffer from it stand somewhere towards the centre of the spectrum of made-up persons. Their dilemma very precisely illuminates Sartre's conviction that, as Hacking puts it, possibility, project, and prison are of a piece in human consciousness.[30] It certainly helps that the syndrome, posing relatively little danger to self or others, has not required orchestration to the same degree by experts. The phobic subject is only on-duty – and so fully describable – when confronted by the phobic object or scene. Significant differences between behaviour on- and off-duty provoke in her or him thoughts about the act of description itself; as indeed do significant similarities between the syndrome displayed by made-up persons known to be phobic and that displayed by made-up persons not so known. During the past 150 years, other comparable projects have been developed out of the possibilities inherent in phobic feeling which considerably enlarge phobia's prison without abolishing it altogether. Aesthetic enquiry figures the instantaneousness lived and felt in phobia in relation to events and forces which include the making-up of persons whose job is to live and feel instantaneousness, but who cannot readily be described as phobic. I want now to describe briefly one such made-up person, who as far as I know evaded description altogether at the time; and indeed has done ever since. I think of this person as a *nauséaste*.

My interest in nausea and its uses has a distant origin in enquiries undertaken some time ago into the social and sanitary reform literature of the 1840s and 1850s, an early advertisement of the emergence of a technological and statistical culture in Britain. What confronted the sanitary reformers, when they began to investigate the slums systematically in the 1830s, was waste: vast accumulations of rotting matter, in stagnant cess-pools and blocked gutters, in mounds of garbage and excrement, in graveyards bulging with corpses. Not altogether surprisingly, the rhetoric of sanitary reform developed around the idea of nausea. The nausea felt by the reformer did not just serve to represent the reality of the slums to a middle-class audience. Like the phobic symptom, it was a feeling to keep intact, as an achievement or personal motif, a guarantee of singularity.[31] I discuss its uses in nineteenth-century philanthropy and social commentary, in Chapter 4, and in the philanthropic stoicism displayed by the officer-class on the battlefields of the First World War, in Chapter 6.

There is some reason to think that this sort of behaviour coalesced, in European literature and culture in the 1860s, into a made-up person to rival the figure installed by Charles Baudelaire's charismatic essay on 'The Painter of Modern Life' (1863) as the high priest of modern transience and contingency, the *flâneur*. In a book on the idea of mess in nineteenth-century art and fiction, I described the crystallization of the figure of the *nauséaste* in literary Naturalism.[32] Here, I want to suggest that this particular made-up person enjoyed a long and vigorous life after Naturalism, and one deserving of greater critical scrutiny than it has so far received. For Walter Benjamin, the *flâneur* was a kind of detective, a connoisseur of social types, a physiologist who botanized on the asphalt in the name of pleasure as well as science.[33] According to Baudelaire, the *flâneur*'s stroll establishes a 'cult of the self', a mobile narcissism continually reinforced by skills comparable to those of the detective and the physiologist.[34] The *nauséaste* might be regarded as an anti-detective or anti-physiologist. Detective and physiologist convert material traces into meaning; the *nauséaste* stands transfixed.

It may well have been Joseph Conrad who re-invented the *nauséaste* for genre fiction, in *The Secret Agent* (1907), a novel that can't quite bring itself to ironize sleuthing out of existence. Chief Inspector Heat's day had begun with a visit to the scene of the explosion at Greenwich, and then the hospital morgue, to view the bomber's corpse.

> The Chief Inspector's eyes searched the gruesome detail of that heap of mixed things, which seemed to have been collected in shambles and rag shops.
> 'You used a shovel,' he remarked, observing a sprinkling of small gravel, tiny brown bits of bark, and particles of splintered wood as fine as needles.

'Had to in one place,' said the stolid constable. 'I sent a keeper to fetch a spade. When he heard me scraping the ground with it he leaned his forehead against a tree, and was as sick as a dog.'

The Chief Inspector, stooping guardedly over the table, fought down the unpleasant sensation in his throat.

The keeper, failing to rise to the occasion, is a true *nauséaste*. He sees matter rather than meaning. Heat, in the morgue, certainly does not spare himself the stimulus to unpleasant sensation. 'And meantime the Chief Inspector went on peering at the table with a calm face and the slightly anxious attention of an indigent customer bending over what may be called the by-products of a butcher's shop with a view to an inexpensive Sunday dinner.' He, however, is able to fall back on the 'trained faculties of an excellent investigator, who scorns no chance of information'. Those faculties help him to fight down the unpleasant sensation in his throat; and they are on full alert when he disentangles from the heap of 'mixed things' on the slab a strip of velvet with a triangular piece of dark blue cloth hanging from it. He has his clue.[35]

It is generally assumed that the shock detective fiction delivers is strictly hermeneutic. What we confront when the detective arrives at the scene of the crime is not a corpse so much as a ripening enigma. The enigma provokes interpretation rather than nausea: as the pursuit of meaning heats up, any unpleasantness initially provoked by 'gruesome detail' soon evaporates. The detective's domain, as Slavoj Zizek has pointed out, is the domain of *meaning*, not of 'facts'. The crime-scene is 'by definition "structured like a language"'.[36] It requires a display of hermeneutic prowess. But we need also to take into account the almost inevitable presence at the scene of someone other than the detective, someone altogether lacking in hermeneutic prowess. What exactly is that person doing there? After a few genteel preliminaries, Dorothy Sayers's *Whose Body?* (1923) unveils a body in a bath, in the suburban apartment belonging to an architect, Mr Thipps (henceforth 'poor little Thipps'). The body's metamorphosis from material trace into sign-system begins almost immediately on the arrival of Lord Peter Wimsey, as the detective deploys his monocle 'with the air of the late Joseph Chamberlain approving a rare orchid'. In the brief interval between Wimsey's first glimpse of the body in the bath and his application of the monocle, poor little Thipps feels obliged to leave the room. '"If you'll excuse me," he murmured, "it makes me feel quite faint, it reely does".'[37] Poor little Thipps is about to barf. His nausea brings into play, at the inaugural moment of detection, a curiosity about matter which Wimsey's brilliance will soon overshadow, but never quite eclipse. Such moments recur in detective fiction of all kinds, whether hard- or soft-boiled.[38] Their persistence testifies to the strength of our desire to know what the world might look like if it had neither meaning nor value for us, in that brief and blissful interval before interpretation begins. Holly-wood has acknowledged as much by incorporating what one might call the barf-scene into *film noir*. There's a memorable barf-scene in Richard Marquand's *Jagged Edge* (1985), for example, when the District Attorney first enters the bedroom where a publishing magnate's wife lies battered to death. By now, the convention has become so well established that the Coen brothers' *Fargo* (1996) even includes a meta-barf-scene. Police chief Marge Gunderson, inspecting the overturned car which contains one of the victims in a multiple homicide, announces that she's going to barf; but what turns her stomach is morning sickness, not the sight of blood.

Of course, the person of the *nauséaste* could not have been made up retrospectively had it not been for Jean-Paul Sartre's brilliant philosophical descriptions of various kinds of behaviour more Naturalist than Naturalism itself. Nausea, Sartre argued, is the very 'taste' of contingency. Roquentin, in *Nausea* (1938), is, though he is never described as such, a *nauséaste*: a man almost overcome by enduring ontological revulsion. 'The grey thing has just appeared in the mirror. I go over and look at it, I can no longer move away.'[39] What he sees in the mirror is his own image, evidently; but the image no longer functions *as* an image. It fails to present him to himself. It fails to acknowledge that search for meaning and value which is the great aim of consciousness, and its only justification. Roquentin is brought face to face with physiognomy's obverse. The mirror lowers him, outside of himself, into his own estranged flesh.[40] This wrenching self-estrangement later develops into a nauseous ontology, when the root of a chestnut tree which Roquentin happens to be inspecting suddenly loses its 'harmless appearance' as an abstract category, as an identifiable object in the world. The root appears to decompose in front of him. The 'veneer' of shape and identity melts, 'leaving soft, monstrous masses, in disorder – naked, with a frightening, obscene nakedness'.[41] Where consciousness hollows out a negativity into which it can withdraw, being (physiognomy's obverse) coagulates and solidifies into a mass or mess 'glued to itself'. In *Being and Nothingness* (1943), Sartre installed slime (*le visqueux*) as the ultimate glue, the nauseous essence of being. Slime, he wrote, appears to us not only as an object or substance, but as a relation, in which we are always already implicated, to the world. To exist is to get stuck. Slime, in which we are always already stuck, is the world's 'ontological expression'.[42]

These essays are not philosophical.[43] But they owe their inspiration if not their method to the remarkable studies of partially disabling affect which existential phenomenology began to conduct from the late-1920s onwards, with a view to taking philosophy closer to a grasp of lived experience: Heidegger's analysis of fear and anxiety, in *Being and Time* (1927);[44] Levinas's analyses of shame, in 'De l'evasion' (1935), and of fatigue, in *De l'existence a l'existant* (1947);[45] Sartre's analyses of hatred, in *The Transcendence of the Ego* (1937), and of fear and horror, in *Sketch for a Theory of the Emotions* (1939).[46] These feelings in some way disable or exceed consciousness, without damaging it beyond repair, as trauma would. They are as close as we can reasonably expect to get to how the world might appear if we were to stop having ideas about it. Of course, that appearance does hold for us a meaning and a value. But the starkness of the meaning and value thus generated mark the moment of their generation out as a crisis in the dialectic of illusion and disillusionment which constitutes lived experience. The moles on a woman's neck are seen starkly, the quid of tobacco is touched starkly, and so on. Heidegger, Levinas, and Sartre pursue their analyses of disabling affect in the name of ontology. 'Being,' Sartre claims, 'will be disclosed to us by some kind of immediate access – boredom, nausea, etc., and ontology will be the description of the phenomenon of being as it manifests itself; that is, without intermediary.'[47]

By the late 1940s, commentators like Emmanuel Levinas had begun to argue that Sartre did not go nearly far enough in his denunciations of the philosophy of consciousness. Levinas thought that the contingencies laid bare by horror are a whole lot nastier than those laid bare by mere nausea. It is of his or her subjectivity, he argued, that the subject is stripped, in horror. 'The subject is depersonalized. "Nausea", as a feeling of existence, is not yet depersonalization; whereas horror turns the subjectivity of the subject, its particular nature as *being*, inside out.'[48] Horror, so to speak, trumps nausea; and has itself since been trumped again and again, in that further raising of the depersonalization stakes which has culminated, after aporia, abjectness, and the rest, in trauma theory's cultivation of the unrepresentable past. Today, we read Sartre and his contemporaries, if we read them at all, as an anticipation of or feint towards Derrida, Foucault, and Kristeva.[49] We return to Paris in the 1930s primarily in order to find contexts for Paris in the 1960s and 1970s. It might just be, however, that Paris in the 1930s was more interesting than Paris in the 1960s and 1970s; and that Sartre and his contemporaries demand reconsideration in terms which are neither exactly their own nor exactly those of their variously disappointed successors. The approach these essays develop is that of enquiry into the representation of a range of stark behaviours including phobia and nausea. These, it's worth noting, sometimes appear separately, and sometimes in mutual relation. *The Secret Agent*, the text which invented the *nauséaste* for genre fiction, also includes an agoraphobe. The bomb-toting Professor, apparently intended to demonstrate through his appearance and mentality the degenerationist theories of Cesare Lombroso and Max Nordau,[50] in fact suffers from an intense dread of the 'mass of mankind mighty in its numbers' which looks a lot like agoraphobia. 'Often while walking abroad, when he happened to come out of himself, he had such moments of dreadful and sane mistrust of mankind.' Dreadful *and sane* mistrust: that, exactly, is the note of the feelings whose representation in literature and film I explore here. Impervious to fear, the Professor fears doubt, or mistrust. Agoraphobically, he thinks of the 'refuge of his room, with its padlocked cupboard, lost in a wilderness of poor houses, the hermitage of the perfect anarchist.' That hermitage alone will fortify him once again against the 'despicable emotional state' he endures in the crowded street.[51]

Phobia and nausea are experiences ordinary in content if not in form (that is, in the intensity with which they possess some people as a syndrome, and most of us at one time or another). The phobic or nauseating object or scene is itself (for most people most of the time) utterly commonplace. Ordinariness is now a topic on a number of agendas, and the best way to situate my argument in relation to these agendas is to touch briefly on the most ambitious and productive of them, that developed by the philosopher and film theorist Stanley Cavell in a series of influential books and essays.[52] For Cavell, ordinariness can only be acknowledged in and through the overcoming or endurance of scepticism. Scepticism he understands as the product and expression of trauma; or, historically, as the product and expression of an 'unhinging of our consciousness from the world' – as original sin, as a fall from grace.[53] For example, the intricate thematic index to *Contesting Tears* directs us to treatments of scepticism with regard to the following conditions: astonishment, emptiness, excess, homosexual panic, madness, nihilism, panic, torture. *Contesting Tears* is a book about melodrama, so these associations are by no means inappropriate. But Cavell does consistently code doubt as extraordinary, and the acknowledgement through which doubt might be overcome as an overcoming in and through ordinariness. He has described himself as continuing Romanticism's work. Indeed, his commitment to 'the task of bringing the world back, as to life,'[54] connects his reflections on the overcoming of doubt to Geoffrey Hartman's proposition that trauma theory will finally lay bare the imaginative processes which shaped the poems of Wordsworth and Coleridge.[55] For Cavell, as Simon Critchley puts it, philosophy is a 'descent' into the 'uncanniness of the ordinary'.[56]

The essays brought together in this book first appeared in a variety of publications, under the sway of a variety of preoccupations and emphases. They have been revised minimally, almost always in order to avoid the repetition of material. They are anti-Romantic in tendency. They deal in ordinary doubt, in dreadful and sane mistrust. They propose that phobia is above all *canny*.

Notes

1 'First Hates: Phobias in Theory', in *On Kissing, Tickling, and Being Bored: Psychoanalytic Essays on the Unexamined Life* (London: Faber and Faber, 1993), 5–21, pp. 16–17.

2 *Early Greek Myth: A Guide to Literary and Artistic Sources*, 2 vols. (Baltimore: Johns Hopkins University Press, 1996). 1. 80.

3 'The Phobia', reprinted in *The English Lyceum, or, Choice of Pieces in Prose and Verse* (Hamburg: J.W. von Archenholtz, 1787), 84–92, pp. 86–7. Hydrophobia, a symptom of rabies when transmitted to a human being, had long been an object of medical discussion.

4 Joy Melville, *Phobias and Obsessions* (Harmondsworth: Penguin, 1978); Fredric Neuman, *Fighting Fear: An Eight-Week Guide to Treating Your Own Phobias*

(London: David and Charles, 1985); Richard Stern, *Mastering Phobias: Cases, Causes, and Cures* (Harmondsworth: Penguin, 1995); Raeann Dumont, *The Sky Is Falling: Understanding and Coping with Phobias, Panic, and Obsessive-Compulsive Disorder* (New York: W.W. Norton, 1996); Elaine Sheehan, *Anxiety, Phobias & Panic Attacks* (London: Vega, 1996); Andrea Perry, *Claustrophobia: Finding Your Way Out* (London: Worth Publishing, 2008); Helen Kennerley, *Overcoming Anxiety: A Self-Help Guide Using Cognitive Behavioural Techniques* (London: Robinson, 2009).

5   *Understanding Phobias* (New Lanark: Geddes and Geddes, 2000), 7–8. For a wide-ranging survey of what is known about the diagnosis, epidemiology, and treatment of the syndrome, see Mario Maj et al., eds, *Phobias* (Chichester: John Wiley & Sons, 2004). See also Isaac M. Marks's influential *Fears, Phobias, and Rituals: Panic, Anxiety, and their Disorders* (Oxford: Oxford University Press, 1987).

6   *Collected Letters*, ed. Earl Leslie Griggs, 6 vols. (Oxford: Clarendon, 1956–1971), 2. 774.

7   *Attachment and Loss: Volume 2: Separation: Anxiety and Anger* (Harmondsworth: Penguin, 1985), 299. Emphases in the original.

8   Balint writes perceptively about ordinary experience in *Thrills and Regressions* (London: Karnac, 1959), but his terminology for those who advance towards ('philobat') or retreat from ('ocnophil') excitement is a bit of a mouthful.

9   'Historical Ontology', in *Historical Ontology* (Cambridge, MA: Harvard University Press, 2002), 1–26, p.1.

10 'Making Up People', in *Historical Ontology*, 99–114, pp. 108, 113. See also his *Rewriting the Soul: Multiple Personality and the Sciences of Memory* (Princeton: Princeton University Press, 1995).

11 *City Planning According to Artistic Principles*, trans. George R. Collins and Christiane Crasemann Collins (London: Phaidon Press, 1965), 45. For a 'postmodern' version of Sitte's argument, which eschews both his antiquarianism and his commitment to 'artistic principles', see Paul Carter, *Repressed Spaces: The Poetics of Agoraphobia* (London: Reaktion, 2002).

12 Anthony Vidler, 'Psychopathologies of Modern Space: Metropolitan Fear from Agoraphobia to Estrangement', in Michael S. Roth, ed., *Rediscovering History: Culture, Politics, and the Psyche* (Stanford: Stanford University Press, 1994), 11–29.

13 'A Berlin Chronicle', in *Selected Writings*, trans. Rodney Livingstone and others, ed. Michael W. Jennings, Howard Eiland, and Gary Smith, 4 vols. (Cambridge, MA: Harvard University Press, 1996–2003), 2. 595–637, p. 619.

14 'Wound Culture: Trauma in the Pathological Public Sphere', *October*, 80, 1997, 3–26, p. 18.

15 'Trauma, Psychiatry and History: A Conceptual and Historiographical Introduction', in Micale and Lerner, eds, *Traumatic Pasts: History, Psychiatry and Trauma in the Modern Age* (Cambridge: Cambridge University Press, 2001), 1–27, pp. 1, 10.

16 Roger Luckhurst, *The Trauma Question* (London: Routledge, 2008), 19. See also Micale and Lerner, 'Trauma, Psychiatry and History'; and Ruth Leys, *Trauma: A Genealogy* (Chicago: Chicago University Press, 2000). For Hacking, the trauma subject is a made-up person: 'Historical Ontology', 17–20.

17 *Post-Traumatic Culture: Injury and Interpretation in the Nineties* (Baltimore: Johns Hopkins University Press, 1998), 2, 17.

18   'On Some Motifs in Baudelaire', in *Illuminations*, ed. Hannah Arendt, trans. Harry Zohn (London: Fontana, 1970), 157–202, p. 165.

19   *Trauma Question*, 64.

20   Micale, 'Jean-Martin Charcot and *les névroses traumatiques*: From Medicine to Culture in French Trauma Theory of the Late Nineteenth Century,' in Micale and Lerner, eds., *Traumatic Pasts*, 115–39.

21   *Studies in Hysteria* (Harmondsworth: Penguin, 1974), 58.

22   'Introduction to Psychoanalysis, Trauma and Culture I', *American Imago*, 48.1, 1991, 1–12, p. 7.

23   Ibid., 3.

24   Allan Young, *The Harmony of Illusions: Inventing Post-Traumatic Stress Disorder* (Princeton: Princeton University Press, 1995), 13.

25   *Trauma Question*, chs. 2–5.

26   Beulah McNab, *Perceptions of Phobia and Phobics: The Quest for Control* (London: Academic Press, 1993).

27   Rosemary Randall, 'Phobia and Object Relations Theory', in Siân Morgan, ed., *Phobia: A Reassessment* (London: Karnac, 2003), 91–112, pp. 92–3.

28   *Understanding Phobias*, 10. It is surely appropriate that William James should have been enlisted in the study of phobia: Wendy K. Silverman and Willam M. Kurtines, *Anxiety and Phobic Disorders: A Pragmatic Approach* (New York: Plenum Press, 1996).

29   'Making Up People', 108–11. See Sartre, *Being and Nothingness*, trans. Hazel E. Barnes (London: Methuen, 1957), 59–60.

30   Ibid., 231.

31   I discuss the rhetoric of sanitary reform from this point of view in 'The New Historicism and the Psychopathology of Everyday Modern Life', *Critical Quarterly*, 42, 2000, 36–58; reprinted in William A. Cohen and Ryan Johnson, eds., *Filth: Dirt, Disgust and Modern Life* (Minneapolis: University of Minnesota Press, 2005), 30–48.

32   *Cooking with Mud: The Idea of Mess in Nineteenth-Century Art and Fiction* (Oxford: Oxford University Press, 2000), Ch. 6.

33   *Charles Baudelaire: A Lyric Poet in the Age of High Capitalism*, trans. Harry Zohn (London: Verso, 1983), 36, 39–41.

34   'The Painter of Modern Life', in *The Painter of Modern Life and Other Essays*, trans. Jonathan Mayne (London: Phaidon, 1964), 1–40, pp. 9, 27.

35   *The Secret Agent: A Simple Tale*, ed. John Lyon (Oxford: Oxford University Press, 2004), 65–6.

36   'Two Ways to Avoid the Real of Desire', in *Looking Awry: An Introduction to Jacques Lacan through Popular Culture* (Cambridge, Mass.: MIT Press, 1991), 48–66, pp. 53, 57.

37   *Whose Body?* (London: Coronet Books, 1989), pp. 17–18.

38   See my 'Fascination and Nausea: Finding Out the Hard Way', in Warren Chernaik, Martin Swales, and Robert Vilain, eds., *The Art of Detective Fiction* (Basingstoke: Macmillan, 2000), 21–35.

39   *Nausea*, trans. Robert Baldick (Harmondsworth: Penguin Books, 1965), 30.

40   Alain Buisine, *Laideurs de Sartre* (Lille: Press Universitaire de Lille, 1986), 95–9.

41   *Nausea*, 183.

42   *Being and Nothingness: An Essay on Phenomenological Ontology*, trans. Hazel E. Barnes (London: Routledge, 1969), xli, 604–11.

43   This is perhaps the point at which to note that the consolidation of phobic feeling into collective pathology, as in homophobia, racial phobia, and so on, is a topic requiring a different kind of analysis from the one I propose here. I do, however, discuss phobic feeling as itself a mode of resistance to racial phobia, in 'Fanon's Nausea', *Parallax*, 11, 1999, 32–50.

44   *Being and Time*, trans. John Macquarrie and Edward Robinson (Oxford: Blackwell, 1962), 228–35.

45   *De l'evasion* (Montpellier: Fata Morgana, 1982); *De l'existence a l'existant* (Paris: Fontaine, 1947), 41–52.

46   *The Transcendence of the Ego: An Existentialist Theory of Consciousness*, trans. Forrest Williams and Robert Kirkpatrick (New York: Noonday Press, 1957), 62–8; *Sketch for a Theory of the Emotions*, trans. Philip Mairet (London: Routledge, 1994), 66–91.

47   *Being and Nothingness*, xxiv–xxv.

48   *De l'existence a l'existant*, 100.

49   This is the case, for example, with Denis Hollier's elegant and instructive *Absent without Leave: French Literature under the Threat of War*, trans. Catherine Porter (Cambridge, MA: Harvard University Press, 1997).

50   Norman Sherry, *Conrad's Western World* (Cambridge: Cambridge University Press, 1971), 274–8.

51   *Secret Agent*, 61.

52   For example, *Pursuits of Happiness: The Hollywood Comedy of Remarriage* (Cambridge, MA: Harvard University Press, 1981), *Themes Out of School: Effects and Causes* (San Francisco: North Point Press, 1984), and *In Quest of the Ordinary: Lines of Skepticism and Romanticism* (Chicago: Chicago University Press, 1988); *Contesting Tears: The Hollywood Melodrama of the Unknown Woman* (Chicago: University of Chicago Press, 1996). See also Simon Critchley, *Very Little ... Almost Nothing: Death, Philosophy, Literature*, 2nd edn. (London: Routledge, 2004), and *Things Merely Are: Philosophy in the Poetry of Wallace Stevens* (London: Routledge, 2005); and Andrew Klevan, *Disclosure of the Everyday: Undramatic Achievement in Narrative Film* (Trowbridge: Flick Books, 2000).

53   *The World Viewed: Reflections on the Ontology of Film* (Cambridge, MA: Harvard University Press, 1979), 22.

54   *In Quest of the Ordinary*, 52–3.

55   'On Traumatic Knowledge and Literary Studies', *New Literary History*, 26, 1995, 537–66.

56   *Very Little ...*, 139.

1

Household Clearances in Victorian Fiction

The deathbed apart, there are few more scenes more profoundly disturbing in nineteenth-century fiction than household clearance, or the process of 'selling up': the identification of domestic material goods for sale at auction, either *in situ*, or elsewhere. Of course, we shouldn't be surprised at this, if the Victorians took the idea of home anything like as seriously as they made out. How could such a violation or wilful sacrifice of domesticity *not* prove as profoundly disturbing to those who witnessed it as to its victims? How could it not constitute a traumatic event? But I want to argue that scenes of household clearance in nineteenth-century fiction possess a density and an edge which at once falls short of and exceeds any shock they might have administered to the sensibilities of the house-proud. Such scenes expose to critical view an aspect of existence otherwise generally understood, then as now, not to require or to benefit from illumination. Illuminate it, however, they most certainly do. For the collapse of domestic arrangements was not thought to involve a collapse of the symbolic order as a whole, of literature's will to represent. The scenes render dismay and loathing as critique's inaugural moment, rather than its extinction in trauma. They belong to ontology.

Some Household Clearances

Chapter 17 of Thackeray's *Vanity Fair* describes the sale by auction of the possessions of John Sedley, a City of London merchant who has gone bankrupt. The chapter begins with Thackeray, in Bunyanesque mood, contemplating the moral to be drawn from the advertisements for sale by auction which at that time covered the entire back page of the *Times*. Here is an example, from the *Times* of 10 March 1847 (the part of the novel containing Chapter 17 appeared in *Punch* in May 1847).

> Bedford row.
> MESSRS. DEBENHAM and STORR will SELL by AUCTION, upon the Premises, 11, Chapel-street, Bedford row. To morrow, March 11. at 12. by order of the Executors of the late Miss Burrows, all the capital HOUSEHOLD FURNITURE, a handsome rosewood drawing room suite in blue damask, comprising chairs, sofa, card, loo, and occasional tables, what-nots, and

Davenport, Brussels carpets, or-moulu suspending lamp, noble chimney and pier glasses, two superior Spanish mahogany pedestal sideboards, (one of them with plate-glass door and back,) a set of mahogany extending dining tables, an eight-feet Spanish mahogany winged wardrobe, handsome toilet and wash stands with marble top, four-post and French bedsteads, and suitable bedding, numerous kitchen requisites, cut glass, china, &c. may be viewed on the day previous to and on the morning of sale, when catalogues may be obtained upon the premises; of Mr. Handisyde, 55. Lamb's Conduit-street; and of Messrs. Debenham and Storr, auctioneers and valuers, King-street, Covent-garden.[1]

All that remains of Miss Burrows is the faint trace of the meaning these objects might once vividly have held for her; and the auctioneer's insinuating prose (a *handsome* rosewood drawing-room suite, two *superior* Spanish mahogany pedestal sideboards) does its level best to rub that out. Even so, who, Thackeray asks, witnessing 'this sordid part of the obsequies of a departed friend', could fail to feel 'some sympathies and regrets'?[2]

Still, pathos, or moral enquiry, was by no means all he was after. The melancholic rumination on advertisements gives way to a much spikier account of the goings-on in a house which could be any house whose owner has died recently, or lost a lot of money, including the Sedley mansion in Russell Square:

How changed the house is, though! The front is patched over with bills, setting forth the particulars of the furniture in staring capitals. They have hung a shred of carpet out of an upstairs window – a half-dozen of porters are lounging on the dirty steps – the hall swarms with dingy guests of oriental countenance, who thrust printed cards into your hand and offer to bid. Old women and amateurs have invaded the upper apartments, pinching the bed-curtains, poking into the feathers, shampooing the mattresses, and clapping the wardrobe drawers to and fro. (*VF* 201)

There is a new energy in the writing, here. Something has stirred within Thackeray's elegiac tone, so that he now finds it hard to distinguish between dismay at all the pinching and poking and racial hatred. The dingy guests of oriental countenance *swarming* in the hall seem by their actions to justify a measure of social and cultural pest-control. Two years after this instalment of the novel was published, Thackeray's friend Lady Blessington had to sell up, ignominiously. He couldn't resist taking a look.

I have just come away from a dismal sight – Gore House full of Snobs looking at the furniture – foul Jews, odious bombazeen women who drove up in mysterious flies wh. they had hired, the wretches, to be fine as to come in state to a fashionable lounge – Brutes keeping their hats on in the kind old drawing-rooms – I longed to knock some of 'em off: and say Sir be civil in a lady's room.[3]

The contempt, sharpened by personal allegiance, is now all-embracing. Indeed, it barely stops short of fury. What, exactly, has provoked it? The contempt hesitates, as such feelings often do, between absorption in existence as such and a compensatory symbolic adjustment to or complaint about the unfairness of it all. Both kinds of feeling merit description as phobia. One is a compulsive and compelling disquiet, the other an ideology. Critically, they need to be kept apart.

In the novel, if not the letter, Thackeray's account of what happens when a person's worldly goods are prepared for auction is unrelentingly particular. This is a household turned inside out for inspection, laid bare in its material being; indeed, understood as matter. And it's hard not to sense, at the same time as the fierce moral indignation, a certain relish. Thackeray may not like the invasive bargain-hunters, who pinch bed-curtains, poke pillows, prod ('shampoo') mattresses, and clap wardrobe drawers to and fro; but he likes describing their penetration into the very substance of objects customarily rendered to all intents and purposes invisible by habitual use. He enjoys as a writer the brutality he deplores as a moralist. Whatever may have motivated it, the description seems utterly unforgiving. It is hard to see how there could be any redemption for those who pinch and prod, or keep their hats on in kind old drawing-rooms. Indeed, so intense is the feeling produced in him by the spectacle that Thackeray, in the novel at any rate, draws back a little from it. For the resumption of the narrative, in a lengthy account of the sale of the Sedley family's possessions, cherished and uncherished, does at least hold out the hope that something may yet be saved from the wreckage. Chapter 17 of *Vanity Fair* is entitled: 'How Captain Dobbin Bought a Piano'. The piano Captain Dobbin buys is Amelia Sedley's; he will restore it to her, without advantage to himself, as soon as he gets the chance (*VF* 221–3). We could even say that narrative itself, by resuming at all, by advancing purposefully, and so demonstrating that purpose is conceivable, in literature if not always in life, has got the novel out of the hole into which too bleak a description had dug it.

Some Theories

How might we explain what is revealed in and through scenes of household clearance? It would seem to be a topic tailor-made for object studies, or 'thing-theory'. In such scenes, objects predominate. But I am not convinced that thing-theory can help us, here. What troubles me about that mode of enquiry is its ineradicable preoccupation with subjectivity.

Object studies could be said to take its bearings from Max Weber's claim, in an essay of 1916, that 'culture will come when every man knows how to address himself to the inanimate simple things of life. A pot, a cup, a piece of calico, a chair . . .' To address oneself to the simple things of life, Weber goes on, is at once to touch them lovingly and to see them with a 'penetrating' eye; in seeing them, we see ourselves. 'What first reads like the effort to accept things in their physical quiddity,' Bill Brown has observed of

Weber's thesis, 'becomes the effort to penetrate them, to see through them, and to find ... within an object ... the subject.' For Brown, it would seem, the subject is all there is to find 'within' objects. The texts he discusses in his study of the 'object matter' of American literature are texts which 'ask why and how we use objects to make meaning, to make or re-make ourselves, to organize our anxieties and affections, to sublimate our fears and shape our fantasies.'[4]

Object studies, thus conceived, has both an historical and a phenomenological or psychoanalytic dimension. Among the theorists Brown has in mind as discoverers of the subject in objects are Heidegger, Lacan, and Bachelard. Peter Schwenger, in his book about melancholy and physical objects in literature and painting, adds Sartre, Blanchot, and Baudrillard to the list. Schwenger's topic is the distinctive feeling generated in and by the subject's perception of an object. 'This perception, always falling short of full possession, gives rise to a melancholy that is felt by the subject and is ultimately *for* the subject.' Failing to grasp the object fully, even as we perceive it, we fail to grasp ourselves as fully perceiving subjects. The subject's 'embodiedness in the world' will never achieve even that 'degree of focus' which perception grants the object. Out of that failure, Schwenger concludes, arises the melancholy which has proved the stimulus to so much still-life art and literature, as well as to the activities of collecting, classification, and connoisseurship.[5]

Thackeray, contemplating the back page of the *Times*, with its serried catalogues of objects in limbo, grows melancholic. But at the moment when he begins to imagine a particular household turned inside out by the prospect of auction, his mood alters. What arouses him, now, what engages him, are the consequences of a ferocious pinching and poking. The attention he devotes to the pinching and poking is as little melancholic as the activity itself. We could say that he has held melancholy back, for Dobbin's subsequent purchase of the piano. Melancholy belongs to narrative. The description of household clearance yields some other feeling altogether.

By contrast to the phenomenological or psychoanalytic approach, the historicist approach emphasizes the reader's attribution of social and political meaning to objects the literary text invites her or him at once to look at (by describing them in detail) and to overlook (by doing no more than describe them). Elaine Freedgood has recently argued that many of these objects, although inconsequential in the text's 'rhetorical hierarchy', turn out to have been 'highly consequential in the world in which the text was produced'. Her primary example is the 'old mahogany' furniture which Jane Eyre installs in Moor House, the home of the Rivers siblings, who have taken her in after her departure from Thornfield. Understood in historical context, Freedgood claims, the mahogany tells a story of 'imperial domination' strikingly at odds with the novel's 'manifest narrative', from which empire is expunged by Bertha Mason's suicide.[6] Jane Eyre's furniture, then, which the novel's 'manifest narrative' at once looks at and overlooks, had a hidden social and political meaning. But for whom? What subject, melancholy or otherwise, what set of anxieties about empire, is to be found 'within' the old mahogany? To that question, which her own argument everywhere raises, Freedgood has no answer. It's a shame, perhaps, that Miss Burrows, proud possessor of 'two superior Spanish mahogany pedestal sideboards (one of them with plate-glass door and back)' and an 'eight-feet Spanish mahogany winged wardrobe', did not quite live long enough to read *Jane Eyre*. Thackeray, a connoisseur of the back page of the *Times*, could easily have incorporated such specification, and with it a hint of social and political meaning, into the account he gave of household clearance in *Vanity Fair*. He chose instead to think about mattresses and wardrobes in general, and what might happen to them when inspected vigorously. No more than melancholy do the histories of deforestation and slavery appear to be the point of the account. His compulsive and compelling disquiet enquires into existence as such, rather than in the meaning and value attributed to it, for better or for worse.

Genre as Context

Freedgood is right, I think, to conceive of a 'rhetorical hierarchy' which in large measure determines what the reader can or cannot make out of the objects a novel at once looks at and overlooks. But rather than use an historical knowledge of the production of an object or substance in order to unsettle the hierarchy which has (in theory) hitherto obscured its significance, we should investigate the history of the formation of that hierarchy: that is, the history of the development of the novel as a genre. Under what generic conditions have objects appeared as objects in the literary text? And did that appearance, at its most complete, depend upon a fundamental re-ordering of the elements of fiction?

'Narrate or Describe?' Georg Lukács asked, in an essay of 1936 which charts the novel's sorry decline into Naturalism, from Scott and Balzac to Flaubert, Zola, and beyond. Lukács understood that decline as a re-ordering of the elements of fiction, to the point where description predominated over narrative. Revising this account slightly, we could say that Naturalist doctrine encouraged a particular kind of description, of a more or less de-populated environment, of objects without (or so it might seem) a subject. A predominance of description of that kind could be thought to affect adversely the novel's capacity to articulate meaning and value. 'Narration establishes proportions,' Lukács observed, 'description merely levels.'[7] It fails to sort the significant from the insignificant. Where there is proportion, one person understood in relation to another, person and environment conceived as foreground and background, as in Scott and Balzac, there can be meaning. And where there is meaning, there can be value (moral, social, political). I want to retain Lukács's distinction, even though the tendency among theorists now is to insist that description, too, narrates.[8]

Lukács, as we have seen, located the fall into description somewhere between Balzac and Flaubert. But Henry James was surely not the first, and has not been the last, to marvel at Balzac's 'mighty passion for *things*'. For Balzac, James wrote, 'mise-en-scène' mattered as much as 'event'.[9] Mise-en-scène, or description, was the mode in which objects without a subject began to appear, on a grand scale, in the literary text. It is not that there are no things in eighteenth-century fiction. It is rather that the things there are there lack physical or sensuous texture.[10] They are not described in the sort of detail which would enable them to emerge as objects (relatively speaking) without a subject.

In eighteenth-century fiction, objects emerge as objects in and through the temporary suspension of narrative. Narrative's failure to establish proportion, for whatever reason, creates an opportunity for a performance of levelling. Heroes and heroines who have been brought low by misfortune or miscalculation, who are at an impasse, about whom there is for the moment nothing further to say, often find themselves in the company of objects whose existence does not depend on whether or not they have attracted that young person's attention. As the protagonists sink, so the novel sinks with them, from narrative to description. And those objects – described in detail, with full regard for physical, sensuous texture – are, more often than not, objects in a state of disrepair or decay: they have themselves been levelled. Defoe's Robinson Crusoe, contemplating the shipwreck which he alone has survived, remarks that the only sign he ever saw of his dead comrades was 'three of their Hats, one Cap, and two Shoes that were not Fellows'.[11] Not a great deal of sensuous texture there, perhaps: but Crusoe has observed the shoes closely enough to know that they are not fellows. Richardson's Clarissa Harlowe, after escaping from the brothel in which she had been raped, ends up in a bailiff's house, under arrest for debt, in surroundings so sordid that Belford cannot resist describing them to Lovelace in almost sumptuous detail.[12]

Protagonists brought low in this fashion would have to include Fanny Price, in *Mansfield Park* (1814), whose lengthy visit to her family in Portsmouth, in Chapter 46, forces her to acknowledge that her life has reached an impasse. Fanny feels the loss of Mansfield Park's moral and physical comforts acutely; she expects to hear at any moment that Edmund Bertram, the man she loves, has engaged himself to Mary Crawford; while Henry Crawford, a man she does not love, courts her assiduously. Austen renders this impasse by ceasing to tell us what is going on in her head, and instead showing us what she sees: the 'stains and dirt' brought forward by the 'sickly glare' of sunlight through the parlour window.

> She sat in a blaze of oppressive heat, in a cloud of moving dust, and her eyes could only wander from the walls, marked by her father's head, to the table cut and notched by her brothers, where stood the tea-board never thoroughly cleaned, the cups and saucers wiped in streaks, the milk a mixture of motes

floating in thin blue, and the bread and butter growing every minute more greasy than even Rebecca's hands had first produced it. Her father read his newspaper, and her mother lamented over the ragged carpet as usual, while the tea was in preparation, and wished Rebecca would mend it; and Fanny was first roused by his calling out to her, after humphing and considering over a particular paragraph: 'What's the name of your great cousins in town, Fan?'[13]

What 'brings forward' stains and dirt that might otherwise have slept on unnoticed is the frustration of narrative desire: of Fanny's desire for Edmund, of the reader's desire for crystallizing event. There is melancholy, here, to be sure, as Fanny's eyes 'wander' from one stain to another. But it is not a melancholy provoked by the stains themselves, which are too much the outcome of other people's habitual actions, and other people's habitual feelings about those actions, for Fanny to find herself in them.

Fanny's eyes level down to matter or stuff already levelled down to the point where there is no proportion in it any longer. The hiatus is soon at end. Austen, feeling, perhaps, on her own part, and on our part, that narrative desire has been frustrated for long enough, supplies an event. The butter is not a moment greasier before Mr Price broadcasts the news of Henry Crawford's elopement with Maria Rushworth. Edmund is free again! Fanny will be able to resume immediately the 'active indispensable employment' she craves.

These examples from Defoe, Richardson, and Austen make me want to insist on the negative function of a certain kind of description: the description, itself a levelling down, of objects levelled down to matter or stuff. Such descriptions are a description of the world as it will be like when we are no longer here to see it (when for us there is no longer any narrative desire to be frustrated). They oblige us to conceive the indifference of a subject to objects which are already indifferent to it. They are prospective, and therefore not melancholic. The prospect almost excludes meaning and value altogether. That almost exclusion defines the nature and scope of nausea's critique.

Commodity Fetishism

With Balzac, James said, the book fills up with things. But what kinds of things? There are, to be sure, descriptions in the nineteenth-century novel after Balzac of the equivalent of pairs of shoes that don't match, where the not matching is the point, and streaky cups and saucers, where the streakiness is the point. But there are also descriptions, by the yard, of arrays of objects whose significance is not in doubt: for example, of objects which stand forth primarily in and through their potential exchange-value. The social and cultural transformation which above all made new work for description was the establishment in nineteenth-century life and literature of the commodity as the object *par excellence*. Novels began to fill up with commodities.

The objects described in detail in eighteenth- and early-nineteenth-century novels are often objects laid low by accident or neglect. A commodity, by contrast, is an object raised in and through its preparedness for exchange – its abstraction from the sensuous human activity of which it is the product – to the status of an idea. Marx's chapter on commodity-fetishism in *Das Kapital* defines commodification as a form of transcendence, so that the common household table stands not only with its feet on the ground, but, in relation to all other commodities, 'on its head,' evolving out of its wooden brain 'grotesque ideas'.[14] Studies of nineteenth-century commodity culture have taught us that the commodity 'steps forth as commodity,' in Marx's phrase, in shop-window, exhibition hall, and novel alike, by reason of its self-transcendence. According to Thomas Richards, it was the Great Exhibition of 1851 which demonstrated 'once and for all that the capitalist system had not only created a dominant form of exchange but was also in the process of creating a dominant form of representation to go along with it.'[15] Commodification turned things into signs. Object studies has on the whole sought to distance itself, in its concern for the objectness of objects, from such accounts of the 'culture of consumption'.[16] But we may need to return to them if we are to understand the objectness of the objects on view in a household clearance, objects, I shall argue, at once newly consumable and already beyond consumption.

Andrew Miller has argued that *Vanity Fair* imagines more thoroughly than any other Victorian novel the 'fetishistic reduction of the material environment to commodities, to a world simultaneously brilliant and tedious, in which value is produced without reference either to the needs or to the hopelessly utopian desires of characters.' According to Miller, Thackeray's main interest lay in the stimulus provided by the display of private possessions at public auction to the recirculation not only of wealth but of 'significance'. Jos Sedley's 'significance' certainly suffers some recirculation when a portrait of him on an elephant is put up for sale, and eventually knocked down for half a guinea, amid much ribaldry, to Rawdon and Becky Crawley. There is a reduction, here, from one kind of significance to another, from cherished possession to mere commodity. In theory, it is possible to restore value and meaning to objects thus reduced by means of moral action. Some young stockbrokers buy back 'one dozen well-manufactured spoons and forks at per oz., and one dozen dessert ditto ditto' on Mrs Sedley's behalf; while Captain Dobbin, hopelessly in love with Amelia Sedley, fiancée of his best friend and fellow-officer George Osborne, bids, as we have seen, for her piano. As Miller points out, objects can gain a 'lonely meaning' for Thackeray's characters through 'an allegorical process in which they seem to prefigure a distant realm of satisfaction'. However, such 'libidinal' transcendence of an object's commodity-status rarely proves anything other than a delusion.[17] When Amelia learns, many years later, that it was Dobbin who bought the piano on her behalf, not George Osborne, as she had always supposed, it at once ceases to have any value for her (*VF* 758–9).

I'm not sure that 'libidinal' quite covers the nature and extent of Mrs Tulliver's emotional investment in her silver tea-pot, in George Eliot's *The Mill on the Floss* (1860), but there's a kind of loneliness to that, too, which the novel explores during an extended account of the consequences of Mr Tulliver's bankruptcy. The Tullivers will have to sell up, and a chapter entitled 'Mrs Tulliver's Teraphim, or Household Gods' shows her seated in the store-room inspecting her 'laid-up treasures'. Eliot pokes gentle fun at Mrs Tulliver's abiding anxiety that the silver tea-pot will end up in the local inn, 'being scratched, and set before the travellers and folks – and my letters on it – see here – E.D. – and everybody see 'em'.[18] But there is a serious concern, too, with the potential loss of the history sedimented in personal possessions, a history which can easily come to mean either too little or too much. The title of the chapter refers to Judges 18:14–20, in which armed men forcibly remove 'household gods', the ephod and the teraphim, from the house of their possessor. In this case, the moral action required to restore meaning and value will indeed prove biblical in scope. However, a necessary emphasis on the auction as a system for the recirculation of wealth and significance should not be allowed to obscure the intensity of the interest shown by writers like Thackeray and Eliot in what precedes it: in the curious condition of abandonment which afflicts a household awaiting clearance.

We have already witnessed Thackeray's distress, in life and in literature, at such dismal sights. Eliot, concerned though she is above all to explore the moral implications of being sold up, or having the bailiff in the house, none the less takes trouble to register the nauseous sensation it induces. The first thing Tom and Maggie Tulliver notice when they return home on the fateful day is an overpowering smell of tobacco. 'There was a coarse, dingy man, of whose face Tom had some vague recollection, sitting in his father's chair, smoking, with a jug and glass beside him.'[19] Dismal sights can usually be held at distance: an odour is already inside us by the time we notice it. Thackeray and Eliot were not alone in thinking that such physical revulsions mattered.

There is a vivid instance in Charles Reade's *Hard Cash* (1863).[20] Despite his novel's title, Reade was not interested primarily in the recirculation of value and meaning, any more than he was in melancholy, or the social and political history of objects. What interested him was rawness, or stuff: the matter in material culture.

> Jane Hardie had found Albion Villa in the miserable state that precedes an auction; the house raw, its contents higgledy-piggledly. The stair carpets, and drawing-room carpets, were up, and in rolls in the dining-room; the bulk of the furniture was there too; the auction was to be in that room. The hall was clogged with great packages, and littered with small, all awaiting the railway carts; and Edward, dusty and deliquescent, was cording, strapping, and nailing them at the gallop, in his shirt sleeves.[21]

Albion Villa and its inhabitants have been brought down low, into a 'miserable state'. The misery inhibits narrative. That failure becomes the opportunity for description: for a description of objects without (or so it might seem) a subject. Reade finds a suitably down-to-earth term for this misery. The *OED* defines 'higgledy-piggledly' as a vocal gesture, the word conforming to the thing described: 'whether founded on *pig*, with some reference to the disorderly and utterly irregular fashion in which a herd of these animals huddle together, is uncertain, though examples show that such an association has often been present to persons using it.' Even the chief human being on the scene, dusty and deliquescent, appears to have been reduced to matter.

Scenes of household clearance imagine the object's double reduction: from household god to commodity; from commodity to matter, or stuff. The first reduction deprives objects of their past, of that surplus of meaning and value they have acquired since their purchase: of everything but their exchange value in the here and now. It can, of course, be quite brutal, as in the case of Mrs Tulliver's silver tea-pot. But the transaction at issue does no more (or no worse) than replace the meaning and value a commodity has had for one person by the meaning and value it will sooner or later have for another. It thus remains possible to see how, under favourable circum-stances, or as a result of charitable intervention, its original meaning and value might be restored to it. In *Vanity Fair*, the young stockbrokers buy back Mrs Sedley's spoons for her. In Elizabeth Gaskell's *Cranford* (1853), some 'friends in need' step in to spare Miss Matty, who has been ruined by the crash of the Town and County Bank, from recourse to the auctioneer.[22]

As often as not, however, in the scene of household clearance, a second reduction accompanies, and violently exacerbates, the first. This second reduction, enforced by the ruthless scepticism of the bargain-hunters who thumb curtains, prod mattresses, and clap wardrobe drawers to and fro, deprives the objects awaiting disposal not only of their past, but of their future as well. It demonstrates that these still radiant commodities have, beyond a certain point, no future at all. The thumbing and prodding threatens to expose them as the waste-matter they will before very long become. The reduction from commodity to waste-matter which household clearance distinctively fosters is not just the assault of one system of value and meaning on another. It is an assault on the very possibility of systems of value and meaning. Since this is literature, it's likely that the the assault will have been mounted, ultimately, on behalf of meaning and value, or in the name of critique. That's what the world looks like when you stop having ideas about it, such scenes announce; and, furthermore, it's no bad thing to be reminded of the imminence of that hiatus. One of literature's great assets is its ability *almost* to squeeze the meaning and value out of existence. To grasp the significance of that achievement, we will need more than the new ways of thinking about objects that thing-theory has to offer. We will need a way to think about objects *as they cease to be objects*.

I have proposed a generic context, because it may well be that a shift in the relation between narrative and description in the nineteenth-century novel recreated in modern terms the always useful illusion of a direct insight into the stuff of existence, into what happens when meaning and value appear to come to an end. To demonstrate as much would require a far more systematic account than I have been able to offer here of how and why narrative abruptly gives way to description, in the texts at issue. I would like to conclude, however, by suggesting that in the nineteenth-century as in the eighteenth-century novel, the stuff of existence gets laid bare at precisely the moment when the pressure to generate meaning and value is (for a variety of reasons) at its most intense; and nowhere more so than in novels which concern the moral and sentimental education of a young man of indeterminate origins. The topic of such novels is nothing less than the emergence and gradual self-definition during the nineteenth century of a professional or non-capitalist middle class.[23] At especially low points in their as yet none-too-brilliant careers, these young men find themselves after one fashion or another unable altogether to avoid the dismal sight of a household clearance. It happens to Pip, in Dickens's *Great Expectations* (1861); to Will Ladislaw, in Eliot's *Middlemarch* (1870–1), and to Jude, in Hardy's *Jude the Obscure* (1895).[24] All three feel thoroughly sick.

These episodes, in texts by writers as diverse as Dickens, Eliot, and Hardy, can surely be taken to indicate both the pervasiveness and the intrinsic interest of the scene or trope of household clearance. Indeed, they give that scene or trope an additional twist. In each case, the household whose clearance the young men witness is not their own, evidently, since a household is something they can still only aspire to. The event – or, rather, the levelling description it brings about – draws attention to the very specific problem of identity which afflicts those whose capital is symbolic through and through: those who only have their own integrity to sell, rather than muscle, or the contents of a bank account. For aspirants to professional status, at that particular moment in history, the dialectic of necessary illusion and necessary disillusionment which constitutes *Bildung*, or moral and sentimental education, must have appeared thoroughly perplexing. Nausea is vigorously at ontological work in these levelling descriptions of the spectacle of clearance. Its persistence suggests that disillusionment is necessary in *Bildung*, rather than merely the result of avoidable error. Whether that makes the whole experience less painful than it might be to a Mrs Tulliver, or more so, is of course open to debate.

Notes

1   *Times*, 10 March 1847, 12.
2   *Vanity Fair: A Novel without a Hero*, ed. John Sutherland (Oxford: Oxford University Press, 1983), 200. Henceforth *VF*.
3   *Letters and Private Papers*, ed. Gordon N. Ray, 4 vols. (Cambridge, Mass.: Harvard University Press, 1945–6), 1. 532.
4   *The Sense of Things: The Object Matter of American Literature* (Chicago: Chicago University press, 2004), 12, 4.

5   *The Tears of Things: Melancholy and Physical Objects* (Minneapolis: University of Minnesota Press, 2006), 2–3.

6   *The Ideas in Things: Fugitive Meaning in the Victorian Novel* (Chicago: University of Chicago Press, 2006), 2–3.

7   Georg Lukács, 'Narrate or Describe?', in *Writer and Critic and Other Essays*, ed. and trans. Arthur Kahn (London: Merlin Press, 1970), 110–48, pp. 127–8, 131.

8   Mieke Bal, 'Over-writing as Un-writing: Descriptions, World-Making, and Novelistic Time', in Franco Moretti, ed., *The Novel*, 2 vols. (Princeton: Princeton University Press, 2006), 1. 571–610.

9   'Honoré de Balzac', in *Literary Criticism: French Writers, Other European Writers, The Prefaces to the New York Edition*, ed. Leon Edel and Mark Wilson (New York: Library of America, 1984), 31–68, pp. 49–50.

10 Cynthia Wall, 'The Rhetoric of Description and the Spaces of Things', in Dennis Todd and Cynthia Wall, eds., *Eighteenth-Century Genre and Culture: Serious Reflections on Occasional Forms* (Newark: University of Delaware Press, 2001), 261–79.

11 *Robinson Crusoe*, ed. J. Donald Crowley (Oxford: Oxford University Press, 1983), 46.

12 *Clarissa, or the History of a Young Lady*, ed. Angus Ross (Harmondsworth: Penguin Books, 1985), 1064–5.

13 *Mansfield Park*, ed. Kathryn Sutherland (Harmondsworth: Penguin Books, 1996), 362–3.

14 *Capital*, trans. Ben Fowkes, 3 vols. (Harmondsworth: Penguin Books, 1976), 1. 163–4.

15 *The Commodity Culture of Victorian England: Advertising and Spectacle, 1851–1914* (Stanford: Stanford University Press, 1990), 3.

16 For example, Brown, *Sense*, 13.

17 *Novels behind Glass: Commodity Culture and Victorian Narrative* (Cambridge: Cambridge University Press, 1995), 9, 21, 202, 205–6, 35.

18 *The Mill on the Floss*, ed. A.S. Byatt (Harmondsworth: Penguin Books, 1979), 281, 294.

19 Ibid., 280.

20 Other instances well worth investigating would include Anthony Trollope, *Framley Parsonage*, ed. P.D. Edwards (Oxford: Oxford University Press, 1980), 527; and Gustave Flaubert, *Madame Bovary* (Paris: Gallimard, 1972), 377.

21 *Hard Cash*, new ed. (London: Chatto and Windus, n.d.), 306.

22 *Cranford*, edn. Elizabeth Porges Watson and Charlotte Mitchell (Oxford: Oxford University Press, 1998), Ch. 14.

23 A topic I discuss at greater length in *Paranoid Modernism: Literary Experiment, Psychosis, and the Professionalization of English Society* (Oxford: Oxford University Press, 2001), ch. 3. The classic account is Harold Perkin, *The Origins of Modern English Society 1780–1880* (London: Routledge & Kegan Paul, 1969).

24 *Great Expectations*, ed. Charlotte Mitchell and David Trotter (Harmondsworth: Penguin Books, 1996), 473–4; *Middlemarch*, ed. David Carroll and Felicia Bonaparte (Oxford: Oxford University Press, 1997), 574; *Jude the Obscure*, ed. Patricia Ingham (Oxford: Oxford University Press, 1985), 72.

2

The Invention of Agoraphobia

The last three decades of the nineteenth century were phobia's *belle époque*. During this first phase of full investigation there was, it must have seemed, no species of terror, however febrile, which could not talk its way immediately into syndrome status. In 1896, Théodule Ribot spoke of psychiatry's inundation by a 'veritable deluge' of complaints ranging from the relatively commonplace and self-explanatory, such as claustrophobia, to the downright idiosyncratic, such as triskaidekaphobia, or fear of the number 13.[1] Twenty years later, in his *Introductory Lectures on Psychoanalysis*, Sigmund Freud was to respond with similar impatience to the list of phobias drawn up by the American psychologist Stanley Hall: Hall had managed to find 132.[2]

There are two emphases worth noting, for our present purposes, in the turn-of-the-century psychiatric literature on phobia. First, the doctors expressed surprise at the disproportion or asymmetry, in phobia, between stimulus and response. There is a consistent emphasis in Freud's thinking about the disorder on the scale and density of the precautions thus erected against danger. Phobia's anticathexis, he observed, takes the shape of a proliferating defensive system. In 1900, in *The Interpretation of Dreams*, he compared this system to a frontier fortification.[3] In 1916, in the *Introductory Lectures*, no doubt mindful of recent innovations in military science, he compared it to an entrenchment. However, elsewhere in the same lecture he spoke of the danger confronted in phobia as 'tiny'.[4] For Freud phobia was both immense, in its power to engender avoidance, and utterly trivial. It was a Hindenburg Line built to repel an army of one. Freud was by no means alone in emphasizing the disproportion between stimulus and response in phobia. Most psychiatrists regarded the disorder as a perverse singling out, more or less at random, of an object or event to be afraid of. Charles Féré, for example, in *The Pathology of Emotions* (1892), distinguished between two kinds of 'morbid emotivity', one 'diffuse and permanent, the other induced only under particular conditions which always remain the same for the individual in question.[5] These conditions, Féré insisted, have no meaning for anyone except the person who finds them unendurable. A favourite diversion among commentators was to make lists of celebrities unhappily transfixed in this way by the mere force of circumstance. Thus Féré, citing B.A. Morel: ' "Who has not heard," says Morel, "of the febrile fits which were produced in the savant Erasmus at the sight of a plate of lentils? ... King James II trembled at the sight of a naked sword: and the sight of an ass, if the chronicle of the time can be believed, sufficed to cause the Duke of Epernon to lose consciousness" '.[6] Other stalwarts included Hobbes (fear of darkness), Pascal (fear of precipices), and Francis Bacon, who experienced syncope during eclipses of the moon.

The second emphasis to be noted in the psychiatric literature is a distinction between those phobias which produce fear and those which produce disgust. Ribot, for example, included in the first group the fear caused by anything from the prick of a needle to illness or death, and in the second group the disgust caused by contaminations of one sort or another. The latter he termed 'pseudophobia'. Phobia and pseudophobia are both forms of aversion, but forms which conduce to different kinds of behaviour: flight, in one case; disgust, or nausea, in the other. In nausea, Ribot said, 'the organism cannot escape by movement in space from the repugnant body which it has taken into itself, and goes through a movement of expulsion instead.'[7] It would also be possible, Ribot argued, to classify phobias and pseudophobias in accordance with the sensations which constitute the basis of the anxiety aroused. Thus, agoraphobia tends to be connected with sight, the fear of contamination with touch and smell.

According to Adam Phillips, the phobic person 'submits to something akin to possession, to an experience without the mobility of perspectives.' It is a secular, bodily possession. 'A phobia, like virtually nothing else, shows the capacity of the body to be gripped by occult meaning; it is like a state of somatic conviction.'[8] Yet a disproportion or asymmetry persists, between the intensity of the conviction provoked and the unassumingness of the object which provokes it. If that asymmetry proves hard to ignore, might we not say that the 'technique' enforcing it has entered into consciousness? Phobia's somatic convictions are knowingly whimsical, or canny. Its constitutive asymmetry might be thought to permit, after all, a certain 'mobility' of point of view. What the phobic person has learned through phobia is that incapacity is not the same thing as non-existence, although it sometimes feels like it.

In 1871, the Berlin psychologist Carl Otto Westphal offered the first comprehensive account of the nature and possible causes of a disorder to which he gave the name 'agoraphobia', because its symptoms arose at the moment when the sufferer was about to set off across an open space, or along an empty street, and were at their most intense wherever there was no immediate boundary to the visual field. Among Westphal's patients was a shopkeeper who could not bring himself to cross a street or square if the shops in it were closed, and could not travel by omnibus, or attend the theatre without feeling acute anxiety, accompanied by rapid palpitations of the heart.[9] By 1876, the French psychiatrist Legrand du Saulle was able to produce a synthesis of extensive enquiries into what he termed *peur des espaces*. Legrand was keen to emphasize the syndrome's ubiquity: panic might strike anywhere, on bridges and ferries, as well as in city streets and squares. He characterized the onset of an attack as a hesitation at a boundary: the transition between street and square, the edge of a pavement, an upstairs window overlooking a limitless expanse. Here, the sufferer, unable either to advance or to retreat, begins to tremble, or shiver, or breaks out in a sweat. Legrand's patients included a Madame B., who found that she could not cross the boulevards and squares of Paris alone, was fearful of empty restaurants, and even needed help in mounting the wide staircase to her apartment. Once inside, she was unable to look out of the window. She had filled her rooms with furniture in order to take the edge off their spaciousness.[10]

In 1898, Dr J. Headley Neale, a physician at the Leicester Infirmary and Fever House, and himself an agoraphobe, offered a vivid account of the disorder in an article in the *Lancet*. The onset of agoraphobia is so sudden and so fierce, Neale explained, that it seems like the end.

> I stop; the heart seems seized in an iron grip. I feel as though I were going down into the earth and the earth were coming up to meet me. There is no semblance of giddiness or faintness in these attacks, it is more a feeling of collapse as though one were being shut up like a crush hat or a Chinese lantern. I have a strong inclination to cry out and I feel that I must fall, so I lay hold of, and steady myself by, the palings.

In Neale's case, the attack passed in a couple of seconds, giving way to embarrassment. '"Anyone looking out of his window will think I'm drunk," flashes through my mind, so I drop a book or stoop to tie a shoelace and then hurry homeward, restored by the consciousness that I am not dead.'[11] Not being dead, and knowing it, is one thing that can usually be said for the agoraphobe.

There would seem to be as much disproportion in an inability to cross a square or boulevard, or to climb the stairs to one's own apartment, as there is in an aversion to lentils. But *is* there? Agoraphobia has been said to constitute the most disabling of all phobias.[12] Once we recognize that the spaces which bring it on are not just topographically open, but *public*, a social as well as a physical expanse, we can surely agree that there is a great deal in them to disable. Indeed, some commentators now argue that the disorder is a product of the 'fearfulness experienced by most women in public settings'.[13]

These analyses restore a certain proportion between stimulus and response. In them, agoraphobia disappears as a category. It is the environment which must be held responsible for causing panic, not individual perversity. The wonder is now not that some of us sometimes can't step through the front door, but that any of us ever do. My concern here is with nineteenth-century commentaries, both psychiatric and literary, on agoraphobia. As the record of what happened to J. Headley Neale and many others amply demonstrates, the medical profession had no doubts about the disorder's existence; and no doubts, either, about the disproportion within it between stimulus and response. Open spaces enjoyed the same status, in psychiatric debate, as the plate of lentils.

In his vivid discussion of terror in *The Principles of Psychology* (1890), William James distinguished between 'pathological fears', on one hand, and 'certain peculiarities in the expression of ordinary fear', on the other. The first category includes 'cadaveric, reptilian, and underground horrors', as well as the feelings provoked by 'caverns, slime and ooze, vermin, corpses, and the like'.[14] James, we might think, has been reading too much Gothic fiction. But he needed his caverns and corpses in order to define by contrast the 'ordinary' fear manifest in agoraphobia. Ordinary, but 'odd'. James thought that evolution had rendered agoraphobia, once a survival strategy, redundant in human beings (though not in the domestic cat). Its oddness, in his view, lay in the disproportion it sustained between stimulus and response. Caverns and corpses, on the other hand, were worth worrying about.

Like the psychiatrists upon whose work he drew, James understood that agoraphobia's asymmetry rendered it negotiable. Knowing that the open public space holds no terrors for other people, the agoraphobic person makes out of their untroubled progress across it an enclave. He or she moves out into the void behind a vehicle, or in the centre of a group. Those who cannot avail themselves of company, Neale observed, carry a stick or umbrella which at each step they plant at some distance from themselves in order thus to increase the 'base line of support'.[15] Such people behave like small children, Freud was to remark rather huffily: all we have to do to relieve them of their anxiety is to accompany them across the square.[16]

But one might also want to say that agoraphobes know how to put the disproportion which structures their feelings of panic to good use. One of Westphal's patients, a priest, experienced an overwhelming anxiety whenever he had to leave the protection of the vaulted ceiling of his church, but was able to walk in the open beneath an umbrella.[17] The most interesting case of all, perhaps, widely circulated in the literature, concerns a cavalry officer who was unable to cross open spaces when dressed as a civilian, but did so with ease when in uniform, or on horseback.[18] Here, it is not companionship, but performance, which saves the agoraphobe from his anxiety. Putting on a show, one accompanies oneself across the open space. The priest and the cavalry officer have learned to measure non-existence against mere incapacity. In what remains of this essay I want to ask whether the invention of agoraphobia might have made it possible for writers not just to examine these intriguing states of perverse bodily possession, but to grasp their usefulness, as a form of knowledge, to the possessed; and thus to become a little less sure than William James evidently was about the difference between the trivial and the non-trivial.

George Eliot and Agoraphobia

The news about agoraphobia spread rapidly. 'Dr C. Westphal has an article on Agoraphobia,' the *Journal of Mental Science* reported in 1873: 'by this he means the fear of squares or open places.'[19] The English philosopher G.H. Lewes, hard at work in the early 1870s on a series of books about the relationship between mind and body, had in his library an issue of the *Psychiatrisches Centralblatt* which contains a brief summary of the debate about Westphal's findings. There is unfortunately no evidence to suggest that George Eliot ever took this particular volume down from the shelves. She may not have needed to. In 1870, she travelled with Lewes to Berlin and Vienna. 'Mr Lewes,' she reported,

> has had a good deal of satisfaction in his visits to laboratories and to the *Charité*, where he is just now gone for the third time to see more varieties of mad people, and hear more about Psychiatrie from Dr Westphal, a quiet, unpretending little man, who seems to have been delighted with George's sympathetic interest in this (to me) hideous branch of practice. I speak with all reverence: the world can't do without hideous studies.[20]

Whether the branch of practice in which Lewes took such a sympathetic interest included an enquiry into agoraphobia is impossible to say. But Eliot knew that literature, like the world, couldn't altogether do without hideous studies. Gwendolen Harleth, in *Daniel Deronda*, the novel she began to write in 1874, suffers from what could perfectly well have been described at the time as agoraphobia.

Gwendolen Harleth has long been a focus of debates about gender in nineteenth-century fiction. The consensus appears to be that Eliot chose to characterize her as an hysteric, and that this characterization can best be understood as an allegory of her 'imprisonment within social forms'.[21] Jane Wood, in a recent study which usefully connects *Daniel Deronda* to Lewes's enquiries into the relationship between mind and body, concludes that Gwendolen is to some extent a product of the 'rhetoric of hysterical neurosis'.[22] And yet, although Gwendolen is sometimes described as behaving hysterically, the only symptom of hysteria she ever exhibits is the choking sensation brought about by the thought of what her husband might do to her, and that is always rendered figuratively. Unlike the hysteric, she suffers in mind rather than in body, and is able, to a large extent, to keep her fits under control.

There may be grounds for thinking that Eliot wanted to try out rhetorics other than that of hysteria in designing her novel. The *Daniel Deronda* notebooks include extracts from Sir James Paget's lectures on neuromimesis, a disease which the eminent physician was careful to distinguish from hysteria.[23] These extracts are followed immediately by a list of important events in the 1860s, some of which find their way into the novel. Neuromimesis is not Gwendolen's problem; but she does suffer from a nervous disorder to which – like neuromimesis, unlike hysteria – men were at that time thought to be as susceptible as women.

Consider the scene, a crux for arguments concerning the rhetoric of hysteria, in which Gwendolen, posing as Hermione in a *tableau vivant*, collapses when a panel in the wall opposite her springs open, revealing a macabre picture.[24] The psychiatric textbooks maintained that in hysteria 'the patient yields herself up to, and is overcome by bodily and mental impressions, such as we see in no other disease; there is, therefore, no attempt at concealing or suppressing the paroxysms.'[25] By contrast, after the initial shock has worn off, Gwendolen still has 'self-consciousness enough to aim at controlling her signs of terror'.[26] This terrifying experience leads to a discussion of her 'liability' not to hysteria, but to something like agoraphobia.

> She was ashamed and frightened, as at what might happen again, in remembering her tremor on suddenly feeling herself alone, when, for example, she was walking without companionship and there came some rapid change in the light. Solitude in any wide scene impressed her with an undefined feeling of immeasurable existence aloof from her, in the midst of which she was helplessly incapable of asserting herself. (*DD* 63–4)

Limitlessness, the absence of boundaries, is Gwendolen's problem. We might note the specificity of the conditions under which these 'fits of spiritual dread' (63) are likely to occur: for example, when she is walking alone, 'and there came some rapid change in the light'. Such sensitivity to minute variation is characteristic of the syndrome. As Neale pointed out, a 'sudden noise' or a 'flash of bright sunlight upon a white pavement' will often induce an attack.'[27] Eliot does seem to want the danger confronted in Gwendolen Harleth's fits to be, as Freud put it, 'tiny'.

Like the cavalry officer who was to feature so prominently in the psychiatric literature on agoraphobia, Gwendolen overcomes this dread through performance. Riding to hounds, she feels 'as secure as an immortal goddess' (*DD* 72); while her skill at archery fills her with 'joyous belief in herself' (102). Then there is, of course, the rather more complicated performance at the roulette-table, with which the novel opens (7–14). The understanding of agoraphobia available in scientific circles in the 1870s would have made sense of the dialectic of outward triumph and inward helplessness that is said to characterize her. What difference might it make, then, to think of her as an agoraphobe?

After Gwendolen's marriage, explicit references to agoraphobia drop away. The fears which beset her in the wedded state are distinctly 'pathological', in James's terms. She soon comes to think of the mastery Grandcourt exerts over her as reptilian (*DD* 423–4), for example. The damage done to the 'texture' of her nerves is such that she can no longer defy him. 'Her husband had a ghostly army at his back, that could close round her wherever she might turn' (447–8). And close it does, at moments of crisis. 'His words had the power of thumb-screws and the cold touch of the rack' (680). Like James, Eliot finds in Gothic fiction – or in Gothic fiction's successor, the sensation novel – a way to talk about serious terror. Agoraphobia's triviality disqualifies it from commentary on the feelings which afflict Gwendolen once she has been lifted away from the 'petty empire' of her girlhood (441). However, that 'undefined feeling of immeasurable existence aloof from her' does rancorously persist; and it could be said to produce knowledge, of a kind, as well as rancour.

Take Chapter 54, for example, in which Grandcourt fatally rows Gwendolen out into the bay at Genoa. During this climactic event, the terminology of imprisonment, torture, and strangulation itself tightens almost unbearably. And yet the manuscript incorporates a deleted motto from Coleridge's *Ancient Mariner*: 'Alone, alone, all all alone/Alone on a wide wide sea/And never saint took pity on/My soul/Coleridge.'[28] Gwendolen thinks of this 'dual solitude in a boat' as one of the subtlest tortures her husband has yet devised for her (*DD* 678). For her, the scene of their marriage is configured not as a dungeon, but as a vast empty space. After the event, she describes what has happened as though it were a renewal of agoraphobia. 'I had stept into a boat, and my life was a sailing and sailing away – gliding on and no help – always into solitude with *him*, away from deliverance' (695). There is at any rate nothing figurative about the paralysis which grips her when her husband tumbles into the water.

To confront patriarchy, in this novel, is to confront not just a tyrannical ordering and regulating principle, a deployment of rack and thumb-screw, but a vast emptiness, a lack of boundaries, or boundedness. Grandcourt has been from the beginning an empty grand court. He embodies that immeasurable existence whose aloofness has always troubled Gwendolen. The most frightening thing about him is his indifference, and his refusal ever to be explicit, or to descend into detail (*DD* 595). Just about the only mistake he ever makes is to get his henchman Lush to inform Gwendolen about the content of his will; the explicitness of this humiliation revives in her, for a moment, a 'defiant energy' (595–601). In every other respect, the marriage has been from the start a dual solitude on a wide, wide sea. Chapter 54 opens with a reference to Madonna Pia, in Dante's *Purgatorio*, taken by her husband to his castle, and there disposed of (668). The bad medieval husband locks his wife up in a castle; the bad modern husband leaves *his* to stew in her own agoraphobia.

Gwendolen, of course, has always relied on Daniel Deronda to accompany her across empty space. The only 'definite help' she can find, in the 'vast silence' which surrounds her on Grandcourt's yacht, a silence unbroken except by her husband's breathing, is in the thought of Deronda, and of the 'direction' he might give her (*DD* 674). However, from quite early on in the novel, Deronda himself has been associated, in an oblique fashion, with empty space. Gwendolen's reluctance to sell the necklace he had redeemed for her is said to derive from the same 'streak of superstition' as her agoraphobia (276). There has always been a contrast between their respective destinies, 'hers narrowly personal, his charged with far-reaching sensibilities' (621). Eliot fully endorses the scope of those (masculine) sensibilities. But she also allows us to see, from the point of view of

agoraphobia's whimsicality, the damage they do. For Deronda's announce-
ment of his political mission, in the novel's penultimate chapter, puts
Gwendolen back out to sea again.

> There was a long silence between them. The world seemed getting larger
> round poor Gwendolen, and she more solitary and helpless in the midst. The
> thought that he might come back after going to the East, sank before the
> bewildering vision of these wide-stretching purposes in which she felt herself
> reduced to a mere speck. (803)

The bad husband and the good mentor have conspired to leave poor
Gwendolen where they found her, in thrall to 'fits of spiritual dread'. All
that has changed, under the pressure of bad marriage and good mentor-
ship, is the scope of the dread the fits express: its plausibility. Patriarchy,
unlike sudden changes in the light, is something she has had every reason
to be afraid of.

Gwendolen Harleth's agoraphobia constitutes a point of view unique in
the novel, and quite possibly in Victorian fiction. It enables her to
understand the activities of her husband and the activities of her mentor
as in some respects similar (in effect, if not in intention). This is a radical
thought, and it is hard to imagine many other ways in which a nineteenth-
century novelist could have come at it. If we remember the early episodes of
Daniel Deronda, we remember the significant disproportion between
stimulus and response established, in terms not all that far from the terms
of science, as the primary characteristic of Gwendolen's fits of spiritual
dread. Eliot's familiarity with the terms of science enabled her to propose
both that some of patriarchy's grand schemes require endorsement, and
that they all operate on the basis of a damaging and ultimately
unsustainable distinction between the trivial and the non-trivial.

Esther Lyon's Aversions

Eliot's interest in specific phobia – in phobias of presence as well as of
absence – and in the performances which might release one from it,
predated her encounter with Westphal. In Chapter 5 of *Felix Holt the Radical*
(1866), the hero pays a visit to Mr Lyon, the dissenting minister. Mr Lyon is
defined for us in this scene by the anxiety with which he insists to Felix that
the use of candles made of wax rather than tallow is not an 'undue luxury',
but rather the result of the loathing his daughter feels for the smell of
tallow.[29] Felix, the embodiment of Arnoldian disinterestedness, has
cultivated a staunch indifference to the social aspiration encoded in undue
luxury. This indifference is dramatically at issue in his troubled courtship of
Esther Lyon. When Esther suggests that there is a good way and a bad way
to be refined, Felix condemns refinement out of hand. To Felix, one sort of
'fine ladyism' seems as good, or as bad, as another (*FH* 153). In this and

other respects, Eliot endorses Felix's idealism, just as she will endorse Daniel Deronda's. However, the indiscriminate vehemence of Felix's 'strong denunciatory and pedagogic intention' (150) towards Esther, not to mention his rudeness about almost everything she says and does, prompts a certain scepticism. Is he right, for example, to make no distinction between her various shortcomings? From his point of view, which is the point of view of the Arnoldian best self, a loathing for tallow is as disreputable in its implications as a liking for subtle bonnets. The novel, which is never imprecise about Esther's aversions, gives us reason to disagree with him.

The term the psychiatrists were soon to find for Esther Lyon's aversions was 'mysophobia': fear of contamination. Féré complained that mysophobia 'applies itself sometimes to objects or substances which are really absurd. Trélat cites the case of a female who had a morbid horror of tallow, and all the articles which could contain any of it.'[30] In this case, Eliot's interest in such absurdities clearly precedes their classification as a disorder. But Esther Lyon might none the less be counted among those who learn through an encounter with phobia (or pseudophobia) that incapacity is not quite the same thing as non-existence, although it may sometimes feel like it. Esther's defining limitation has a double aspect. Considered as vanity and snobbishness, it is symptomatic of a woman's 'imprisonment within social forms', and can be eradicated by self-knowledge; considered as phobia, it is an incapacity rather than a symptom, and cannot be eradicated. Eliot, I think, wanted to explore not just limitation, but the difference between one kind of limitation and another. Esther's loathing for tallow does not serve the same heuristic function as Gwendolen's agoraphobia. It does not survive to trouble the making of easy distinctions between the trivial and the non-trivial. But it belongs to the same general enquiry into pathologies of presence and absence. It was an enquiry that Eliot's close involvement in philosophical and scientific debate enabled her to pursue with a vigour and sophistication few other writers could match. Both *Felix Holt the Radical* and *Daniel Deronda* rather wonderfully find political and aesthetic work for ontology to do.

Notes

1   *The Psychology of the Emotions* (London: Walter Scott, 1897), 213.
2   *Introductory Lectures on Psychoanalysis*, trans. James Strachey (Harmondsworth: Penguin, 1973), 446.
3   *The Interpretation of Dreams*, trans. James Strachey (Harmondsworth: Penguin, 1976), 738.
4   *Introductory Lectures*, 459, 457.
5   *The Pathology of Emotions: Physiological and Clinical Studies*, trans. Robert Park (London: The University Press, 1899), 360.
6   Ibid., 362–3.
7   *Psychology of the Emotions*, 213–14.

8   'First Hates: Phobias in Theory', in *On Kissing, Tickling, and Being Bored: Psychoanalytic Essays on the Unexamined Life* (London: Faber and Faber, 1993), 5–21, pp. 16–17.

9   'Die Agoraphobie: eine neuropathische Erscheinung', *Archiv für Psychiatrie und Nervenkrankheiten*, 3, 1871, 138–61.

10 'De la peur des espaces (Agoraphobie des Allemands)', *Annales Médico-Psychologiques*, 34, 1876, 405–33.

11 'Agoraphobia', *The Lancet*, 19 November 1898, 1322–3.

12 See, for example, A.J. Goldstein, *Overcoming Agoraphobia* (New York: Viking, 1987).

13 Maureen McHugh, 'A Feminist Approach to Agoraphobia: Challenging Traditional Views of Women at Home', in J.C. Chrisler, C. Golden and P.D. Rozee, eds., *Lectures on the Psychology of Women* (Boston: McGraw-Hill, 2000), 339–57; Joyce Davidson, '"... the World Was Getting Smaller": Women, Agoraphobia, and Bodily Boundaries', *Area*, 32, 2000, 31–40, and 'Fear and Trembling in the Mall: Women, Agoraphobia, and Body Boundaries', in Isabel Dyck, Nancy Davis Lewis and Sara McLafferty, eds., *Geographies of Women's Health* (London: Routledge, 2001), 213–30.

14 *The Principles of Psychology*, 2 vols. (London: Macmillan, 1890), 2. 420–2.

15 'Agoraphobia', 1323.

16 *Introductory Lectures*, 448.

17 'Agoraphobie', 139–51.

18 William Ireland, *The Blot upon the Brain: Studies in History and Psychology* (Edinburgh: Bell & Bradfute, 1885), 188; Féré, *Pathology of Emotions*, 363.

19 Review of 'Die Agoraphobie', *Journal of Mental Science*, 19, 1873, 456.

20 *Selections from George Eliot's Letters*, ed. Gordon S. Haight (New Haven: Yale University Press, 1985), 373. Letter of 3 April 1870 to Mrs Richard Congreve. Lewes made three visits to the Charité, where Westphal had been on the staff since 1857, on 21 and 28 March, and 3 April.

21 Kate Flint, 'George Eliot and Gender', in George Levine, ed., *The Cambridge Companion to George Eliot* (Cambridge: Cambridge University Press, 2001), 159–80, p. 177.

22 *Passion and Pathology in Victorian Fiction* (Oxford: Oxford Univesity Press, 2001), 158.

23 *George Eliot's* Daniel Deronda *Notebooks*, ed. Jane Irwin (Cambridge: Cambridge University Press, 1996), 352. See Paget, *Clinical Lectures and Essays*, ed. Howard Marsh (London: Longmans, Green, 1875), 180–1. The copy of *Clinical Lectures* in Lewes's library bears the inscription 'G.H. Lewes Esq/with the author's kind regards'. The textbooks available to Eliot and Lewes defined hysteria as a female (or feminine) malady: for example, Moritz Heinrich Rombert, *A Manual of the Nervous Diseases of Man*, 2 vols., trans. and ed. Edward H. Sieveking (London: Sydenham Society, 1853), 2, 81, 84; and Robert Brudenell Carter, *On the Pathology and Treatment of Hysteria* (London: John Churchill, 1853), 34 (this, too, was in Lewes's library).

24 See, for example, Athena Vrettos, 'From Neurosis to Narrative: the Private Life of the Nerves in *Villette* and *Daniel Deronda*', *Victorian Studies*, 33, 1990, 551–79, pp. 570–1; and Evelyn Ender, '"Girls and Their Blind Vision": George Eliot, Hysteria, and History', in *Sexing the Mind: Nineteenth-Century Fictions of Hysteria* (Ithaca, NY: Cornell University Press, 1995), 229–72, pp. 253–4.

25 E.g., Rombert, *Manual*, 2, 84. There was a copy of this book in Lewes's library; the margins of the chapter on hysteria have been marked and annotated in pencil, probably by Lewes himself.
26 *Daniel Deronda*, ed. Terence Cave (Harmondsworth: Penguin, 1995), 61. Henceforth *DD*.
27 'Agoraphobia', 1323.
28 Cited in the Penguin edition (842). The original reads: 'Alone, alone, all, all alone,/Alone on a wide wide sea!/And never a saint took pity on/My soul in agony' (lines 232–5).
29 *Felix Holt, the Radical*, ed. Peter Coveney (Harmondsworth: Penguin, 1972), 139–40. Henceforth *FH*.
30 *Pathology of Emotions*, 373.

3

Naturalism's Phobic Picturesque

Jean Renoir once remarked that realism in film is 'a child of the naturalist school'. The remark has prompted Dudley Andrew to propose that Naturalism itself might best be understood not as a 'school' at all – a late-nineteenth century literary movement – but as an 'impulse'; an impulse, he adds, 'crucial to the cinema from its earliest years'.[1] This essay is an attempt to add further theoretical and historical substance to the idea of a Naturalist 'impulse' in literature and film. I shall try to define a Naturalist aesthetic which remained in use, or at least available for use, even as the movement's various intellectual and ideological provocations came increasingly under challenge, after 1900, or simply fell out of favour. The question I shall ask is not so much 'What was Naturalism?' as '*Why* Naturalism?' Put bluntly, where is the pleasure or the instruction in lengthy blow-by-blow accounts of some of the very worst things that could possibly happen to a person in this life? What is so compelling about epic reluctance to provide even the faintest glimmer of consolation? We're glad it isn't all happening to us, of course. But *Schadenfreude* has its limits, as an aesthetic principle. The resilience and adaptability of the Naturalist impulse suggest that there may be a philosophical dimension to its relentlessness. The hypothesis I shall advance here is that Naturalism's anatomies of deterioration offered a new and vital understanding of the ordinariness of ordinary existence. The understanding persisted because it had by the end of the century taken distinctive shape as an aesthetic: in fiction, at first, and subsequently, and to most enduring effect, in cinema.

Émile Zola, by any reckoning the movement's founding father, and its focus right up until his death in 1902, seems to have regarded Naturalist method as that supplement to the prevailing literary orthodoxy concerning the representation of the real which would once and for all lay bare its inadequacy. Balzac, Zola declared in his 1880 essay on 'The Experimental Novel', had gone beyond mere observational realism in those passages in *La Cousine Bette* (1846) in which he subjects Baron Hulot to a series of tests or experiments in order to determine exactly how the 'mechanism' of a man's passion works. No longer a 'photographer of facts', Balzac has intervened directly to place his protagonist in laboratory conditions over which he maintains absolute control.[2] For Zola, drawing on Claude Bernard's *Introduction to the Study of Experimental Medicine*, the supplement was in the science. Just how closely his practice conformed to his theory has always been a matter for debate.[3]

Certainly, there were other ways to conceive Naturalism's alleged exceeding of the photographic. In an essay first published in *The Wave* on 27 June 1896, Frank Norris firmly distinguished Zola's work from that of a 'realist' like W.D. Howells, whose novels concern 'the smaller details of everyday life, things that are likely to happen between lunch and supper, small passions, restricted emotions, dramas of the reception-room, tragedies of an afternoon call, crises involving cups of tea.' There are no tea-cup crises in Zola's 20-volume Rougon-Macquart cycle (1871–93), an investigation of the degenerative effects of heredity and environment upon the members of a single extended family. To Norris, the experiment Zola conducts – tracing the passage of a genetic flaw (*fêlure*) down the legitimate line of the ruthlessly acquisitive Rougons and an illegitimate line divided between the proletarian Macquarts and the provincial bourgeois Mourets – looked like romance. For the only things that happen to the characters of the 'naturalistic tale' are momentous things. These unfortunates find themselves 'twisted from the ordinary,' Norris said, 'wrenched out from the quiet, uneventful round of every-day life'. For him, the supplement was clearly in the romance. He couldn't see a great deal to distinguish Zola's novels from those of Victor Hugo. 'We have the same huge dramas, the same enormous scenic effects, the same love of the extraordinary, the vast, the monstrous, and the tragic.'[4]

What is most interesting about Norris's argument, however, is that he could not sustain it. In the final paragraph of his essay, he feels obliged to admit that the dramas recounted in Zola's Rougon-Macquart novels are not romantic at all in so far as they take place largely 'among the lower – almost the lowest – classes'. The lower classes feature in Hugo, of course. But Naturalism sought out the lowest of the low. And that's not all there was to its lowness. For Naturalist narrative at its most characteristic gave itself over to enquiries into the brutal reduction of meaning and value to an approximation of mere matter. Norris does not quite put it like that. But his examples have already spoken for him: Nana's face 'distorted to a frightful mask' at death; Jacques Lantier 'ground to pieces under the wheels of his own locomotive'. Meaning and value have not been obliterated altogether; a mask, after all, signifies. But they might just as well have been. In *Nana* (1880) and *La Bête humaine* (1890), the low persons who provoke and suffer the terrible dramas are thereby lowered yet further from some small measure of physical and moral autonomy to what Norris terms 'blood and ordure'.[5] Blood flows freely, in romance. But ordure? The supplement to crises involving cups of tea enacted by such provocation and such suffering cannot be thought of as romantic. Nor was it exactly science.

Naturalism always arises out of, and in the same movement falls below, or deliberately brings down, the prevailing state (and status) of the art of observation. If we are to understand the enduring appeal of dramas worked out in blood *and* ordure, we must first establish the nature and scope of the aesthetic effect they aimed to produce. For the Naturalist impulse is another, and perhaps elucidatory, term for the enduring modern reduction of the meaning and value invested in the idea of beauty to mere (and thus no longer merely 'mere') matter.

Zola's Monet

Émile Zola's writings about art are of great interest, not least because they undo an opposition fundamental to aesthetic theory since Kant: the opposition between a desire for beauty and rank disgust, or between objects distinguished by good taste as worthy of a feeling little short of reverence and that which tastes so bad we feel like throwing up. None is more radical, in this respect, than his review of the 1868 Salon, which extends an immediate response to works shown there into a broader history and defence of Naturalism.[6] The history and defence accord with the literary doctrine he was at that time developing in the preface to the second edition of *Thérèse Raquin*, where he insisted that his aim in writing the novel had been above all scientific.[7] The preface appeared in April 1868; he wrote the review in May. 'Mon Salon' demonstrates that from the outset Naturalism took firm hold of an aesthetic whose force and complexity have not yet been fully acknowledged.

The only painting Claude Monet showed that year (now lost) was *Boats Leaving the Port of Le Havre*. It certainly made an impression on Zola, who thought that Monet had found in the combination of industrial machinery and bad weather the perfect excuse to strike a modern note of sourness. 'We are in the ocean's face, we have in front of us a ship smeared with pitch, we hear the steam's muffled and panting voice, which fills the air with its nauseous fume (*sa fumée nauséabonde*).' Zola, jettisoning sight for sound, and sound for smell, seems to have brought himself to the very limit of aesthetic response. Sight depends upon, and articulates, distance. Sounds, by contrast, are already inside us when we register them. Bad smells intrude more deeply still, right down into the stomach. The only way to get rid of them is to vomit: to throw a bit of ourselves up. Where is the pleasure in that? Zola's next sentence, which returns the argument to the first person, has as its topic not art, but life. 'I have seen these coarse tones, I have breathed in these salty stenches.' Perhaps that is what anti-art does: disable collective appreciation by stirring private memories (something else hard to share brought back up again). Of course, Monet was no Duchamp; he wasn't even a Manet, when it came to scandal. But Zola was happy to report that the jury, put off by the sheer filthiness of the waves in *The Jetty of Le Havre*, the other painting he submitted in 1868, had turned it down flat.[8]

Still, Zola had not set foot in the salon in order to regurgitate salt air. He wrote about painting because writing about painting made it possible for him to consider aesthetic effect in and for itself with a frankness he rarely if ever managed when he wrote about writing. He needed to find art in the nauseous fume, not anti-art. So he drew into the argument another, scarcely comparable, painting by Monet, *Women in the Garden*, which the jury had rejected the previous year.

> Sunlight falls directly onto skirts of a dazzling white; the mild shadow thrown by a tree demarcates on the paths and the sun-drenched dresses a large sheet of grey. It would be hard to imagine a stranger effect.[9]

Zola dwells intently on the strangeness of the aesthetic effect caused by the grey shadow thrown on a white dress. The shadow falling onto grass and pathway merely intensifies the green of one and the brown of the other. The shadow falling on the woman's dazzlingly white dress, by contrast, blots it, even blots it out, altering not just tone but texture. It has been laid on thickly, as close inspection of the canvas reveals. Hence Zola's term for it: 'une grande nappe grise,' a large grey cloth or sheet. The strange effect is an effect of overlay or doubling, of substance where there should be transparency. It is high summer, in *Women in the Garden*, a bucolic scene. Elegant women airily enjoy the abundance of blooms. The shadow falling on them does not alter the mood of the picture. It does not propose drama, or melodrama: an impending doom. Rather, its grey blot has soaked up the very principle of matter's durable opacity. For Zola, the strange effect goes, quite incidentally, and without upsetting the bucolic scene, to the bottom or root of lived experience.

'Mon Salon' has a good deal of the manifesto about it. It was, for example, the first time Zola had spoken of Édouard Manet as a Naturalist.[10] Certainly, there is no shortage of strange effects in the subsequent work of some of the painters Zola continued to champion (he rapidly lost interest in Monet). However, it would be hard to argue that these reflections on the palpability of shadows amounted to a doctrine, let alone a theory. Naturalism in Zola's sense has not turned out to be one of the ways in which the main developments in nineteenth-century art are customarily understood. Zola worked out in theory, with regard to Monet, as he did not do and perhaps could not have done with regard to Balzac or Flaubert, what he was to work out in practice in the Rougon-Macquart novels. There, too, shadows fall palpably, and often to an aesthetic effect the narrative itself could only be thought loosely to require. In *Pot-Bouille* (1882), a story of furtive goings-on in a bourgeois apartment block, a neighbour's permanently half-open door can upset the best-laid seduction plan. But for whose benefit, exactly, is the glimpse afforded through the half-open door of the 'grey light' falling from a window onto a pile of off-white linen?[11] It is a question I shall return to. The answer I propose requires further analysis of literature; but of a literature informed by the theory if not the practice of the visual arts.

Naturalism and the Picturesque

Before Zola, the most lively debates about the part played in aesthetic experience by feelings of disquiet amounting to disgust arose out of the formulation – by William Gilpin, Richard Payne Knight, Uvedale Price, and others – of ideas about the picturesque. In eighteenth-century aesthetic theory, the picturesque was distinguished from the beautiful by its ruggedness and its irregularity, and from the sublime by the fact that it did not provoke awe. How did ruggedness and irregularity come about? Either by accident or by decay, theorists of the picturesque maintained. Accident and decay are among Naturalism's most persistent preoccupations.

As Christopher Hussey demonstrates in a book first published in 1927, but still influential today, seventeenth-century Dutch art had established certain kinds of landscape and certain kinds of object as peculiarly suitable for depiction, although neither beautiful nor sublime. 'Such were old gnarled trees, sandy banks, water and windmills, rough heaths, rustic bridges, stumps, logs, ruts, hovels, unkempt persons and shaggy animals.' The picturesque was an art of descent or sinking. First, it involved a choice of subject-matter (stumps, ruts, unkempt persons) which could be thought to lower the genteel artist and genteel viewer, socially, morally, and physically, by bringing them into contact with things otherwise outside their experience. Secondly, it obliged both artist and viewer to attend to that subject-matter *in detail*. According to Hussey, the picturesque eye 'turns to the scene,' rather than in on itself.[12] Descriptive technique reinforces the original choice of subject-matter in bringing art down.

Perhaps the most adventurous account of this new habit of viewing was that put forward by Uvedale Price in his *Essays on the Picturesque, As Compared with the Sublime and the Beautiful*, first published in 1794, and then more expansively in three volumes in 1810. Price thought that the picturesque in nature and art possessed three qualities capable of stimulating curiosity, 'that most active principle of pleasure': roughness, irregularity, abrupt variation. His essay consists largely of wide-ranging discussions of the objects and scenes in which those qualities are most likely to be discerned by the picturesque eye. It amounts to a lengthy meditation on accident, decay, and general wear-and-tear. Price lingers, for example, on the ruts created by traffic through a sunken lane, or the abrasions accumulated by skin, or the bark of a tree. In human beings and inanimate objects alike, decay *produces* the picturesque. Old age is to one what erosion or weathering is to the other: a death-in-life. Price saw a particular affinity between productive decay and the socially low or marginal. The picturesque, he maintained, is to be found above all among the 'wandering tribes of gypsies and beggars' who 'bear a close analogy to the wild forester and worn out cart-horse, and again to old mills, hovels, and other inanimate objects of the same kind.'[13] 'Age-mark' was the term John Ruskin invented for the truth told by a picturesque concentration on abraded persons in an abraded world. Ruskin began his defence of J.M.W. Turner's commitment to the mode, in Volume 4 of *Modern Painters*, with an account of the 'intense pleasure' he himself always felt at the sight of Calais church in 'its stern wasteness and gloom, eaten away by the Channel winds'. The building could not lay claim to beauty, but was 'useful still, going through its own daily work, – as some old fishermen beaten grey by storm, yet drawing his daily nets'.[14]

Towards the end of the nineteenth century, the picturesque achieved new popularity as a means at once to exploit and to come to terms with the heterogeneity of the modern metropolis. It became an extension of *flânerie* by other means,[15] or an adjunct to middle-class 'slumming': all those activities, philanthropic, sensationalist, or otherwise, 'undertaken by people of wealth, social standing, or education in urban spaces inhabited by the poor'.[16] Like *flânerie*, like slumming, it involved a deliberate transgression of boundaries, a descent into the physical, social, and moral depths. In America, W.D. Howells's rambles through the streets of New York provided the picturesque basis for a new urban realism which let some air in on the teacup tragedies Frank Norris was to mock for their circumspection.[17] The photographs Alfred Stieglitz took between 1893 and 1895 express a similar ambition. 'I loathed the dirty streets,' Stieglitz was to explain, 'yet I was fascinated. I wanted to photograph everything I saw. Wherever I looked there was a picture that moved me – the derelicts, the secondhand clothing shops, the rag pickers, the tattered and the torn.'[18] Stieglitz explicitly invoked the category of the picturesque in presenting his city photographs.[19]

The urban picturesque did for the nineteenth-century urban middle-classes what the rural picturesque had done for the eighteenth-century land-owner wishing to improve his or her estate. It rendered dereliction and class or ethnic diversity as delightfully quaint: as Old World remnants not wholly incompatible with doctrines of progress. But there were always, of course, limits to this inclusiveness. In *Impressions and Experiences* (1896), Howells noted that New York's 'shabby avenues' constituted a 'repulsive picturesqueness' unless seen at an appropriate distance.[20] Exponents of the new urban realism knew where to draw the line.

The picturesque had always been defined as a mode by an internal representational limit. The 1810 edition of Price's *Essays* includes a dialogue between three gentlemen concerning the nature and implications of a theory of art not wholly dependent upon the concepts of the beautiful and the sublime. The gentleman set out to view the paintings in the gallery of a neighbouring country house, the centrepiece of which is Rembrandt's astonishing *Slaughtered Ox* (c. 1638). The gentlemen admire the painting's mellow and harmonious tints enthusiastically, while agreeing that on their way through the estate village they had crossed the road in order to avoid the sight and smell of an ox similarly hung in a butcher's shop. 'Animal disgust, therefore, prevailed in the one case, and not in the other.'[21] Price's main aim was to justify and promote a high taste for low objects (for objects neither beautiful nor sublime). How might an ox hung in a butcher's shop be represented in art without arousing the 'animal disgust' it would arouse if seen and smelt in real life? For animal disgust reduces the noble viewer to the level of the ignoble object viewed. As John Macarthur observes, Price sought above all to distinguish 'an interest in the material object from an interest in the problem of materiality, of the subjection of material to technique'. Picturesque ugliness 'defused' disgust within the 'realm of taste' by subjecting offensive material to technique, and thus demonstrating art's 'productivity', its capacity to raise ugly things to value.[22] Art told the gentleman bent on improving a village on his estate what to do with the butcher's shop: that is, how to incorporate it into a prospect without obliging genteel persons to walk past it on their way to visit a neighbour.

What of Zola? The admiration he expressed for Monet's paintings of Le Havre indicates a belief that artists should not flinch from ugliness. The equally admired shadow falling on a dress in *Women in the Garden* is neither beautiful nor sublime, but rather an effect of accident. The urban realism of a Howells or a Stieglitz fulfils picturesque theory. Zola's Naturalist aesthetic, disavowing the beautiful and the sublime, establishes itself within picturesque theory but operates constantly at or beyond the theory's internal representational limit: the line drawn between an interest in the 'problem' of materiality and an interest in the material object.

Zola liked the cloth-like slabbiness of the shadow falling on a dress in *Women in the Garden*. Uvedale Price would not have done. Price distinguished with great care between deformity, a deviation from usual shape, and mere ugliness, or complete 'want of form'. Deformity might become picturesque, when viewed correctly; ugliness not. One example Price gave of mere ugliness is the 'cold white glare' of what would usually be called a 'fine sheet of water'. To him, the expression 'sheet of water' suggested that the stretch of water at issue could be seen as 'linen spread upon grass', and thus altogether lacking in the variation necessary to create a picturesque effect. If a 'sheety appearance' is what you're after, he proposed, you should have some 'exact imitations' of a lake made up in fabric; and so save a great deal of money.[23] An imitation exact enough to preserve the materiality of the material object would have suited Zola nicely. His is a *perverse* picturesque which consistently fails to separate an interest in the material object from an interest in the problem of materiality.

To that extent, it bears some resemblance to the idea of the 'formless' (*l'informe*) Georges Bataille put forward in the *Critical Dictionary* published in *Documents*, the ethnographic and surrealist journal he launched in 1929. The formless, in Bataille's usage, is not just a term for that which has lost its form. It is rather an act of declassing and declassification which brings objects down in the world by exposing their materiality: the perverse picturesque in action, a way to cross the line Price and others had painstakingly drawn between deformity and ugliness. 'To affirm . . . that the universe resembles nothing at all and is only *formless*,' Bataille wrote, 'amounts to saying that the universe is something akin to a spider or a gob of spittle.'[24] Or, perhaps, an abattoir, a factory for carcasses. In *L'Assommoir*

(1877), Gervaise Coupeau, reduced finally to prostitution ('Elle se moquait d'être la dernière des dernières, au fin fond du ruisseau'), passes a slaughterhouse in the process of demolition: a gap in the wall discloses 'des cours sombres, puantes, encore humide de sang' (R-M 2. 924, 937). The slaughterhouse merits an entry in the Critical Dictionary, accompanied by Eli Lotar's unflinching photographs of carcasses and sweepings of blood.[25]

Bataille's liking for the surreal reminds us that there was more than one version of the perverse picturesque around, in Paris in the 1920s and 1930s. In Naturalism, all is formless; but not all formlessness is in Naturalism. Even so, the Critical Dictionary does demonstrate the durability of a willingness to become absorbed in the absence of meaning and value. That absorption had been made durable by the Naturalist impulse. We must establish how.

Description

The picturesque established itself in Naturalist fiction by means of the elaborate descriptive passages, which were from the outset understood to constitute one of its most easily identifiable features. In the Rougon-Macquart novels, however, the picturesque mode is invariably shadowed by, and more often than not lapses into, something altogether harder to define. In Le Ventre de Paris (1873), for example, two distinct attitudes take shape to the abundance of provision on display at the new food markets built at the beginning of the Second Empire. As David Baguley has pointed out, the painter Claude Lantier 'provides aesthetic distance and is the vehicle for the presentation of each nature morte;' while his friend and companion Florent, an anorexic amateur insurrectionary, feels engulfed by an excess of matter (of food-stuff) which for him has neither meaning nor value.[26] Florent, we might say, finds himself already at the picturesque's internal representational limit. What marks that limit for him, as it had for Zola in front of Monet's Boats Leaving the Port of Le Havre, is an abrupt transition from sight to smell which abolishes distance. Claude Lantier had climbed on to a bench in order to survey and to celebrate the vegetable mountains. Florent, left alone, lingers by the butchers' stalls until the stench of meat convulses him. Towards the novel's end, he stands at the open window of his attic-room looking out over Les Halles, unable even at that height to escape the sickening stench of decayed matter (R-M 1. 583–8, 788–9). Lantier is Zola's pre-eminent flâneur; Florent we might think of as a nauséaste.

In Naturalist fiction, bad sights and worse smells do not necessarily require a nauséaste as vehicle. Writing in the Fortnightly Review in March 1892, Arthur Symons praised Huysmans for his ability to describe with elegant precision novel and unpleasant subjects, such as a cow's carcass.[27] A few years later, in a review of Huysmans's La Cathédrale (1898), Symons returned to his theme, remarking that the author had begun his career by developing so profound a mastery that he could 'describe the inside of a cow hanging in a butcher's shop as beautifully as if it were a casket of jewels.' Uvedale Price would no doubt have approved. Symons, however, went on to observe that the female protagonists of Huysmans's early Naturalist novels – *Marthe, histoire d'une fille* (1876), *La Fille Élisa* (1877), *Les Soeurs Vatard* (1879) – seem frequently to be dispatched on long walks during which 'they would have seen nothing but the arm on which they leant and the milliners' shops which they passed; and what they did not see [is] described, marvellously, in twenty pages.'[28] Here, too, the line drawn within picturesque theory between an interest in the problem of materiality and an interest in the material object has begun to blur; but for a different reason. The distance built into sight has been abolished, not by a foul odour, but by the removal of any mediating figure for whom the objects viewed might conceivably have a meaning and a value. Octave Mouret may glance through a half-open door, in *Pot-Bouille*; but the grey light falling on off-white linen is there for us, not for him. What sense are we to make of it? The moment or scene rendered by Zola's strange effect is utterly singular. It insists, but without expression. Like Nana's mask-like face in death, it signifies – barely.

Phobia

We might extend Lukács's commentary on the decline of the novel (above, pp. 21–2) by proposing that description unhinged from narrative is Naturalism's supplement to that art of observation which requires that the world observed yield an implicit or explicit meaning and a value, if not necessarily for those who inhabit it, then for those who observe them inhabiting it. Description unhinged from narrative is where Naturalism perverts the picturesque, itself an art of observation which, like narrative, or *as* narrative, must at all costs extract meaning and value out of existence. What, then, compels the Naturalist impulse to describe, and when it describes, always to declassify, to affirm that the universe 'resembles nothing at all and is only *formless*'? I want to invoke as a context for that compulsion to describe the emergence in the 1870s of the psychiatric category of phobia. When the physician Édouard Toulouse undertook an enquiry into the nature of genius, in 1896, he chose Zola as his subject; and duly took note, during the course of an exhaustive programme of physical and psychological tests, of his subject's phobias.[29]

On the whole, phobia triggers fear rather than nausea; but neither in the psychiatry nor in the literature of the period was an absolute distinction made between them. Naturalist fears are often nauseous, and its nauseas fearful. A brief account of what Zola and Huysmans did with fear of contamination (an incipient nausea) will demonstrate how they adapted the picturesque to an enquiry into the insistence of the real in and as formlessness. In Naturalist fiction, the fear of contamination measures identity. Zola maintained that the family group at the centre of the Rougon-

Macquart novels has as its prime characteristic a perpetual 'overflow of appetite' into increasingly pathological pleasures.[30] Desire impels it. Zola measured the force of that appetite, not against the countervailing forces of social convention or moral self-awareness, as most other nineteenth-century novelists would have done, but against phobia. Desire defines identity as and when it overcomes the fear of contamination: a fear which is also the knowledge of mortality. The triviality of the objects of that fear is the scandal Naturalism stirred up against the novel as a genre. It is scandalous that there should be nothing left to oppose to appetite except the nausea provoked by the taste (or smell, or touch) of contingency.[31]

Nobody in Naturalist fiction does more to provoke an overflow of appetite than the actress and prostitute Nana. The poem of male desires, Zola called the novel in which she features. Nana conquers and destroys Parisian high society, ruining all the men who fall under her spell, and to most spectacular effect of all the wealthy and respectable Count Muffat, Chamberlain to the Empress. In theory, the barrier over which Muffat's insatiable appetite for Nana flows is that erected by rigid devotional practices and a consistent adherence to law and precept. In fact, all that holds him back is phobia. Of course, a fear of moral contamination is the fuel on which a strict adherence to law and precept customarily runs. Muffat's nausea, however, is physical; and its various objects striking in their triviality. Desire troubles him profoundly because it entails a perpetual submission to contingency understood as death-in-life. The most persevering among Nana's many lovers are the oldest.

Muffat, Nana's protector, and effectively her pimp, suffers more than most. Every time he enters her bedroom he has to open the window so as to flush out the body-smells of the men who have been there before him. On the threshold, an ineradicable blood-stain marks the spot of a suicide-attempt. For the most part, Nana's lovers disregard the stain, taking away a small part of it on their shoes when they leave. Muffat, by contrast, dreads the sight of it, and always steps over it out of a sudden panic that he might crush something alive ('par une crainte brusque d'écraser quelque chose de vivant, un membre nu étalée par terre'). This hesitation is phobic. Once over the threshold, in Nana's presence, desire takes control again ('un vertige le grisait'), and the stain is forgotten. Forgotten, momentarily, but not erased; for this 'age-mark' shown up by the descriptive intensity of Zola's perverse picturesque remains a good deal more vivid than the lives and loves of the men who pass it by without a glance. Zola insists that Muffat's phobic dreads are at once particular (his rivals do not share them) and general (they could perfectly well arise in contexts other than the reckless sexual pursuit of a blonde Venus). When Muffat climbs the stairs to Nana's dressing-room in the theatre, he is forcefully reminded of the tenement houses seen during tours of inspection undertaken as a member of a Charity Committee. A filthy room glimpsed through an open door looks like a barber's shop in a poor district, with its two chairs, mirror, and dressing-table blackened by the grease from combs (*R-M* 3. 316, 128). As so often in Naturalist description, the glimpse through a half-open door is as much for our benefit as for the protagonist's. Reference to the discourse of slumming has generalized Muffat's nausea.

It is worth noting just how far down into formlessness Naturalism's perverse picturesque went in its specification of the phobic object. The threshold of disgust across which Nana's ancient admirers must pass is never more apparent than when, seated in front of the mirror in her dressing-room, she applies cold-cream to her face and arms (*R-M* 3. 120–1). It is cold-cream, rather than boredom or remorse, which brings to an end the revivifying affair enjoyed by the protagonist of Huysmans's *En Ménage* (1881), who cannot get over his discovery in the bathroom of a comb full of hair and, in a heap of dirty linen, a face-cloth greasy with cold-cream ('graissée de cold-cream').[32] It would scarcely be possible to find a more vivid example of the disproportion between stimulus and response in phobia. The cold-cream is all the more obdurate, all that more of an impediment to desire, on account of its banality. It insists: and not least by its survival as an English expression in a French text.

In Naturalist fiction, then, description supplements narrative through-out. Its felt preponderance commits that discourse as a whole to supplementarity. The discourse must be perpetually in excess of realism, or it is nothing at all. Within Naturalist description, the phobic picturesque flaunts its own excesses: of touch, sound, and smell over sight; of disregard for focalization. The phobic picturesque operates both in close relation to narrative, as that which defines the threshold of disgust a character must cross in pursuit of her or his desire, and somewhat apart from it, as that which just happens to catch the reader's eye (and perhaps no-one else's). In *L'Assommoir*, the stench emanating from the dirty linen heaped in the laundry run by Gervaise Coupeau beautifully renders the ineradicable ordinariness of existence. The passionate embrace Gervaise and her husband enjoy 'au milieu des saletés du métier' takes them decisively across the threshold of disgust; it is their first 'fall', the first slackening ('avachissement') of many. The laundry's ordinariness also gives rise to unmotivated effects. Gervaise's admirer Goujet often hangs out there, attentive to her every movement, then lapsing into reverie, until we notice what he no longer can: the light from the open door falling into the street like a piece of yellow cloth unrolled across the ground (*R-M* 2. 729, 735). This strange effect is for our benefit alone.

It is no simple matter to explain the function of the reality effects encountered again and again in the Rougon-Macquart novels, either as narrative threshold or at random, by means of description: the matted grey light, the foul invasive odours, the stains and grease-marks. What, if anything, do these encounters reveal? Jean-Paul Sartre was to insist that the nausea induced by slime, or viscosity, is the very 'taste' of being itself, the very taste of contingency.[33] Despite (or because of) its overt commitment to determinism, Naturalist fiction delivers a new understanding of contingency: of that which might or might not happen, and by its utter unpredictability challenges our capacity to comprehend and shape experience. How? By articulating the disproportion between stimulus and response built into phobia.

In *La Bête humaine* (1890), Zola's rumbustuous tale of sex, murder, and rolling-stock, deputy station-master Roubaud sticks his hand beneath the floor-boards to retrieve the money he has stashed away there. At the bottom of the hole, he feels (or thinks he feels) a dampness, something whose soft texture revolts him: 'une humidité, quelque chose de mou et de nauséabond, dont il eut horreur' (*R-M* 5. 200). Roubaud has reason enough to feel queasy. The larger part of the stash consists of a thousand francs taken from the body of the wealthy magistrate Grandmorin, whom he had stabbed to death (in a railway-carriage, of course) a month or so previously, after discovering that his wife Séverine first had sex with the man at the age of sixteen. The stash has been a source of ghostly horror ever since. He only plans to retrieve some of the money now because the gambling-habit, which has superseded sexual obsession, leaves him with no choice. But the provocation to nausea is no ghost. The notes taken from Grandmorin's body have long since dried out. They cannot be the something damp and soft Roubaud touches. Roubaud's disgust exists wholly in the present. It is an ordinary feeling, not about ghosts, not traumatic.

We all know what it is like to put a hand unexpectedly on something damp and soft in a dark place. We all know that the intensity of the feeling is in no way diminished by the discovery that the object we have put a hand on is in itself quite harmless. The touch seems to lay bare existence itself, or our relation to existence. The ordinariness thus exposed is a *radical* ordinariness, at once particular and universal. It goes to the root of lived experience, to that which is and must always remain fundamental to it. Radical ordinariness is what phobia knows. Trauma has to do with that which disturbs beyond description; phobia with that which disturbs, and yet can be described.

Radical ordinariness is what stuck in George Orwell's mind, after he had gone down a coal-mine in order to write *The Road to Wigan Pier* (1937), as Zola had in order to write *Germinal* (1885). 'The first time I was watching the "fillers" at work,' Orwell wrote, 'I put my hand upon some dreadful slimy thing among the coal dust. It was a chewed quid of tobacco.'[34] The purpose of Orwell's descent into the mine was to turn capitalism upside down, and so reveal the exploitation sustaining it. He badly wanted to get to the bottom of things. But what *is* the bottom of things? I don't suppose that Orwell had pre-eminently in mind the venerable philosophical meaning of 'quid': that which a thing is, its quiddity. His text is none the less an invitation to think in those terms. There is more Sartre to it than Marx, perhaps. Orwell could have become the English Zola.[35] Like Zola, he found in nausea a provocation to politics.

Screening Naturalism

It would be possible to argue, I think, that the Naturalist impulse in literature did outlast Naturalism understood as a literary movement, both in America, where Naturalism has always been regarded as an important point of reference, and in Britain, where it has not; and that the impulse has quite consistently taken the shape of a phobic picturesque. My claim here, however, will be that the phobic picturesque left its mark most substantially, and with the greatest consequences, on cinema; rather than on literature, or indeed on the visual arts.[36]

Norris's *McTeague* (1899), which includes one of the first accounts in fiction of a visit to the movies, is at once thoroughly Zolaesque in its enquiry into *la bête humaine* and ready-made for a phobic cinematography intent on over-adherence to the real, which it duly got, in the shape of Erich von Stroheim's *Greed* (1924). The stench of dirty linen constitutes the threshold of disgust Gervaise Coupeau and her husband cross, in their desire for each other, in *L'Assommoir*. In *McTeague*, a landscape of mud flat, rubbish dump, and gas works which forms the backdrop to the excursion during which Trina and McTeague 'grossly' enjoy their first full embrace. In both cases, the crossing constitutes an irreversible fall. Like Zola, Norris took great care to describe in intricate detail the *saletés* Trina and McTeague are too busy to notice. 'Across the railroad tracks, to seaward, one saw the long stretch of black mud bank left bare by the tide, which was far out, nearly half a mile.'[37]

Graham Greene very much admired the equivalent scene in *Greed*, which outdoes the grimness of the original by locating McTeague's courtship of Trina beside a sewer (with the further embellishment of a close-up of a drowned rat). Greene became a fan of 1930s French poetic realism, and in particular of the moments in it during which contingency obtrudes. He thought that the best scene in Duvivier's *Un Carnet de bal* (1937) was one involving the performance of an illegal operation. 'Nostalgia, sentiment, regret: the padded and opulent emotions wither before the evil detail.'[38] Evil detail is detail rendered by the phobic picturesque. It was the cultivation of evil detail in the cinema of the 1920s and 1930s (not just von Stroheim, but Eisenstein, Hitchcock, Von Sternberg, and others) which gave substance to Jean Renoir's remark that realism in film was a child of the Naturalist school. These were not 'Naturalist' film-makers.[39] But they knew all there was to be known about the phobic picturesque.

As Dudley Andrew notes, Renoir's close family ties to Zola and Paul Cézanne encouraged him to aspire to a career as a writer in the Naturalist mould. 'When it came to developing a narrative cinema that would be social, realist, popular, and artistically innovative, he unhesitatingly turned to Zola as source and model, selling some of his father's canvases to make *Nana*.'[40] Accounts of that film tend to stress its differences from the novel as much as its similarities.[41] But it seems to me that Renoir went to considerable lengths to preserve (and indeed improve upon) Zola's evil detail.

The most notable example is the scene in which Muffat first waits on Nana in her dressing-room in the theatre. Nana is amply supplied with staff, and Muffat at first feels at something of a loss as maid and hairdresser go about their business, which seems largely to consist of gossip. His glance falls on a basin full of dirty water, and then on a broken comb clogged with hair (figs. 1–4). When Nana asks for the comb, Muffat, with a faint smile on his face, picks it up, carefully removes the excess hair, and hands it to her. Neither the bowl nor the comb is in Zola (though the latter, as we've seen, is in Huysmans). But Renoir has undoubtedly found a way to reproduce Zola's insistence on the obtrusion of formlessness in the world Nana so vividly inhabits. In the film as in the novel, an age-mark or material remnant represents the phobic limit Muffat's overflow of appetite will carry him across: a limit more effective than social convention or moral scruple, but nothing like effective enough.

Like von Stroheim's drowned rat, the bowl and the comb are shown in close-up. The technique of 'monstrous enlargement' had always fascinated Renoir.[42] Enlargement was, of course, a technique put to many and varied uses in the cinema of the period, by no means all of them conducive to the Naturalist impulse.[43] But it certainly suited the phobic picturesque. Like phobia, the close-up perversely singles out something to be afraid of, or disgusted by. Like phobia, it blows that which is in itself trivial or harmless up out of all proportion: the bowl of water, the filthy comb, the drowned rat. Radical ordinariness is what the close-up knows. Cinema's automatism, its capacity to see the world as human beings do not see it, could even be said

Figure 1   His glance falls.

Figure 2   on a basin full of dirty water.

Figure 3   and then

to exacerbate and thus to draw attention to the asymmetry between stimulus and response which constitutes phobia's canniness. What the close-up yields, by cutting the object out of any identifiable environment, is precisely too much presence. The close-up does phobia's ontological thinking for it.

Renoir's enduring preoccupation with Naturalism is evident in his adaptations of Flaubert (*Madame Bovary*, 1933), Gorki (*Les Bas-Fonds*, 1936), and Zola again (*La Bête humaine*, 1938).[44] Equally evident, of course, is his

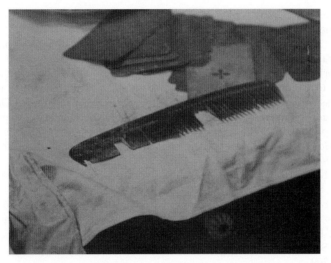

Figure 4   on a broken comb

enduring preoccupation with the picturesque. Naturalism enabled him to work both within and against the picturesque, through phobia's fixated disclosures of radical ordinariness. Boudu seen through a telescope, as he makes his way along the Seine embankment, is the perfect tramp, just what's needed to complete the picture. Boudu brought home, Boudu up close, belligerent, priapic, and stinking, is something else altogether; though, unlike Nana or McTeague, he keeps his charm.

Notes

1   *Mists of Regret: Culture and Sensibility in Classic French Film* (Princeton: Princeton University Press, 1995), 302; citing Renoir, 'Jean Renoir et le réalisme au cinéma', *Ciné-Revue*, 2 December 1955, 12.

2   *Le Roman expérimental* (Paris: Éditions du Sandre, 2003), 15–16; 'The Experimental Novel', in George Becker, ed., *Documents of Modern Literary Realism* (Princeton, NJ: Princeton University Press, 1963), 162–96, p. 166.

3   The case made by Michel Serres to the effect that Zola's Rougon-Macquart cycle is structured throughout in accordance with contemporary scientific theory remains a powerful one: *Feux et signaux de brume: Zola* (Paris: Grasset, 1975). For Serres, however, scientific method has its own supplement, or 'residue', in these novels: the constant re-formulation of mythical 'vignettes' or 'emblems' (bridge, well, labyrinth). See also 'Language & Space: from Oedipus to Zola', in *Hermes: Literature, Science, Philosophy*, ed. and trans. Josué V. Harari and David F. Bell (Baltimore: Johns Hopkins University Press, 1982), 39–53, esp. p. 40. Zola's mythical sensibility had already been examined in considerable detail by Jean Borie, in *Zola et les mythes: ou de la nausée au salut* (Paris: Seuil, 1970).

4   'Zola as a Romantic Writer', reprinted in *Novels and Essays* (New York: Library of America, 1986), 1106–8, pp. 1107–8.

5   Ibid., 1108. This lowering constitutes what David Baguley has termed Naturalism's 'entropic vision': *Naturalist Fiction: The Entropic Vision* (Cambridge: Cambridge University Press, 1990). The ordure in *Les Misérables*, by contrast, is there to exemplify the 'mystery of creation', which transforms productive process into waste and waste back into productive process. See David Pike, 'Sewage Treatments: Vertical Space and Waste in Nineteenth-Century Paris and London', in William A. Cohen and Ryan Johnson, eds., *Filth: Dirt, Disgust, and Modern Life* (Minneapolis: University of Minnesota Press, 2005), 51–77, pp. 59–61.

6   'Mon Salon', in *Écrits sur l'art*, ed. Jean-Pierre Leduc-Adine (Paris: Gallimard, 1991), 191–228.

7   *Thérèse Raquin*, ed. Philippe Hamon (Paris: Presses Pocket, 1991), 261–6; *Thérèse Raquin*, ed. and trans. Andrew Rothwell (Oxford: Oxford University Press, 1992), 1–6.

8   'Mon Salon', 208–9

9   Ibid., 209.

10   Ibid., 199.

11   *Les Rougon-Macquart*, ed. Colette Becker, 5 volumes (Paris: Éditions Robert Laffont, 1991–3), 3. 410. Henceforth *R-M*.

12   *The Picturesque: Studies in a Point of View* (London: Frank Cass, 1967), 11, 84.

13   *Essays on the Picturesque*, 3 vols. (Farnborough: Gregg International Publishers, 1971), 1. 50–1, 25, 80–3, 63.

14   *Works*, edited by E.T. Cook and Alexander Wedderburn, 39 volumes (London, Longmans, Green, 1907), 3. 207, 11.

15   Simon Pugh, 'Loitering with Intent: from Arcadia to the Arcades', in Pugh, ed., *Reading Landscape: Country – City – Capital* (Manchester: Manchester University Press, 1990), 145–60.

16   Seth Koven, *Slumming: Sexual and Social Politics in Victorian London* (Princeton, NJ: Princeton University Press, 2004), 9.

17   Carrie Tirado Bramen, 'William Dean Howells and the Failure of the Urban Picturesque', *New England Quarterly*, 73.1, 2000, 82–99.

18   Cited in Dorothy Norman, *Alfred Stieglitz: An American Seer* (New York: Random House, 1973), 39.

19   Alan Trachtenberg, *Reading American Photographs: Images as History* (New York: Hill and Wang, 1989), 183–9.

20   *Impressions and Experiences* (New York: Harper & Brothers, 1909): 205.

21   *Essays*, 3. 315–16.

22   John Macarthur, 'The Butcher's Shop: Disgust in Picturesque Aesthetics and Architecture', *Assemblage*, 30, 1996, 32–43, pp. 34–6.

23   *Essays*, 1. 188, 315–17.

24   'Formless', in *Encyclopaedia Acephalica*, edited by Alexander Brotchie, translated by Iain White (London, Atlas Press, 1995), 51–2.

25   'Slaughterhouse', in *Encyclopaedia Acephalica*, 72–4.

26   *Naturalist Fiction*, 193–4.

27   'J.-K. Huysmans', *Fortnightly Review*, 51, 1892, 402–14, p. 404. The description he had in mind occurs in 'Claudine', one of the sketches included in *Le Drageoir aux Epices*, ed. Patrice Locmant (Paris: H. Champion, 2003), 99–107, p. 101.

Huysmans was in fact describing Rembrandt's *Slaughtered Ox*, rather than anything he'd actually seen on a city street.

28 *Saturday Review*, 12 February 1898, available at http://www.huysmans.org/cathrev/cathrev4.htm; accessed 03.04.08.

29 *Enquête medico-pschychologique sur la supériorité intellectuelle: Émile Zola* (Paris: Flammarion, 1910), 260.

30 'On the Rougon-Macquart Series', in George Becker, ed., *Documents of Modern Literary Realism* (Princeton: Princeton University Press, 1963), 160–1, p. 161.

31 In some brilliant pages on whiteness in the Rougon-Macquart novels, Serres demonstrates that for some of Zola's protagonists the desire for purification is as strong as any other: *Feux et signaux de brume*, 217–25. The scandal is precisely that it should be a desire like any other, and all too often extinguishable. One December night, Florent looks out of his window to see the roof of Les Halles covered in snow 'd'une blancheur vierge' (*R-M* 1. 788). But the snow melts, and the stench rises. Florent is a purist protected from the world's temptations both by agoraphobia and by the traumatic memory of the death of a young woman in a riot.

32 *Oeuvres completes*, ed. Lucien Descaves, 18 vols. (Paris: G. Crès, 1928–34), 4. 211.

33 *Being and Nothingness*, trans. Hazel E. Barnes (London: Routledge, 1969), 604–15.

34 *The Road to Wigan Pier* (Harmondsworth: Penguin Books, 1989), 20–1. *Germinal* features the apparently limitless supplies of coal-blackened phlegm torn by racking coughs from the throat of a miner called Bonnemort and deposited in the nearest container (*R-M* 4. 29: 377).

35 When he was trying to establish himself as a writer in London in the early 1930s, he frequently offered to review or translate Zola, or indeed any fiction of a Naturalist bent: *Collected Essays, Journalism and Letters*, ed. Sonia Orwell and Ian Angus, 4 volumes (Harmondsworth: Penguin, 1970), 1. 55: 97, 102.

36 Though Julian Bell has briefly sketched a counter-history to turn-of-the-century chromophilia involving 'down-in-the-mouth colourists' like Walter Sickert, William Orpen, and Edward Hopper, and productive ultimately of an 'hegemony of the hueless': 'Eye Candy', *London Review of Books*, 19 July 2007, 7–8. See also David Batchelor, *Chromophobia* (London: Reaktion Books, 2000).

37 *McTeague: A Story of San Francisco*, ed. Jerome Loving (Oxford: Oxford University Press, 1995), 10–11, 66–8.

38 'The Province of the Film: Past Mistakes and Future Hopes', *Times*, 9 April 1928, in *Mornings in the Dark: The Graham Greene Film Reader* (Manchester: Carcanet, 1993), 387–90, p. 389; review of *Un Carnet de Bal* and *Underworld*, *Night and Day*, 9 December 1937, in *Mornings*: 242–4, p. 243.

39 Gilles Deleuze does not discriminate sufficiently in designating as Naturalism's 'heirs' Griffith, von Stroheim, Bunuel, and Renoir: Introduction to *La Bête humaine*, in Zola, *Oeuvres completes*, 15 vols., ed. Henri Mitterand (Paris: Cercle du livre précieux, 1962–1969), 6. 18–19. Lea Jacobs's important discussion of literary naturalism's influence on the way stories came to be told on film quite rightly places substantial emphasis on von Stroheim and von Sternberg, concluding that 'by the late 1920s naturalism provided the framework for most serious, intellectually ambitions filmmaking within the classical Hollywood cinema': *The Decline of Sentiment: American Film in the 1920s* (Berkeley: University of California Press, 2008), 77.

40 *Mists of Regret*, 301. Zola's novels have been adapted over and over again. The 'Select Filmography' provided in Anna Gural-Migdal and Robert Singer, eds.,

Zola and Film: Essays in the Art of Adaptation (Jefferson, N.C.: McFarland, 2005) includes 89 items in all: 33 of these films were made between 1902 and 1920, and a further 22 between 1921 and 1945. And see Leo Braudy, 'Zola on Film: The Ambiguities of Naturalism', in *Native Informant: Essays on Film, Fiction, and Popular Culture* (Oxford: Oxford University Press, 1991), 95–106.

41   Alexander Sesonske, *Jean Renoir: The French Films, 1924–1939* (Cambridge, Mass.: Harvard University Press, 1980), ch. 2; Heather Howard, 'Staging the Courtesan: Taking Zola's *Nana* to the Movies', in Anna Gural-Migdal and Robert Singer, eds., *Zola and Film: Essays in the Art of Adaptation* (Jefferson, NC: McFarland & Company, 2005), 45–61.

42   *My Life and My Films*, trans. Norman Denny (London: Collins, 1974): 52. For an illuminating account of the pivotal role the close-up has played in film theory, see Mary Ann Doane, 'The Close-Up: Scale and Detail in the Cinema', *Differences: A Journal of Feminist Cultural Studies*, 14.3, 2003, 89–111.

43   See, for example, Luis Bunuel, 'The Cinematic Shot', in *An Unspeakable Betrayal: Selected Writings*, trans. Garrett White (Berkeley, CA: University of California Press, 1995), 125–30.

44   For a lucid account of this continuing fascination, see Andrew, *Mists of Regret*, 298–317. On Naturalist *bas-fondmanie*, see Yves Chevrel, *Le Naturalisme* (Paris: PUF, 1982), 98.

4

Feminist Phobia

This essay is dedicated to the simple proposition that women writers have consistently found a use for phobic feeling. It builds in part on previous work in which my topic was the framing of identity through the self-conscious performance of gender in fiction and memoirs published from the 1890s to the 1920s.[1] The emphasis here will be on the potency of the feelings that any kind of performance of the feminine had on occasion to overcome, in Britain during the Edwardian period: feelings, in large part, about patriarchy. Those often nauseous feelings had themselves to be performed self-consciously, in order that their overcoming might not merely result in yet further submission. The feminism at issue is that concern with education, and with the economic and sexual emancipation of women inside and outside marriage, which found a vivid literary focus in the New Woman novels of the 1890s, and their successors, the 'marriage problem' novels of the 1900s and after.[2] My brief, in short, is to uncover the *nauséaste* in the narrator of some of Katherine Mansfield's stories. However, because I believe these feelings to have been socially induced, and thus by implication political in their performance, I begin with two mid-nineteenth century female philanthropists: philanthropy having become by 1860 a means of emancipation for middle-class women, inside or outside marriage.[3]

Some Brothels

In October 1863, a Mission Hall and Soldiers' Institute opened for business in Aldershot, in Hampshire. Aldershot was and is a military town, and in the 1860s it boasted a plentiful supply of souls in need of saving. Some of those souls belonged to the prostitutes who had long been the inevitable concomitant of a standing army. In 1864, the men who ran the Institute's Refuge Committee organized a series of midnight meetings during which strenuous efforts were made to convince these 'outcast women' of the error of their ways. Sarah Robinson, a young woman who worked at the Institute, saw at once that such meetings were next to useless. The motives which prompted outcast women to attend them did not, for the most part, include an overwhelming urge to be cast back in again. Robinson wanted to try a different approach. 'I shut myself up for some hours to pray and think it over,' she recalled in her autobiography, *A Life Record* (1898), 'until my own course, at least, seemed clear, *to go into the girls' own rooms*.'⁴ She meant to be public in private, to reform discreetly.

We know how and to what effect Robinson went into the girls' own rooms both from her own account, and from the account given by Ellice Hopkins, whom she met in 1868 in Portsmouth, where they established a Soldiers' Home, and who subsequently became known in her own right as a resourceful and indefatigable rescue worker.⁵ Robinson's account centres, as so much of the nineteenth-century social reform and slum-visiting literature did, on a rite of initiation: on the revelatory, life-changing moment of encounter between philanthropy's subject and its object. What feelings were at play, on the philanthropist's part, in that encounter?⁶

'Most of the girls were in their beds,' Robinson observed of her first foray into an Aldershot brothel, 'and on the whole received me kindly; but, after a long morning's visiting, I had to hurry back to my room, and for over an hour was violently sick' (*LR* 137–8). As so often in the social reform literature, nausea, at once a gut-feeling and a thesis about the irreparability of the human predicament, configures the philanthropic encounter. The rhetorical function it serves is to establish the philanthropist's singularity as a social being or social performer. The nausea felt by the philanthropist sets her or him apart both from the lower-class men and women whose behaviour has induced it, and from the upper-class men and women who have never known anything like it. 'I could not write the things I saw and heard,' Robinson said, 'and prayed to *forget* them.' The need to forget sights and sounds which cannot be forgotten both impedes philanthropy and in some sense keeps it going. The singularity's the thing. And few things singularize like nausea. To feel nausea was in effect to cease to feel as a pious young woman entering an army brothel might have been expected to feel: ignorant, curious, afraid. Robinson's account of the philanthropic encounter passes rapidly through, or over, any intimidation she may have felt.

> The biggest public-houses owned whole blocks of buildings, each room accommodating two girls, some living luxuriously, others miserably poor, from fourteen years of age up to thirty; some fearfully diseased, unable to leave their beds, supported by the kindness of others. (*LR* 138)

Robinson rather admirably sets aside the figure of the prostitute, discovering in its place individual women with ambitions and dilemmas of their own. Singularized herself by nausea, she is on the look-out for singularity in others. Fearlessness followed by vomiting (followed by a resumption of fearlessness) connects public to private self in ways that weren't otherwise readily conceivable for middle-class women in mid-nineteenth century Britain. The vomit tells her that it is she, and not someone else, who has gone into the girls' own rooms. She needs it, just as the agoraphobe needs a disabling dizziness as well as a re-enabling uniform in order to get across the public square in his or her own way.

In both cases, the feeling is always already social in that it derives from changes in the understanding of public and private space. According to Ellice Hopkins, at the time when Robinson began her work in Aldershot, the prostitutes 'herded together in colonies, as many as a hundred inhabiting a row of small tenements, all communicating with one another internally, by means of passages, and named after the public-house which generally formed the corner house; a state of things which I am thankful to say no longer exists.'[7] Hopkins apprehends, or imagines, something elided in Robinson's account: the den, the row of tenements communicating with one another internally by a passage. This passage evidently fascinated her. In *Active Service: or, Work Among Our Soldiers*, a book written in order to raise money for the Soldiers' Home at Portsmouth, Hopkins further reported that when Robinson began her work in Aldershot the prostitutes 'used to congregate in colonies of 70 to 100 together, occupying whole courts or large blocks of buildings named after the public-house that owned them, and threaded on the inside by long intricate passages connecting the whole.'[8] In Hopkins's eyes, it is the passage threading the tenements together on the inside which makes the space of the brothel utterly distinctive: a space like no other, a labyrinth, a den. We might almost be in Kafka's burrow.[9] There is a literary imagination at work here: an imagination intent on a 'poetics of space'.[10] This imagination does not engage in reverie.[11] Rather, it bears directly on historical circumstance. The space Hopkins has delineated is also a time: a 'state of things' which thankfully no longer exists. Her imagination works with, and in, history. We need to conceive it historically.

Martin Daunton has described how the steep rise in the price of urban land between the 1780s and the 1810s led to a more economical use of the space available. The existing built-up area – notably the courtyards at the rear of houses on the main streets – was exploited ever more intensively through in-filling and sub-division. Developments on the edge of towns and cities reproduced the pattern prevailing in the central districts. 'The result,' Daunton concludes, 'was a promiscuous sharing of facilities in the private domain of the house, a cellular quality of space in the public domain, and a threshold between public and private which was ambiguous and permeable.'[12] Friedrich Engels, writing about Manchester in 1844, found it virtually impossible to convey to his readers the idea of the 'tangle' of dwellings created by this kind of layout.[13] Such was the space Ellice Hopkins imagined Sarah Robinson entering in Aldershot in 1863.

During the course of the nineteenth century, Daunton observes, the 'cellular' layout of these courts, which made it difficult to distinguish between public and private space, gave way to a 'more open texture'. Individual dwellings were sealed off into privacy, while the public domain became a neutral space, or 'connective tissue' made sterile and anonymous.

The threshold between public and private had been redrawn in such a way as to render it less permeable. The change arose in part at least from a concern for public order, for cellularity was a threat at once to hygiene and to respectability. It opened up the city, Daunton observes, 'in order to make it visible for inspection.'[14] In Richard Sennett's terms, the aim was to 'purify' or to 'suburbanize' space, both in new inner-city developments and in the suburbs themselves, and so define it as entirely functional.[15] Baron Haussmann was shortly to realize that aim to spectacular effect in his restructuring of Paris. In Aldershot, in 1863, Sarah Robinson could be thought to have entered not just a space, but a time. The disambiguation enforced by the recent opening up of the city had made the brothel – this domain held between the public and the private, between commerce and domesticity – doubly fascinating. It was there, or rather in going to and fro between different spaces and different times, between the good new open city and the bad old closed city, that one might become independent. Such are the uses to which disorder – and, I would add, phobia – can be put.

Robinson's success in the brothels of Aldershot persuaded Hopkins to try the same tactics in the brothels of Brighton; and she, too, had her rite of initiation, her nauseating rebuff. On her first visit, everything seemed to be going well. She engaged a group of women in earnest discussion, eventually persuading them to kneel and pray with her. Leaving them, she felt that she had at least made an impression. 'The door had not been closed two seconds behind me, as I left, when I heard shrieks of horrid laughter from all four, and fragments of indecent jests, which I in vain strove not to hear.' She went home 'literally bruised and bleeding'. It is worth noting that bricks and mortar played a large part in her conception of the brutal rebuff she had been dealt. She felt, she wrote, as though she had just dashed herself against a 'dead wall'. 'My prayer seemed to have gone no higher than the ceiling' (*VD* 11).

What these metaphors indicate is a considerable investment on Hopkins's part in the poetics of space: an investment which, given its scope and durability, we might even suspect of yielding pleasure. It is the act of entering the labryinth which engrosses her. This is a visitation manual, a how-to book. 'Having fixed upon the house to be visited, do not knock at the front door any more than you would in visiting a public-house, but go boldly in and knock at the door of one of the upstair rooms' (*VD* 18–19). What is engrossing about the brothel is that it is a domain in which the distinction between public and private has not yet been stabilized, set firmly in place. Do not knock at the front door, Hopkins advises, but boldly go in. The boldness, as of a person entering a public-house, was the performance which subdued nausea: subdued it, that is, by acknowledging it.

The going to and fro really made itself felt when the difference in outlook to be negotiated was social as well as moral. A fascinating footnote in *The Visitation of Dens* indicates that the rescue workers did not yet quite know what to do when it came to the 'upper class' of brothel: the kind, that is, which boasted a lockable front door and a servant to open and close it. In such establishments the boundary between public and private had been set at the entrance to the building, and rendered relatively impermeable by protocol. Here one could not go boldly in. The solution Hopkins proposes is an even more deliberate and structured resort to class identity. 'I should suggest all the formalities of a regular call being observed; to dress in one's very best, and to send up one's card, having, if possible, obtained the name, but if not, asking for the lady of the house, and stating that one calls on business' (*VD* 19–20). For the philanthropist, there might well have been a gain, here, in the resumption of formalities. Hopkins and her fellow-workers would no doubt have preferred to dress in their very best. But the gain would also be a loss, I suspect: a loss of the occasion to go boldly in. Different performances yielded different kinds of gratification. In each case, however, gratification must surely have derived from the overcoming of that nausea which set the rescue worker apart from conformity to middle-class attitudes and habits. Rescue work had to be performed among the lowest of the low, and Hopkins knew that it required a self-lowering. 'If you are content to go to this work in the ordinary prayerful frame of mind in which we go into our districts,' she wrote, 'you will be simply paralysed by the evil around you. This work has emphatically to be done on the knees' (17–18). To get down emphatically on your knees, whether to pray or to vomit, was also emphatically to prepare to raise yourself up: to put on a uniform, or grasp an umbrella, in order to cross an empty space, or enter a labyrinth.

Towards Naturalism

In May 1861, a painting in a London gallery provoked a sharp disagreement between two visitors. The visitors were George Eliot, and the writer and political economist Harriet Martineau. The painting depicted a stork killing a toad. Martineau thought it coarse and troublingly amoral. Eliot defended it, on the grounds that art should show the world as it is, rather than as it ought to be.[16] As we saw in Chapter 2, she was subsequently to make brilliant use of phobic and mysophobic response in her fiction to articulate the (by no means insuperable) intellectual and emotional weaknesses afflicting young middle-class women. Oddly enough, in view of the stork/toad *contretemps*, Martineau must count as an important precursor, in this respect, having followed up her *Illustrations of Political Economy* (1832–4) and *Society in America* (1837) with *Deerbrook* (1839), a novel grittily attentive to force of circumstance.[17] The grittiness did not let up, from the 1860s onwards, as more and more women took up social investigation and reform, and as new models of literary realism gained currency.

Beatrice Webb (or Potter, as she then was) joined the Soho Committee of the Charity Organization Society (founded 1869) in April 1883, and in

December 1884 agreed to manage Katherine Buildings, which the East End Dwellings Company had built to house casual labourers and their families, with Ella Pycroft, a country doctor's daughter. She had to abandon her occupation as a rent collector in November 1885, when her father suffered a stroke, and the following year began work as an assistant to Charles Booth, who was laying the foundations for his massive sociological study of London life and labour. Potter's conversion from social work to social enquiry, and her subsequent advocacy of state and municipal socialism, was in large measure a reaction against her experiences as a COS visitor and rent collector. She objected to the emphasis on discipline and surveillance. The COS never granted assistance without prior investigation; a visitor was sent to interview each family, and a case report drawn up. A committee made the final decision. Form 28, carried by all COS visitors, declared that help was only available to those who sought to help themselves. 'Persons of drunken, immoral or idle habits cannot expect to be assisted unless they can satisfy the committee that they are really trying to reform.'[18] The intention was to abolish indiscriminate alms-giving. The effect, Potter complained, was to transform charity-workers into 'amateur detectives'. The COS had failed to learn the lesson learnt by the great sanitary reformer Edwin Chadwick when, in the 1840s, he abandoned his long-running campaign to distinguish the respectable from the unrespectable poor, and began instead to advocate 'positive municipal action in the provision of drainage, paving, water supply, open spaces, improved dwellings, hospitals and what not'.[19]

Potter and Pycroft kept a 'record' of the inhabitants of Katherine Buildings, in which they logged basic information (employment, number of children, dates of arrival and departure, etc.) and explanatory remarks (the reasons for terminating a lease). The record shows Form 28, as it were, in action: an unceasing effort to discriminate the deserving from the undeserving. It also shows how phobic response, when not acknowledged as such, can serve both to sharpen and to intensify forms of social discrimination. A phrase which crops up again and again is 'clean and apparently respectable'. Sometimes the bad sorts were easy to spot. Abraham Morris, a Jewish taylor with a disabled and 'disgustingly dirty' wife, did not last long. 'Room in filthy condition & children uncared for & half starved. Constantly in arrears. Neighbours complained of number of animals kept & smells. Gave them notice to quit – forced them to leave by threat of distraint.' The entry stops short of outright moral condemnation. But the dirt and the stench do seem to have added up, in Potter's eyes, to something more than a failure to pay the rent. These are metonymies poised on the edge of metaphor. Mrs Morris's dirt eclipses the disablement which may well have contributed to it. Keeping animals was always likely to get you into trouble, in Katherine Buildings. One woman, whose husband was a clerk in the Tower of London, brought some bantams back from a visit to Ireland. She promised to send the bantams to the Tower, but instead sent them to the back room, where they disgustingly occupied a washstand.

Her mistake, perhaps, was to create an opportunity for metaphor: animals on the floor bespeak necessity, animals on a washstand innate brutishness. 'Rough, coarse woman, very well to do – Didn't like to be honest.' So *they* had to go, even if they did pay the rent on time. Other fatal indications of lack of social and moral worth apparently included too much scar-tissue. The Bardons, a young couple, 'clean but doubtfully respectable', wanted to move the wife's mother into the Buildings. 'Her landlord advised me not, & her appearance would have been enough. She accounted for the numerous scars on her face by saying that she had always lived in dark places, & so knocked herself about!' The Bardons promptly left, to be near the mother in her dark place.[20] Try as she might, Potter found it hard to think her way past phobia's reinforcements of social and moral discrimination. In November 1886, she went back to Wentworth Buildings, the other East End block she had managed with Ella Pycroft, during Pycroft's absence on holiday. She described in her diary the loathing she felt at the incessant physical mingling, the social and sexual promiscuity, of slum-life. 'Even their careless, sensual laugh, the coarse jokes and unloving words depress one as one presses through the crowd, and almost shudders to touch them.' Potter found the proximity of meeting-places to lavatories in Wentworth Buildings particularly offensive.[21]

Naturalism's first gift to British fiction was a subject-matter, or rather an approach to subject-matter, and a plot. Zola had 'done' peasant life in *La Terre* (1887), slums in *L'Assommoir* (1877), heavy industry in *Germinal* (1885), and so on. His grim environments and plummeting protagonists became archetypes; a powerful stimulus to social criticism in fiction. In March 1887, Potter shared a railway carriage with Sir George Trevelyan. 'I begged him to go into a smoking carriage . . . for had I not in the pocket of my sealskin not only a volume of Zola, but my case of cigarettes! neither of which I could enjoy in his distinguished presence.' The novel was *Au Bonheur des dames* (1883), in which Zola 'did' department stores. Sir George eventually settled down with *The Princess Casamassima* (1886), Henry James's most ambitious attempt at an unpoetic subject. Potter continued to read Zola, as well as George Eliot, with enthusiasm. Like Martineau before her, she even felt on occasion the 'vulgar wish to write a novel'. But sociology seemed to her the more 'worthful' exercise of powers, and she devoted the rest of her life to developing the necessary expertise. 'Meanwhile my diary shall serve for those titbits of personal experience which are representative of the special peculiarities of the different phases of society I pass through.'[22]

The perceived indecency of Zola's fiction meant that fulsome endorse-ments were hard to come by. Yet the New Woman writers who began to make themselves felt during the 1880s found that they could not ignore it altogether. Most nineteenth-century British novels implicitly or explicitly divide the human lifespan into a long rise stretching to the age of 60 or so, and a short (physical) decline. Naturalist fiction envisaged instead a rapid physical rise to the moment of reproduction in the twenties, then a redundancy accelerated by the gradual emergence of some innate physical or moral flaw. Its standard degeneration-plot seemed to many British women writers to fit the case of modern British middle-class manhood only too well. 'Doctors-spiritual must face the horrors of the dissecting-room,' declared 'Sarah Grand' (Frances McFall), one of the leading New Woman novelists, in the preface to *Ideala: A Study of Life* (1888).[23] In the best-selling *The Heavenly Twins* (1893), the heroine's husband discovers to his dismay that her sitting-room is lined with books on subjects such as anatomy and pathology. 'He could not have been more horrified had the books been *Mademoiselle de Maupin*, *Nana*, *La Terre*, *Madame Bovary*, and *Sapho*; yet, had women been taught to read the former and reflect upon them, our sacred humanity might have been saved sooner from the depth of degradation depicted in the latter.'[24] Grand's major preoccupation was with a woman's need for economic, sexual, and spiritual independence within, and conceivably beyond, marriage. In her view, the French realists were the only writers to take full measure of the degradation middle-class marriage had become for a wife dependent in every way on a corrupt and tyrannical husband. For her, as for Zola, individual degeneracy both produced and was produced by the decline and fall of nations. In *The Beth Book* (1897), she proposed political contexts for the intense physical and moral loathing the heroine comes to feel for her husband in the feminist campaigns against vivisection, and for reform of the Contagious Diseases Acts and of the divorce laws.[25]

To be more precise, Beth's loathing for her husband, Dan, a doctor, begins as physical and ends as moral, or even political. He issues detailed bulletins concerning the ailments of his female patients. 'Of two words Dan always chose the coarsest in talking to Beth, now that they were married, which had made her writhe at first.' Equally loathsome is his habit of sitting up until all hours with his cronies, smoking and drinking, and debating 'lewd topics'. As their lives interpenetrate, so Beth's disgust deepens. She objects to his smoking in her bedroom, indeed to his presence in her bedroom. She suffers from 'the smell of alcohol and tobacco, of which he reeked, and from which he took no trouble to purity himself.' When she catches him opening her letters, she endures 'one of those attacks of nausea and shivering which came upon her in moments of deep disgust'. In comparison with these defilements, the social and sexual indignities to which he subjects her – withholding an allowance, an affair with a patient – seem mere pinpricks.[26] To be sure, there is *some* moral complaint in the mixture, about 'lewd topics', and so on. But the nausea which turns Beth decisively against Dan is physical. It is the disgust provoked by Dan's reek which once again surges through her when she discovers a dog strapped to the table in his surgery. The feeling, forcefully articulated in the 1890s by a militant political campaign against vivisection, now has public as well as private force. Beth leaves home. Ontological thinking has decided her fate: her feminism.

Cynics

Rather oddly, in view of Dan's behaviour, Beth never sues for divorce. She simply leaves both Dan and nausea behind to live on her own in London. By the 1890s, however, conduct likely to cause acute mental suffering, such as to injure health and endanger reason, had long since amounted to cruelty in the estimation of the law.[27] Beth could well have petitioned successfully for legal separation. Many abused wives did.

'The case is an exceedingly filthy one,' the *Times* observed about *Craigie v. Craigie* (1895), 'and most of its details are utterly unfit for publication.'[28] Reginald Walpole Craigie, a clerk at the Bank of England, had married Pearl Richards on 16 July 1887. He was 29, she 19; they had one son, born on 16 August 1890. Early in 1891, she left him, and returned to her father's house. The petition she filed on 12 April 1894 listed sixteen charges against him, including habitual adultery, physical violence, and consistent unkindness. He had, among other things, sworn at her, hit her, thrown her books into the fire, and infected her with venereal disease. The most explosive charge was that contained in paragraph 18 of the petition. 'That on numerous occasions when the said Reginald Walpole Craigie has been in bed with me he has insisted, notwithstanding my strong and repeated objections, on my taking part in filthy and disgusting practices which were most offensive to me and rendered me ill.' On 15 June 1894, the petitioner was asked to furnish further and better particulars of the nature of these practices. On 4 July 1894, Reginald Craigie responded by claiming that his wife had condoned any acts of adultery and cruelty he might have committed. He also claimed that 'on several occasions the Petitioner, while refusing to render the Respondent marital intercourse as hereinafter mentioned, herself suggested and offered to take part in the practices in the said paragraph 18 of the said petition referred to.'[29] Pearl Craigie, accompanied by her father and a nurse, gave evidence at the trial. She was awarded a decree nisi, with costs.

After she left her husband in 1891, Craigie began to develop a career as a writer, adopting the pseudonym 'John Oliver Hobbes'. In the early 1890s, she published a series of novellas which understandably take as their subject courtship and marriage, or more often mis-marriage. These novellas reflect upon the anxieties endured by many women at the time, and they do so in ways, which vary significantly the formula of the New Woman novel. The difference lies in their tone: a cynicism which feeds off, and displaces, expressions of physical loathing.[30] The first of these tales, *Some Emotions and a Moral* (1891), announces in its opening sentence the moral around which emotions are to circulate: "'Ideals, my dear Golightly, are the root of every evil. When a man forgets his ideals he may hope for happiness, but not till then.'" [31] Golightly, an idealist to the end, commits suicide rather than seduce his best friend's wife. But it is the women, in Craigie's tales, not the men, who go lightly, or go Wilde: who learn through bitter experience that ideals are at the root of every evil. Craigie could not stop imagining female cynics. There must be as much heartless flirtation in her books as in those of any other writer in an age dedicated to heartless flirtation. For her, marriage was cynicism's laboratory. She was by no means alone among women writers of the period.

Prominent in the turn-of-the-century school of cynicism were Violet Hunt and Ada Leverson. The heroine of Hunt's *A Hard Woman* (1895) is a professional flirt, hardened by pride and some impressively metallic dresses. One of her flirtations goes disastrously wrong, leaving her penitent and heavily in debt. Her husband forgives her, but he has himself fallen in love with another woman, a 'type-writer girl' and aspiring actress who lives in a slum occupied by 'professional independent women', 'free lances'.[32] The result is a stand-off between two types of modern woman, and unhappiness all round. Hunt championed the second type in *The Workaday Woman* (1906), and the first in *Sooner or Later: The Story of an Ingenious Ingenue* (1904), which vents the bitterness she felt after two unsatisfactory relationships with older men. Ada Leverson married young, and unhappily; when her husband emigrated to Canada, she did not go with him. Such action as there is in her novels tends to involve muddled courtship, mis-marriage, and the petering out of minor flirtations. The tone of *Love's Shadow* (1908), the first in a trilogy chronicling the marriage of Edith and Bruce Ottley, is light, and sometimes marvelously waspish, but the plot turns on the bullying of women by morally and intellectually inferior men: Bruce Ottley, a humourless bore and hypochondriac, was based on Leverson's husband, Ernest. Born in the 1860s, united by the experience of sexual and emotional intimidation, Craigie, Hunt, and Leverson were feminists, but not New Women.

When one character in Craigie's *A Study in Temptations* takes a gloomy view of the world, another advises him not to get his nose in an artificial manure heap and think he is studying nature. "'If you take Zola for your gospel and the gospel for fiction, God must help you".[33] Getting her own nose in an artificial manure heap was a temptation Craigie knew well, and one which, like Sarah Grand, she for the most part avoided. However, the sensationalism for which Craigie had little time flourished unapologetically – and with it a new figure, a figure from Zola – in the work of Eliza Gollan (1856–1938), who published as 'Rita'. Rita's *A Husband of No Importance* (1894), the story of a wife who devotes herself full-time to literature, was an overt attack on the New Woman novel. She achieved popular success with *Souls* (1903), a satire, more violent in tone than Craigie's or Leverson's, on the corruption of High Society. *Saba Macdonald* (1906) draws on the bitter experiences of her unhappy first marriage, to a German composer of popular music. But it is in the authentically rancid *Queer Lady Judas* (1905) that the female *nauséaste* puts in her first appearance in English fiction. Cécile de Marsac, widow of a Parisian *roué*, arrives in London to establish herself, under the name of Madame Beaudelet, as a beautician and *masseuse*. Her first client, the spectacularly ugly Lady Judith Vanderbyl, turns out to be Lady Judas, famous *modiste*. The two women form an alliance in loathing. The disgust they feel for the physical and moral foulness their expertise helps to alleviate or obscure, and for their own part in the deception, is unrelenting. Nausea constitutes their horizon. 'This is a book OF WOMEN, FOR WOMEN, BY A WOMAN,' Rita declared in the preface. 'They may hate it for its truth, but each and all in their "looking glass" hours will acknowledge that it is true. For his own sake, and for the sake of some cherished illusions, no "mere man" should be bold enough to read it.'[34] Whether it amounts to a feminist book is another question.

In the summer of 1909, Katherine Mansfield was deposited by her mother, who had travelled from New Zealand for the purpose, in the little Bavarian spa town of Bad Worishofen. She shortly moved out of her hotel into the Villa Pension Muller, which was to provide the setting and the title of her first collection of stories, *In a German Pension* (1913). Mansfield's cousin and friend Elizabeth von Arnim, had already made a successful literary career out of witty assaults on German arrogance, philistinism and misogyny. Von Arnim's first marriage, to a German nobleman who died in 1910, was troubled by differences of age and nationality, and by her distaste for childbearing: feelings which found expression in the dark and lucid *The Pastor's Wife* (1914). Her second, even more disastrous marriage, to Earl Russell, provided the theme of the yet darker *Vera* (1921). Von Arnim's friendship with Mansfield connects the school of cynics to female Modernism.

In von Arnim's novels, the Germans are for the most part buffoons, albeit buffoons intent on world–domination.[35] Mansfield chose the same targets. But she wasn't simply out to bash the Hun. Several of the pension stories were first published in *The New Age*; and they belong, as Lee Garver has shown, to the journal's critique of Fabian socialism's centralizing tendencies. Mansfield was certainly no Beatrice Webb. What the narrator of *In a German Pension* most objects to among her fellow-guests is a perceived fondness for state regulation, and for motherhood in all its forms. Garver compares the political attitudes implicit in her own behaviour to the individualist feminism advocated by Mansfield's friend – and *New Age* contributor – Beatrice Hastings.[36] The politics of *In a German Pension* should not be over-stated. But there is plenty of attitude in the sly observations. That attitude I would describe as a cynicism produced by and in turn producing phobia. Mansfield was against the kinds of social and moral purification programme, now taking a statist and even eugenic turn in Britain as well as in Germany, of which Ellice Hopkins and Sarah Robinson had been the product, and which they had by their going to and fro implicitly put to the test. The descriptive detail in her stories is a way of observing that since such programmes never work in physical terms – and we have phobia to tell us that they don't – they are unlikely to work in social, political, and moral terms either. Mansfield's Germans preach cleanliness, but are themselves, and really through no great fault of their own, in the most literal sense unclean. The very first story in the collection, 'Germans at Meat', gives us soup on a waistcoat, a woman who picks her teeth with a hairpin, and a man who cleans his ears with a table napkin. Surfaces and apertures become a contaminated space where self and world mix promiscuously. The story reverts at the end to von Arnim territory, with banter about invasion–scares and England's degeneracy. But its bodily emphasis has opened up a margin for the expression of less easily classifiable anxieties. Subsequent stories explore that margin, presenting, among other *frissons*, a tie dunked in coffee, and a waiter who cleans his nails with the edge of a concert programme.[37] This is ontological thinking. And it forms the basis for an individualist feminism.

The narrator of *In a German Pension* would qualify on most counts as a *nauséaste*. Her nausea goes against the grain of what we now take to be the preoccupations and methods of the most innovative women writers of the time. Thus, the reaction provoked by Germany in the Mansfield's narrator is very different from that provoked in Dorothy Richardson's Miriam Henderson, in *Pointed Roofs* (1915). Germany proves less of an ordeal for Miriam, who has gone there to teach English, than might have been expected: and certainly not the land of spillage and self-evacuation depicted by Mansfield. The success of her first class signifies not so much in itself as because it removes 'an obstacle to gladness which was waiting to break forth.'[38] Gladness waiting to break forth is very much the subject of the early volumes of *Pilgrimage*, and Germany counts only insofar as it hinders or encourages the breaking forth.

At one point, Miriam has her hair washed by an intimidating German woman. Gripped by nausea, she places her head in the bowl. 'Then her amazed ears caught the sharp bump-crack of an eggshell against the rim of the basin, followed by a further brisk crackling just above her. She shuddered from head to foot as the egg descended with a cold slither upon her incredulous skull.' The sound of the egg breaking is wonderfully rendered, as if by some extraordinary disembodied act of attention. But the shudder doesn't last long. By the time the egg reaches it, Miriam's skull is already 'incredulous': no longer a surface upon which the world leaves its mark, but a seat of consciousness. Soon 'warmth' and 'ease' return to her 'clenched body'. She emerges from the ordeal 'glowing and hungry', identified once again by appetite, not revulsion. Miriam's appetite for life swallows Germany whole. Sitting in a Delikatessen, surrounded by the girls from her school, she feels 'securely adrift'.[39] In Mansfield's stories, by contrast, no-one is ever *securely* adrift.

These differences of emphasis perhaps lay behind the scepticism Mansfield expressed on occasion about women writers like Richardson and May Sinclair. The scepticism is evident enough, for example, in her review of Sinclair's *Mary Olivier: A Life* (1919). *Mary Olivier* is a book about desire, about getting what you want. Desire, which seeks out difference, makes Mary different. 'Restlessness. That was desire. It must be.' When all her potential lovers have proved unsatisfactory, or left her, and her mother, who claimed her from them, has died, she still does not give up on desire. Instead, she converts desire itself into a form of fulfilment. 'She had gone through life wanting things, wanting people, clinging to the thought of them, not able to keep off them and let them go.' Now she rejects other-generated 'ecstacy' in favour of self-generated 'happiness'. The advantage of this arrangement, the novel concludes, is that there 'isn't any risk' to it.[40]

Mansfield expressed astonishment at the fervour with which Mary Olivier pursues happiness, 'running into the room where Papa on his dying bed is being given an emetic, to see if it is on the counterpane, running out to see if it is in the cab that has come to take Aunt Charlotte to the Lunatic Asylum, and then forgetting all about it to stare at "Blanc-mange going round the table, quivering and shaking and squelching under the spoon".'[41] Mansfield felt, I think, that this strident 'passion for life' is in fact curiously passionless; and that Mary Olivier, because she never really sees the horror of mad Aunt Charlotte or vomiting Papa (and it took a true aficionado to spot the disgusting blanc-mange, which plays a *very* small part in the novel), never sees life at all. To Mansfield, such experiences were important in themselves, and not merely as obstacles to gladness. Mary Olivier, whose favourite authors are Shelley and Whitman, finds 'a secret and terrible enchantment' in 'the ugliest facts'.[42] By contrast, Mansfield's protagonists find only ugliness in the ugliest facts.

There is some evidence to suggest that, had she lived longer, Mansfield would have become the most formidable cynic of them all. '*Je ne parle pas français*', a story first published in 1920 by the Heron Press in an edition of one hundred copies, is the next best (or worst) thing to a manifesto for cynicism. The narrator is a twenty-six-year-old Parisian, Raoul Duquette, author of three books: *False Coins*, *Wrong Doors* and (quintessential Mansfield topic) *Left Umbrellas*. Sexually initiated at the age of ten by an African laundress, Duquette is thoroughly corrupt, an idler, a gigolo, a pimp, and bisexual to boot. The story concerns his encounter with an English friend and lover, Dick Harmon, and a woman called Mouse, whom Dick has brought to Paris, and abruptly abandons; it is she who can't speak French. Duquette promises to return to the hotel in which Mouse has been abandoned, but never does. Sarah Henstra has engagingly compared Duquette to Dr Matthew Dante O'Connor, the drunken, conniving, transvestite narrator of Djuna Barnes's *Nightwood* (1936). The critical consensus, Henstra notes, is that these male narrators imagined by women should be understood as 'examples of masculinity gone awry, against which the awakening feminist consciousness of the stories asserts itself'. But such readings cannot account for the 'vexed interplay' in their utterances of 'mischief, exhilaration, discomfort, and sorrow'. Better, Henstra argues, to regard those utterances as performative than as symptomatic. 'Barnes and Mansfield have created in Matthew and Raoul narrative voices that expose and challenge the social and discursive limits on the construction of the self.'[43] This is persuasive and illuminating. But it doesn't quite take fully enough into account the most striking formal feature of '*Je ne parle pas français*'.

The story cordons off narrative from description. It begins and ends in description. Duquette sits in a dirty little café, observing in a self-conscious fashion the owner seated on a stool with her face perpetually to the window, and the scarcely more active waiter.

> When he is not smearing over the table or flicking at a dead fly or two, he stands with one hand on the back of a chair, in his far too long apron, and over his other arm the three-cornered dip of dirty napkin, waiting to be photographed in connection with some wretched murder. 'Interior of Café where Body was Found.' You've seen him hundreds of times.

Thus far, the story is no story at all, but an exercise in the phobic picturesque, and one that concludes with a flourish Zola would surely have approved of. Tempted to create a *vignette*, the writer reaches over to the next table for some writing materials. 'No paper or envelopes, of course. Only a morsel of pink blotting-paper, incredibly soft and limp and almost moist, like the tongue of a little dead kitten, which I've never felt.' The all-seeing literary imagination founders in the abject touch of something soft and limp and moist: something rather like the soft moistness Roubaud encounters, in Zola's *La Bête humaine*, when he sticks his hand beneath the floor-boards (above, p. 52). What literature comes down to, through description, is radical ordinariness. However, just as the detective discerns the outline of a clue in the mangled remains on a slab in the morgue, so Duquette notices at the bottom of the page of blotting-paper (already it's a page, not a 'morsel'), written in green ink, the phrase 'Je ne parle pas français'. Meaning blossoms. 'There! It had come – the moment – the *geste*.' The phrase recalls Mouse, and the occasion of their first meeting, and then the whole sorry story of abandonment and failure of nerve. The rest is melancholia. Or not quite, because in concluding the text reverts from past to present, from narrative to description.

> I must go. I must go. I reach down my coat and hat. Madame knows me. 'You haven't dined yet?' she smiles.
>
> 'No, not yet, Madame.'
>
> I'd rather like to dine with her. Even to sleep with her afterwards. Would she be pale like that all over?
>
> But no. She'd have large moles. They go with that kind of skin. And I can't bear them. They remind me somehow, disgustingly, of mushrooms.[44]

Phobia could not have announced itself more clearly. This really is what the world looks like when you stop having ideas about it.

'*Je ne parle pas français*' is a manifesto for cynicism, and one which should by now have received a great deal more attention than it has done. It proposes two distinct portraits of the artist: as melancholic, immured in the past; and as *nauséaste*, face to face, at altogether too close a range, with the present. It asks us to assess the uses of narrative, perpetually *a la recherché du temps perdu*, against those of ontological thinking as evinced in and by description. There is no easy choice, of course. But Mansfield has made it abundantly clear what is at issue. And it is descriptive levelling, not the *geste*, or significant moment, which has the last word.

No school of cynics appears to have rallied to this manifesto. I want, however, to conclude by suggesting that an alertness to phobic feeling in literature might assist critically in the revaluation of unduly neglected writers. Where there is phobia, there is often something of interest going on, something that criticism has hitherto failed to identify. That seems to me to be the case with regard to the fiction of Penelope Gilliatt, a writer who has disappeared without trace from the histories of post-war British literature, of which there are many. Gilliatt was a cinephile who wrote extensively and with considerable shrewdness about film, in the *New Yorker* and elsewhere.[45] Her long engagement with the work of Jean Renoir, greatest of all Naturalist directors, resulted in a provocative and entertaining book.[46] In an essay on the portrayal of eccentricity in film from Buster Keaton to Tony Hancock, she declared her admiration for 'unharassed copers'.[47] In her novels and short stories, however, the copers are rarely unharassed. Indeed, more often than not the coping at once produces and is produced by the harassment.

Gilliatt's first novel, *One by One* (1965), imagines, three hundred years after the Great Plague, a London swept by a lethal epidemic and cut off from the rest of the country. It concerns the increasing revulsion felt by Joe Talbot, a vet who has volunteered to work in a plague-hospital, for his pregnant wife Polly, who still loves him passionately, and her response to it. What is the source of Joe's revulsion? Their snatched phone conversations, after she has left London, taking their cat with her, turn on the reasons he might have for not communicating with her.

> 'Are you all right?'
> 'Fine.'
> 'You sound as if there's someone in the room.'
> 'No, I'm on my own.'
> 'Joe, cats aren't carriers, are they?'
> 'Not as far as we know. But people have different phobias.'
> 'Like you about sending letters, even though everyone else does.'
> 'Not from a hospital,' he said stubbornly.

Does Joe want to protect Polly from risk, or has he stopped loving her? His mood doesn't improve when an old conviction for homosexual behaviour comes to light. In the end, unable to cope any longer with the harassment, from sexual guilt, from the dead and dying, he falls into depression, and jumps off a window-ledge. Polly, by contrast, *is* a coper. She survives because she understands that the coping is inextricable from the harassment. Severe agoraphobia pulls her through.

> When Joe killed himself I didn't know how to manage. I thought I couldn't. Then it was like being in solitary, I got the trick of it. You have a month of agony, two months, when it's more than you can stand, and then something happens because of the isolation. Your blood thins, I suppose. It becomes almost all right, it goes away from you a little, as long as you don't let anyone near you.[48]

As the novel ends, Polly is about to put on the performance which will overcome her agoraphobia. She, perhaps, is Gwendolen Harleth's true successor.

Notes

1 'Lesbians before Lesbianism: Sexual Identity in Early Twentieth-Century British Fiction', in Billie Melman, ed., *Borderlines: Genders and Identities in War and Peace, 1870–1930* (London: Routledge, 1998), 193–211.

2 All scholars of the period owe a debt to the path-breaking work of Martha Vicinus. See, in particular, *Independent Women: Work and Community for Single Women 1850–1920* (Chicago: University of Chicago Press, 1985). On the New Woman novel, see Sally Ledger, *The New Woman: Fiction and Feminism at the Fin de Siècle* (Manchester: Manchester University Press, 1997).

3 Frank Prochaska, *Women and Philanthropy in Nineteenth-Century England* (Oxford: Clarendon Press, 1980); *The Voluntary Impulse: Philanthropy in Modern Britain* (London: Faber and Faber, 1988); 'Philanthropy', in F.M.L. Thompson, ed., *The Cambridge Social History of Britain 1750–1950*, vol. 3 (Cambridge: Cambridge University Press, 1990), 357–93.

4 *A Life Record* (London: James Nisbet, 1898), 137. Henceforth *LR*.

5 And this despite her partial disablement. She suffered from curvature of the spine, and spent most of her adult life buckled into a surgical 'support': Jennie Chappell, *Noble Work by Noble Women* (London: S.W. Partridge, 1900), 70.

6 The question of motive has not been consistently addressed in the social history of philanthropy. David Owen's *English Philanthropy 1660–1960* (Cambridge, MA: Harvard University Press, 1965), the first major survey of the field, is primarily a study of institutions, though it does include a 'gallery' of heroic benefactors whose motives are regarded as beyond remark. Brian Harrison immediately took Owen to task for neglecting the part philanthropy played in the lives of its advocates. The 'psychological condition' of the Victorian philanthropist, Harrison maintained, demands investigation: 'Philanthropy and the Victorians', *Victorian Studies*, 9, 1966, 253–74. The next generation of historians, much taken with the concept of 'social control', tended to regard benevolence as one of the ways in which a dominant middle-class asserted its hegemony. Prochaska's work on philanthropy in general, and on women philanthropists in particular, can be regarded as in part a reaction against the then prevalent emphasis on social control. There has been some emphasis on pleasure: for example, Harrison, 'Philanthropy and the Victorians': 259–60;

Prochaska, 'Philanthropy': 360. But terms in which such pleasure might be understood historically have not yet been adequately defined.

7   *The Visitation of Dens: An Appeal to the Women of England* (London: Hatchards, 1874), 8. Henceforth *VD*.

8   *Active Service: or, Work Among Our Soldiers*, revised ed. (London: Hatchards, 1874), 11.

9   'The Burrow', in *The Great Wall of China and Other Works*, ed. and trans. Malcolm Pasley (Harmondsworth: Penguin, 1991), 185–218.

10 Hopkins was the accomplished if derivative author of a novel – *Rose Turquand*, 2 vols. (London: Macmillan, 1876) – and a volume of poems: *Autumn Swallows: A Book of Lyrics* (London: Macmillan, 1883).

11 As, for example, is the nonetheless penetrating discussion of rooms and houses in Gaston Bachelard, *The Poetics of Space*, trans. Maria Jolas (Boston: Beacon Press, 1994).

12 'Housing', in F.M.L. Thompson, ed., *The Cambridge Social History of Britain*, 3 vols. (Cambridge: Cambridge University Press, 1990), ii, 195–250, p. 202.

13 *The Condition of the Working Class in England* (London: Panther, 1969), 81.

14 'Housing', 203–4.

15 *The Uses of Disorder: Personal Identity and City Life* (New Haven: Yale University Press, 2008), 83.

16 R.K. Webb, *Harriet Martineau: A Radical Victorian* (London: Heinemann, 1960), 39.

17 For an excellent account of *Deerbrook* in particular and Victorian 'high realism' in general, see Philip Davis, *1830–1880: The Victorians* (Oxford: Oxford University Press, 2002) *The Oxford English Literary History*, vol. 8, ch. 9.

18 Carole Seymour-Jones, *Beatrice Webb: Woman of Conflict* (London: Allison and Busby, 1992), 79.

19 *My Apprenticeship* (London: Longmans, Green, 1926), 200–05.

20 *Katherine Buildings: Record of the Inhabitants during the Years 1885–1890*, British Library of Political & Economic Science, Miscellaneous Collection, 43, 25, 115, 148.

21 *Diary*, ed. Norman and Jeanne Mackenzie, 2 vols. (London: Virago, 1986), 1. 185–6. For a comparable response, see Edith Hogg, 'On the Fur-Pullers of South London', *Nineteenth Century*, 42, 1897, 734–43.

22 Ibid., 1, 198, 298.

23 *Ideala: A Study of Life*, 3rd edn. (London: Richard Bentley, 1889), viii.

24 *The Heavenly Twins* (Ann Arbor: University of Michigan Press, 1992), 104.

25 I describe these contexts, and what Grand made of them in the novel, in *Cooking with Mud: The Idea of Mess in Nineteenth-Century Art and Fiction* (Oxford: Oxford University Press, 2000), 267–86.

26 *The Beth Book* (London: Virago, 1980), 355, 380–1, 344, 381–2.

27 As I demonstrate at length in *Cooking with Mud*, 278–86.

28 *The Times*, 4 July 1895, 3.

29 *Craigie v. Craigie* (1895): PRO divorce files, J77/534/16319.

30 *Cooking with Mud*, 286–89.

31 *The Tales of John Oliver Hobbes* (London: T. Fisher Unwin, 1894), 2.

32 *A Hard Woman*, 2nd edn,. (London: Chapman and Hall, 1896), 35, 138.

33 *Tales*, 216.

34 *Queer Lady Judas* (London: Hutchinson, 1905), ii.

35   See, for example, *Elizabeth and Her German Garden* (1898), *Fraulein Schmidt and Mr Anstruther* (1907), *The Caravaners* (1909), and *Christine* (1917).

36   'The Political Katherine Mansfield', *Modernism/Modernity*, 8.2, 2001, 225–43.

37   *Short Stories* (New York: Ecco Press, 1983), 37–9, 47, 68.

38   *Pilgrimage*, 4 volumes (London: Virago, 1979), 1. 56.

39   Ibid., 1, 60, 88.

40   *Mary Olivier. A Life* (London: Virago, 1980), 228, 378, 380.

41   'The New Infancy', in Bonnie Kime Scott, ed., *The Gender of Modernism*, (Bloomington: Indiana University Press, 1990), 312.

42   *Mary Olivier*, 289.

43   'Looking the Part: Performative Narration in Djuna Barnes's *Nightwood* and Katherine Mansfield's *"Je ne parle pas français"'*, *Twentieth Century Literature*, 46.2, 2000, 125–49, p. 126.

44   'Je ne parle pas français', in *Selected Stories*, ed. Angela Smith (Oxford: Oxford University Press, 2002), 142–67, pp. 143–5, 167.

45   Her writings about film have been collected as *Unholy Fools: Wits, Comics, Disturbers of the Peace: Film & Theater* (New York: Viking Press, 1973); *Three-Quarter Face: Reports & Reflections* (London: Secker & Warburg, 1980); *To Wit: In Celebration of Comedy* (London: Weidenfeld & Nicolson, 1990).

46   *Jean Renoir: Essays, Conversations, Reviews* (New York: McGraw-Hill, 1975).

47   'Optics: Intent on the Marginal', in *To Wit*, 134–58, p. 135.

48   *One by One* (London: Secker & Warburg), 114–15.

5

Modernist *Toilette*: Degas, Woolf, Lawrence

One of the least remarked contributions to the first, seismic issue of Wyndham Lewis's *BLAST* (June 1914) was 'Pastoral', a short poem by Ezra Pound which begins with an act of observation:

> The young lady opposite
> Has such beautiful hands
> That I sit enchanted
> 　　　While she combs her hair in décolleté.

The speaker goes on to explain that he feels no embarrassment at all in watching the performance so closely.

> BUT God forbid that I should gain further acquaintance,
> For her laughter frightens even the street hawker
> And the alley cat dies of a migraine.[1]

The poem may well be unremarked because it is unremarkable: one of a series of squibs Pound and Eliot produced during this period, in which the speaker cruises or is cruised by (as if!) a beautiful young woman whose imminent display of vulgarity will absolve him of any obligation to approach her – while at the same time justifying expressions of contempt calculated to repair any damage the encounter may have done to his self-esteem.[2] Pound's upper-case 'BUT' indicates that there is no way back, in this particular pastoral scene, to the straightforward pleasure of looking. Some rather ropey jokes about street hawkers and alley cats will have to do instead.

And yet the idea of *toilette*, the action or process of washing and grooming, especially when it involved a woman, was evidently of sufficient interest to Eliot for him to want to incorporate two such scenes into *The Waste Land* (1922).[3] In 'A Game of Chess', an evening *toilette* is in progress: a woman seated at a dressing-table brushes her hair out into 'fiery points', before engaging an interlocutor we take to be her husband in desultory, tortured debate.[4] But that wasn't the half of it. In the summer of 1921, Eliot had written a 72-line pastiche of Pope's *The Rape of the Lock* which chronicles the morning *toilette* of a wealthy socialite called Fresca, who, aroused from a dream of 'pleasant' rape, takes breakfast in bed, attends to her correspondence, and then draws a 'steaming bath'.[5] The pastiche was to have served as an introduction to 'The Fire Sermon', until Pound struck it out.

Toilette clearly appealed, as a modern idea, and not just to experimental poets. It also held sway in Hollywood. Cecil B. De Mille's *Old Wives for New* (1918) was the first of a series of quasi-satirical social dramas to address the already fashionable topic of the decline of bourgeois marriage as an institution. In these dramas, the new wife might or might not turn out to be the same as the old one: what mattered was that she should modernize herself, or make herself over, first and foremost by the purchase of a new and more daring wardrobe, and the behaviour to go with it. De Mille understood make-over to involve a great deal of *toilette*: of preparation, at the beginning or the end of the day, for the performance of a new role. To be sure, husbands were also required to spruce themselves up a bit, which largely meant not dropping cigar-ash all over the place. But it was the wives who bore the burden of modernization. The good old wife has not only to make herself over in public, but also to develop in private the eye-wateringly modern habits of the bad new other woman who has for the time being got the good old husband under her spell. The bad new other woman generally has three modern things going for her: synthetic perfumes, an ample supply of jazz records, and a complicated art deco machine for dispensing cigarettes. Eliot's bourgeois wife, seated at a dressing-table lavishly strewn with jewels, at least has a decent supply of synthetic perfumes. Jazz features in the conversation which ensues ('O O O O that Shakespeherian rag'), but it would seem to emanate from the hitherto silent husband, rather than from his not yet entirely made-over wife. Is he trying to tell her something? De Mille's Fresca-equivalent was the spoiled-brat daughter in *Male and Female* (1919). Aroused from *her* dream of pleasant rape, Lady Mary (Gloria Swanson) takes a bath first, and then, by way of an intertitle sporting a sanitized quotation from *The Rape of the Lock*, some breakfast, brought to her by a small but insurrectionary entourage. The purpose of *toilette*, in Jazz Age representations, was makeover. Make-over required the application of techniques of grooming whose modernity was crucial to the illusion made, the image in the mirror.

It would be an exaggeration to say that grooming was all the rage in literary London in the years immediately after the end of the First World War. But the topic does seem to have attracted a fair amount of interest in Modernism's feeder magazines. In a poem published in the Chicago magazine *Poetry*, Harold Monro, owner of the Poetry Bookshop in Blooms-bury, imagined a man standing at a window, as Pound had done in 'Pastoral', inspecting a house across the road where a ghostly presence 'will comb out her languid hair'.[6] The December 1919 issue of *Coterie*, which at that time included Eliot, Lewis, Richard Aldington, and Nina Hamnett on its Editorial Committee, had a particularly high *toilette*-count. Eliot's Harvard friend Conrad Aiken contributed a poem which reconstructs the last hours ('She sat by a mirror, braiding her golden hair . . .') of a beautiful corpse laid out on a slab in the morgue.[7] Elsewhere in the same issue, a short story by Aldous Huxley begins with a description of another young woman in the process of combing her hair in *décolleté*. This one gets someone else to finish the job for her.

> 'Harder, harder!' cried Ninon, turning round to look at him over her shoulder. 'You'll never get the tangles out unless you comb harder.'
> 'But doesn't it hurt?' Coligny was horrified at the prospect of inflicting pain on his mistress.
> 'Of course not, if you're not clumsy.'[8]

The emphasis remains on *décolleté*, in this scene. Huxley, however, has outdone the poets in his detailed attention to process, or labour: to the aptitude and the sheer physical and emotional energy required to force a particular instrument through a particular material object.

In 'Of Modern Poetry' (1940), Wallace Stevens declared that the modern poem

> must
> Be the finding of a satisfaction, and may
> Be of a man skating, a woman dancing, a woman
> Combing. The poem of the act of the mind.[9]

Female *toilette* might appear to have been summoned as no more than one inter-changeable version of ordinary experience among several: a man skating, a woman dancing, a woman combing. But Stevens singles it out by doing explicitly what Huxley had done implicitly. He draws attention to process, to aptitude and energy. In ordinary usage, 'to comb' is a transitive verb; Stevens has rendered it intransitive, and thus an idea with a fascination all its own. He has further isolated that idea by enjambement. A woman's combing stands out, as a topic for the modern poem, beyond a man's skating or a woman's dancing. Its isolation as an idea enables Stevens to complete his own treatise on modern poetry, as 'combing' finds an echo in 'poem'. The combing somehow already *is* the act of the mind, as its (still) potential subject-matter.

This essay has two aims. First, I shall argue that an attention to process or labour, recommended by Stevens for the modern poem, but equally if not more evident in modern prose fiction, was what put the Modernism into Modernist *toilette*. Some writers of the time conceived an affinity between such attention to process or labour and the emphasis on technique required by Modernism's efficiency (or literary hygiene) programmes.[10] *BLAST*, after all, had undertaken to 'BLESS the HAIRDRESSER' for making 'systematic mercenary war' on Mother Nature; while one of the first things Katherine Mansfield did when she became assistant editor of *Rhythm*, in June 1912, was to introduce an advertisement for the salon run by her friend Ida Constance Baker, who specialized in 'SCIENTIFIC HAIR-BRUSHING AND FACE TREATMENT'.[11] Combing, however, can be a messy business, since it tends to displace waste-matter, rather than remove it altogether. The detritus extracted from a head of hair attaches itself to the instrument of extraction: *sale comme un peigne*, the French say, dirty as a comb. Modernist representations of the technique exercised in *toilette* derive from and comment upon a late-nineteenth-century concern with (or phobic captivation by) mess as contingency's signature.[12] The essay's second aim is to explore the political and aesthetic consequences of such an understanding of *toilette* as the exercise of aptitude and energy to uncertain – that is to say, by no means purgative – effect. In 'Pastoral', Pound opposes élite masculine abstraction to commonplace feminine mess-making in ways which have come to be regarded as characteristic of the High Modernism of the 'Men of 1914'. But there was another kind of experiment. Some writers and artists (male and female) made common cause, through the choice of *toilette* as topic, with a process which generates both illusion and disillusionment: the dirt without which there would be no possibility of image, and the image without which there would be no possibility of dirt. My intention is to provoke enquiry into that kind of experiment by examining representations of female *toilette* by a trio of Modernists assembled, as I hope to show, not quite at random: Edgar Degas, Virginia Woolf, and D.H. Lawrence.

Toilettes de Venus: Degas and Striation

Stevens would probably not have felt so confident in his identification of a woman combing as a possible topic for the modern poem if images of *toilette de Venus* had not been for so long a mainstay of canonical Western art. In paintings by Titian, Rubens, Velasquez, and many others, the goddess, in varying degrees of *décolleté*, gazes into a mirror held by an amenable attendant, winged or unwinged. She designs and prepares her sexuality. And yet in the vast majority of these paintings the traditional *instruments* of design and preparation – the brush and comb, the perfume, the make-up – have been occluded. Venus studies the effect she will have on others, an effect whose causes we need not enquire into. How much help, after all, does a goddess need? So it was, as far as I can tell, with some notable exceptions, up until the middle of the nineteenth century. Even after the goddess had become an ordinary woman obliged to do without attendants – as in Jacques-Louis David's *Venetian at Her Toilette* (1860), or Édouard Debat-Ponson's more bohemian *Gypsy at Her Toilette* (1896) – the emphasis remained on social and sexual persona: on the femininity thus got into shape, rather than on its shaping. The mirror was still the major prop: as instrument and emblem of a crucial moment in the preparation of a persona between its manufacture in private and its first public appearance. The look in the mirror has already put causation (the preparatory *work*) behind it; and confidently anticipates effect.

It is true that work does sometimes enter the picture. Dante Gabriel Rossetti's *Lady Lilith*, of 1868, from one of his own poems, is one of the most unabashedly sensuous of all nineteenth-century representations of *toilette*'s mirror-stage. In Talmudic legend, Lilith was Adam's first wife, a *femme fatale* who abandoned him when he denied her equality. Rossetti has given her full, rose-red lips, and long, thick, luxuriant hair whose sheer abundance is a sexual invitation.[13] Gazing into the mirror she holds in front of her, she prepares herself to be irresistible. As J.B. Bullen observes, Rossetti has translated the threat Lilith poses in the literary and mythological accounts into an 'act of self-contemplation' given an added frisson by the figure's contemporaneity. Rossetti's Lilith is a *femme fatale* of the sort it might just be possible (as if!) to encounter in the modern upper-class boudoir or bedroom.[14] In her right hand, she clasps a comb big enough to hitch to a tractor. But the activity which concerns Rosetti is not the work which has gone into the preparation of a social and sexual persona so much as the indolent pleasure taken in calculating its effect. 'And still she sits', as he put it in the poem from which the painting derives,

> young while the earth is old
> And, subtly of herself contemplative.
> Draws men to watch the bright web she can weave
> Till heart and body and life are in its hold.[15]

Lilith's separateness or self-enclosure, as she gets ready for seduction, is the source of her power. Nineteenth-century visual representations of *toilette* subordinate comb to mirror.

So, too, do the novels. In Chapter 15 of George Eliot's *Adam Bede* (1859), humble Hetty Sorrel tries to establish, with the aid of a shilling looking-glass, what she will need to look like if she is to secure the affections of the local squire, Captain Donnithorne. She pushes her soft, silken hair backward, to 'make herself look like that picture of a lady in Miss Lydia Donnithorne's dressing-room.' The hair forms a dark curtain, throwing her round, white neck into relief. 'Then she put down her brush and comb, and looked at herself, folding her arms before her, still like the picture.' For Eliot, there is poignancy in this subtle self-contemplation, rather than excitement. Poor vulnerable Hetty Sorrel cannot boast the 'heavy, massive' armature of a Lilith. But what concerns Eliot, as it was to concern Rossetti, is above all the 'lovely image' sent back by the glass.[16] Brush and comb appear and disappear without attracting much attention in their own right.

The proposition I want to advance here is that Stevens's emphasis on the activity of combing reflects an awareness of a new approach to *toilette* taken by the modern painting as well as the modern poem (and the modern novel). If you start to look closely at a range of Impressionist and post-Impressionist pictures of *toilette*, from Mary Cassatt's *The Toilette* (1891) through Pablo Picasso's *The Toilette* (1906), Pierre-Auguste Renoir's *Woman Combing Her Hair*, and Pierre Bonnard's *The Toilette* (both 1908), to George Grosz's *Toilette* (1927), you notice an increasing reluctance to reveal to the viewer what the subject sees in the mirror. These women do not appear to be subtly of themselves contemplative in quite the same way as Rossetti's Lilith. As mirror and mirror-image become harder to grasp, so the brush or comb with which the woman works emerges into prominence. Already, in 1877, in *Before the Mirror*, Édouard Manet had displaced the mirror from its accustomed position in 'pictorial thematizations of the feminine', as Carol Armstrong notes. Point of view and an abbreviated style of notation combine to curtail the image it yields. 'And so what is given to the gaze in *Before the Mirror*,' Armstrong continues, 'is given entirely in the form of suggestive but insufficient glimpses, and mediated prominently through self-announcing facture.' *Before the Mirror* may well have been a response to Berthe Morisot's *Young Woman at Her Toilette*, painted some time between 1875 and 1880, and one of a series of works depicting women at the mirror which suggest a meditation on her own acts of 'self-preparation' rather than on the 'thematics of the courtesan'. Indeed, the facture of *Before the Mirror* could be understood as a reference to a style of brush-work associated with Morisot's work since the mid-1870s: a feminine style itself thought to have revived the eighteenth-century French Rococo of Boucher and Fragonard.[17]

Manet's choice of subject-matter, in *Before the Mirror*, has produced and been produced by both a change of individual style, in relation to his hitherto characteristic manner, and a new consciousness of the gendering of style in general, in Paris in the 1870s. Such conjunctions had happened before, of course. In Giovanni Bellini's *Young Woman at Her Toilette* (1515), a young woman looks into a small handheld mirror in order to arrange her headdress, while a larger mirror on the wall behind her reflects the scene.[18] Beside her, on the window-ledge, is a vase containing ceruse, a cosmetic made out of white lead; the sponge she has used to apply the cosmetic to her face and body rests in the vase's neck. Bellini has identified a woman's artful painting of her face and body with the art of painting itself. The vase, placed on the threshold between the scene's interior and exterior spaces, stands for the painter's palette: it contains the substance (white lead used as a pigment) which enables art to mirror nature. The elevation of *colore* over *disegno* in Venetian painting of the period was often discussed in terms of gender: Michelangelo, for example, condemned Titian's colouring as effeminate. Bellini could be said to have feminized his art (his control over nature) by identifying its medium with cosmetics and its methods with the application of make-up: the crystal vase itself symbolizes the female body. This is not feminism: the headdress the woman arranges is a *reticella* indicating her status as a married woman. She paints herself cosmetically as an act of obedience to her husband: for Bellini, to paint her painting herself is to acknowledge and celebrate that proper subordination.

François Boucher's *Madame de Pompadour at Her Toilette* (1758) shows Madame de Pompadour, Louis XV's favourite, and a power at his court, though by this time no longer his mistress, seated before a dressing-table strewn with the accoutrements of the *toilette*. She looks out at us: one hand holds an open box of rouge, the other a cosmetic brush laden with colour which she is about to apply to her cheeks. 'Tonalities of white and pink dominate the composition,' as Melissa Hyde notes: 'the delicate pallor of her alabaster skin and the rosiness of her cheeks and lips are variously echoed in her gown and mantle, the cameo, table, and powder-puff.' Boucher, like Bellini, has understood the artful application of make-up as a form of art-making. The debates about the relative importance of colour and design which had raged in sixteenth-century Italy were still raging in eighteenth-century France. Boucher, in fact, may have gone considerably further than Bellini in identifying the (implicitly male) art of portraiture with the (implicitly female) arts of the toilette. In some areas of the canvas Boucher's oil paint imitates Pompadour's cosmetic paint with an odd exactness: for example, in the pinkish dusting of colour on the brush, and on her cheeks. Where exactly does make-up stop and depiction start? Who, Hyde asks, has 'painted' Pompadour's lips? The painting posits an impossibly close vantage-point for the spectator: we see as if situated on the table-top itself. Could the image presented be understood as Pompadour's image seen in a mirror? Hyde describes the painting as a 'pseudo self-portrait'. Boucher's representation of Pompadour as left-handed marks a significant departure both from the norms of eighteenth-century painting and from his own previous depictions of her: but it would be consistent with self-portraiture. Boucher has gone beyond Bellini in imagining that the subject of his portrait has painted herself twice over: cosmetically, and then, by means of a long look in the mirror, as virtual self-portraiture. Hyde's conclusion is that the painting deconstructs 'the categories of woman as object and male painter as subject, by conflating the positions of the two.'[19]

It may be that the popularity of the *toilette* as topic enabled some painters, male and female, to continue to conflate those positions. *Madame de Pompadour at Her Toilette* has been seen as an 'appropriate pictorial precedent' for Georges Seurat's *Young Woman Powdering Herself* (1890). Of course, the choice of *toilette* as topic did not in itself ensure a conflation of painter and painted. The difference between *Madame de Pompadour* and *Young Woman Powdering Herself* is that, while both paintings depict kept women, Boucher's model was the rich and powerful companion of a king, who stares boldly out at the viewer, while Seurat's was his clandestine working-class lover, Madeleine Knobloch, who keeps her eyes down. Madame de Pompadour is about to powder her face, Knobloch her breasts. For Seurat, the woman depicted is 'all breast'.[20]

The *toilette* scene could easily become a mammary sub-genre. In 1880, Manet had exhibited *Before the Mirror* in a one-man show in the galleries of La Vie Moderne along with, among other things, an 1878 pastel, *Woman Fixing Her Garter*, the subject of which leans forward to secure a clasp at her knee in such a way that her breasts spill out over the rim of her bodice. The securing of garters had served as bounty for the (male) spectator at least since Boucher's *Toilette* of 1742, and would continue to do so in a variety of visual media including photography, posters, and cartoons: a fact of which the punters in the bar of Ormond Hotel in Dublin, in the 'Sirens' episode of James Joyce's *Ulysses*, are forcibly reminded when Miss Douce, after much 'bending, suspending, with wilful eyes', sets free 'sudden in rebound her nipped elastic garter smackwarm against her smackable a woman's warmhosed thigh'.[21] Clearly, such displays of breast and thigh merely reinforce the category of 'woman as object'. It took an emphatic feminism to counteract them. Julia, in H.D.'s semi-autobiographical *Bid Me to Live* (1960), finds in the wholly palpable step-by-step articulations of morning *toilette* – 'fastening the garter-belt and tightening the stocking-web into the rubber-lined garter-catches, four' – a definiteness otherwise lacking in her life after her husband Rafe has returned to the front line.[22] I still want to maintain, nonetheless, that the representation of female *toilette* could and did encourage in some male painters and writers to interest themselves in, and even to imitate, the humdrum technical activities of washing and grooming.

The 'Suite of female nudes bathing, washing, drying, wiping themselves, combing their hair or having their hair combed', which Edgar Degas submitted to the eighth and final Impressionist exhibition in Paris in 1886, became the benchmark for modern representations of *toilette*. By the end of the 1880s, two subjects had begun to absorb Degas's energies almost to the exclusion of everything else: ballet, and the female nude. Between 1885 and the early years of the twentieth century, he produced around 250 pastels and oil paintings of the female nude, as well as charcoal studies, prints, sculptures in wax and clay, and photographs. He returned again and again, as Richard Kendall puts it, 'to the same set of visual challenges: a distracted bather drying her neck, a head of chestnut hair against pale flesh, a nude reaching for a comb or towel.' Kendall has argued in exhaustive and illuminating detail that the work Degas did from 1890 onwards in a variety of media constitutes a profound shift of emphasis from documentary to expressive ambition, from 'spectacle' to 'neutrality'. Setting and personnel, so full of (salacious) narrative implication in the images he made of the female nude from the mid-1870s to the mid-1880s, more or less dissolve away. Massively at the centre of the later images is a woman's routine self-absorption into the physical activities of *toilette*: a self-absorption as massive when there is someone else in attendance, to comb hair, or deliver a towel, or a cup of tea, as when there is not. In these images, a 'jigsaw of colour' tightens around the central figure, Kendall observes, locking her into its design. Her isolation is less theatrical than it had been, 'more directly expressed in the pastes and patterns of the work of art itself'. The 'physical stuff' of which the picture is made 'both defines and embodies' its essence: the idea of a figure in 'viable movement', its actions locating it in self-absorption into humdrum routine. Kendall suggests that the shift of emphasis thus exemplified may have had something to do with the 'tempering influence' of artists like Mary Cassatt and Berthe Morisot, who was close to Degas personally and professionally in the years before her death in 1895. Degas, Kendall adds provocatively, 'represented *himself*' in the late nudes. His 'attentive rituals' mirrored the activities of the models who posed for him as women engaged in *toilette*. 'Even the prosaic acts of drawing and posing, of stretching to make a mark with the "feminine" medium of pastel or reaching for a towel, modeling wax or grasping a sponge, have their irresistible analogies, merging the functions of portrayer and portrayed.'[23]

The suite of nudes submitted to the Impressionist exhibition of 1886 did not in fact include any images of women 'combing their hair or having their hair combed'. Degas amply made up for the omission. From around 1890 onwards, the motif inspired a profusion of brilliant drawings, pastels, oil paintings, lithographs, and wax sculptures. The women undergoing *coiffure* appear from a variety of angles and distances. Some are decorously clothed, some not. Almost all are 'solemnly engaged' in a *toilette* that seems to provoke in them various feelings ranging from indolence to near-desperation.[24] As they loom massively in (or out of) the image, so too does the detail of the activity of *toilette*: the force in play, the instrument (brush or comb) through which it has been transmitted, the whole conversion of physical-emotional cause into physical-emotional effect. If there is a mirror, in these images, it exists as no more than an implied presence beyond the frame. Luxuriant though the hair on display often is, it has been disabled as bounty for the viewer by the sheer prominence of the instrument in the process of passing through it. That instrument in each instance declares the fact of labour, of nature's dependence upon culture. On one side of it stands crude raw material; on the other, the finished product. Degas's radicalism lay in his understanding of female *toilette* as a technical activity which, however commonplace, involved effort and skill. That emphasis on technique neutralised spectacle. If there is makeover here, it is not discernibly for anyone else's immediate benefit.

In Degas's representations of *coiffure*, the comb (or brush) rules, in more than one sense. It dominates, and it straightens. On one side, an unholy tangle; on the other, alignment. In pastels like *Woman Combing Her Hair* (1890–2), now in the Musée d'Orsay, the contrast drawn between the stretch of hair above the comb and the stretch below it could not be clearer. Areas of neat striation visible immediately above and below the hand pinioning the stretch of hair already combed insist on the difference made by technique, by the application of effort and skill. These areas consist, of course, of the marks made by Degas with brush or stick. We might ask of them the question we asked of Pompadour's lips. Whose work is it? Once again, attention to the technical activity of *toilette* has altered the technical activity of art itself. In another pastel, *Woman at Her Toilette* (1889), now in the State Hermitage Museum in St Petersburg, the striations produced by combing find a visual rhyme in the striations the painter himself has produced in order to represent the rucking of a garment, or a hair-brush's array of bristles. In Kendall's terms, both pastels are transitional: as much documentary as expressive in style. *Woman at Her Toilette*, in particular, while stripped of narrative implication, none the less sets the scene carefully. We see a young woman seated in an armchair in front of a dressing-table on which various familiar items predictably stand. It is the rhymed striations, above all, which impose upon the scene set in documentary fashion the 'pastes and patterns of the work of art itself', and so merge the functions of portrayer and portrayed. The woman striates with a comb, the artist with a brush, crayon, or stick. It is the close resemblance between these activities that provides the basis for Degas's feminized experimentation. The recognition that technique constitutes without wholly defining the illusion which is our bodily self-image (in these cases, a woman's bodily self-image) has produced or been produced by the recognition that technique constitutes without wholly defining the illusion which is the work of art. The attention Degas devoted to *coiffure* from the late-1880s onwards would in itself justify Stevens's sense that a woman combing was a fit subject for the modern poem – or painting, or sketch, or indeed novel.

Combing (in) Words

Degas died in 1917: he went on producing work that was seen and admired by contemporary artists until at least 1912. 'In no other country outside France did Degas's art have such a direct and turbulent effect as that which it produced in England,' Kendall observes, 'and in few other contexts did the transition between his early and late phases create such confusion.' Among British artists influenced by Degas, he lists Philip Wilson Steer, William Rothenstein, Laura Knight, John Copley, David Bomberg, Duncan Grant, and Vanessa Bell, whose *The Tub* (1917) 'brings an awareness of Cubism and the innovations of Matisse to one of Degas's most distinctive themes, defusing the intimacy of his pastels in broad expanses of colour.'[25] His staunchest and most authoritative champion was Walter Sickert, who reworked his motifs inventively in English idiom: the music hall stood in for the café-concert, Camden Town for Montmartre, and so on. One of the least noticed of these reworkings is a sketch entitled 'The Comb', which appeared in *The New Age* in January 1912, and which shows a mother vigorously addressing her daughter's unruly mound of hair. The scene does not lack for striation; and it duly provoked a measure of controversy. Writing in *The New Age* in June 1912, Huntly Carter complained about Sickert's preference for titles likely to 'make the fastidious squirm'. '"Slops", "Wash and Brush-up", "The Chest of Drawers", "The Sofa", "The Comb",' Carter felt, 'try the patience of the poetical, whose taste does not allow them to go travelling all over the house from bedroom to washhouse in search of art emotions and inspiration.' Even more scary, in his view, was the 'method of treatment' Sickert had adopted in these drawings. 'There is no strength or distinctness in them. The lines have shriveled up, the subjects have lost their distinct shapes.'[26] Style, it appears, had once again been inflected by choice of motif.

Figure 5   John Sloan, Combing Her Hair. Etching. Private Collection

As it was, too, in other countries outside France. Three pictures by
Degas were exhibited at the decisive Armory Show in New York in
1913, including the late pastel *After the Bath* (c. 1890–3), now in the Norton
Simon Foundation in Pasadena. As Kendall points out, Degas's composi-
tional techniques and still-provocative urban themes had already influenced American painters such as Edmund Tarbell, William Merritt
Chase and Everett Shinn. [27] John Sloan, for one, had been assiduous
in trying the patience of the poetical as Sickert. Sloan knew Ezra Pound – in
August 1910, they went to Coney Island together – and there is something
of Pound's 'Pastoral' in his etching *Night Windows* (1910), which he once
referred to as 'Man on roof (looking at girl dressing)'.[28] A later etching,
Combing Her Hair (1913), reveals as forceful an interest in striation as
anything by Degas or Sickert (fig. 5). These are connections well worth
developing further.

Figure 6 Edgar Degas, Woman at Her Toilette. Pastel. Copyright: Tate, London 2009

Sickert wrote extensively about art in the London periodicals from the 1880s through to the 1930s, peppering his commentary with sage hints dropped by the master ('Monsieur Degas said to me in 1885 a thing I have never forgotten ...').[29] When the *Burlington Magazine* published Sickert's obituary of Degas in November 1917, it supplied black-and-white reproductions of an early oil painting, *Portrait of a Lady Seated before a Window Overlooking the Tuileries Garden* (1871), and a late pastel, *Woman at Her Toilette* (c. 1894), currently in the Tate Gallery in London (fig. 6).[30]

The latter exemplifies the 'bonding of image and technique' Kendall has so persuasively defined in the depictions of *coiffure*. 'Here pastel is used both to describe and unify, its cascades of yellow, blue, and ginger flowing across the disparate components of the scene and conjuring up rhythms and incident, dignity for the maid and agitation for her mistress.'[31]

The most cascade-like of these cascades is that constituted by the mistress's long chestnut hair, through which she propels a comb, while turning her head in the opposite direction to glimpse the cup of tea held out to her by the maid. The effect of cascade in fact depends on the striation produced by the combing's fierce downward movement, as the liquid mass of hair tumbles from the plateau of her shoulders and arms – a rock-formation held monumentally in place by upright wedges of gingery blue whose vertical thrust has been reinforced by that of the enormous vase on the dressing-table, and extending up along the maid's right arm and shoulder – to meet the junction of wall and floor. That striation wrought in and by the picture's 'physical stuff' is Degas's gesture of comprehension of the 'viable movement' a person is to be known by, unremarkable yet hard to mistake. He might be William Carlos Williams at the Passaic River Falls, wondering what to do with his poem:

> I must
> find my meaning and lay it, white,
> beside the sliding water: myself –
> comb out the language – or succumb

- whatever the complexion.[32]

There was much to be learned from cascades.

Woman at Her Toilette was shown (as *La Toilette*) at an exhibition in the Burlington Fine Arts Club between November 1917 and March 1918. In May 1918, when a large collection of work by Degas went on sale in Paris, Roger Fry acted as an advisor to C.J. Holmes, then Director of the National Gallery, who was planning some modest acquisitions on behalf of the Gallery of Modern Art (now the Tate). Fry told Holmes that he regarded the picture shown at the Burlington – *Woman at Her Toilette* – as the 'greatest type of Degas'.[33] Before writing to Holmes, Fry got in touch with Maynard Keynes, who in March 1917 had bought a Cézanne still life owned by Degas. In April 1918, Virginia Woolf went with Roger Fry to Keynes's house in Gordon Square to see the picture. Her sister, Vanessa Bell, was also present. 'Nessa left the room and re-appeared with a small parcel about the size of a large slab of chocolate. On one side are painted six green apples by Cézanne. Roger very nearly lost his senses.'[34] This was a period of intense debate in Bloomsbury about the visual arts. Degas does not seem to have caused as much excitement as Cézanne, but there is no reason to think that he was ignored. After all, Woolf thought of Sickert as her 'ideal painter'.[35] By March 1918, she had written over 100,000 words of her second novel, *Night and Day*, which she was to finish before the end of the year. A week after Fry had nearly lost his senses over Cézanne, she told Vanessa she had been writing about her all morning, and had 'made her wear a blue dress'.[36] Vanessa was the model for Katharine Hilbery, in *Night and Day*. As far as I know, Woolf never saw *Woman at Her Toilette*, in which there is a great deal of blue, but no blue dress. But Degas's accomplishments in that and other representations of a woman combing none the less seem to me to offer a way to think about what Woolf was trying to accomplish in a scene in the novel in which a blue dress features prominently.

In 'A Sketch of the Past', Virginia Woolf described *Night and Day* as one of only two of her novels (the other being *The Years*) to address 'non-being': that is, everyday activities performed more or less automatically, like washing, or cooking dinner, or repairing the broken vacuum cleaner.[37] In Chapter 26, twenty-two-year-old Cassandra Otway has just arrived in London to stay with her cousin Katharine Hilbery, whom she greatly admires, in Cheyne Walk, in Chelsea. We're told, bluntly, perhaps rather too bluntly, that where Katharine is simple, solid, and direct, Cassandra is complex, vague, and evasive. 'In short, they represented very well the manly and the womanly sides of the feminine nature.' Katharine's glamour crystallizes as Cassandra watches her dress for dinner.

> The face in the looking-glass was serious and intent, apparently occupied with other things besides the straightness of the parting which, however, was being driven as straight as a Roman road through the dark hair. Cassandra was impressed again by Katharine's maturity; and, as she enveloped herself in the blue dress which filled almost the whole of the long looking-glass with blue light and made it the frame of a picture, holding not only the slightly moving effigy of the beautiful woman, but shapes and colors of objects reflected from the background, Cassandra thought that no sight had ever been quite so romantic.[38]

What seems to interest Woolf in this scene is the split between Cassandra's romantic vision of Katharine and the feat of engineering Katharine accomplishes with brush and comb as she drives a parting straight as a Roman road through her hair, while apparently occupied with other things. The earlier blunt distinction in terms of manliness and womanliness has been restated as a difference between kinds of attention, or kinds of engagement with self and world. The clumsiness of the phrasing in the sentence which describes Katharine's labours with the comb ('occupied with other things besides the *straight*ness of the parting, which, however, was being driven as *straight* . . .') intensifies an emphasis on Katharine's concentration: the parting, or rather its exact accomplishment through technique, has become an end in itself. The writer, we might think, has in this instance not found it easy to comb her thought syntactically: *her* technique is also at issue. The next sentence, by contrast, fills smoothly up with Cassandra's admiration, itself immediately comprehensible as aesthetic response: the blue dress's blue light converts the mirror into a picture. In Woolf, as in Degas, an apprehension of *toilette* as work requiring solemn engagement has provoked a small technical disturbance, a change of approach. That apprehension makes all the difference between the *toilette* scenes in *Adam Bede* and *Night and Day*. Hetty Sorrel performs both roles: she is Katharine Hilbery, working intently with comb and brush, *and* Cassandra Otway, gazing in rapture at the beauty thus produced. Roman roads do not feature in her plans for those 'dark hyacinthine curves'. What Eliot had brought together in imagining Hetty through her awareness of a picture (that is, the work done by way of self-preparation, and an understanding of the effect it will have on others), Woolf prises apart. That change of emphasis offers one way to think about a certain kind of Modernism.[39]

Broken Combs, and a Handbreadth of Mirror

Reviewing the 1886 Impressionist exhibition, J.-K. Huysmans had noted that Degas's bathers 'must stoop in order to mask their bodily waste by grooming themselves'.[40] The *toilette* scene could be understood as drawing attention to the very residues of matter which the activity itself was designed if not to eradicate, then at least to remove temporarily, or to disguise. Hence, perhaps, Huntly Carter's feeling that Sickert should not have chosen titles such as 'Wash and Brush-up' or 'The Comb'. Hence, perhaps, the bitter misogyny animating Eliot's Fresca fragment (or, indeed, De Mille's). Although neither Degas nor Sickert depicted the instrument of *toilette* as in itself an object of disgust, others did. Huysmans, for example, worked the phrase *saleté de peigne* into his novel *Les Soeurs Vatard* (1879) in order to describe how a working-class woman lets herself go when she has no lovers to prepare for.[41] It is the consequences of *toilette*, rather than boredom or remorse, which brings to an end the otherwise revivifying affair enjoyed by the protagonist of *En ménage* (above, p. 51). The encumbered bathroom does not necessarily amount to evidence of sluttishness, or moral failure, on the woman's part. The comb and face-cloth are after all only doing their job, which is to move dirt from one place to another. Rather, the protagonist's phobic response has produced a new knowledge: of the facts of life, of the necessary disillusionment that awaits at the far end of each necessary illusion. In Naturalist fiction, the broken, clogged comb constitutes the threshold which illusion (desire) must cross if it is to transcend disillusionment (phobia), however briefly.

One British writer greatly preoccupied by the mutual implication of phobia and desire was D.H. Lawrence. In Lawrence's neo-Naturalist Edwardian divorce-drama *The Trespasser* (1912), Siegmund, about to break the 'bonds' of marriage by embarking on an affair, returns home to the accustomed domestic debris, which he surveys with 'disgust' from the vantage-point of his armchair. Leaning back, he feels something in the way: a small teddybear, and 'half of a strong white comb'. 'This was the summary of his domestic life: a broken, coarse comb, a child crying because her hair was tugged, a wife who had let the hair go till now, when she had got into a temper to see the job through.'[42] The problem (the reason why Lawrence did not write any more novels like this one) lies in the allegory. The broken comb has ceased to be a fact of life: the moment at which phobia permits us to understand desire as what it is, a necessary illusion. Instead, it tells a story: the story of someone else's failure. Siegfried blames his disillusionment on the wife who had let their child's hair go till now, and then got into a temper. Phobia would have told him that a broken comb, like Virginia Woolf's broken vacuum-cleaner (another dirt-magnet), is just a piece of equipment awaiting repair. Siegfried is here the Benjaminian allegorist discerning the 'natural history' of a marriage in the 'ruin' constituted by a broken comb: the ruin being for Benjamin the point in existence at which death has dug out most deeply the 'jagged line of demarcation between physical nature and meaning'.[43] A similar natural history unfolds in De Mille's *Old Wives for New*: the Siegmund-like protagonist has a nasty turn when he discovers the messes his wife has left in the wash-basin, including a clogged comb (fig. 7).

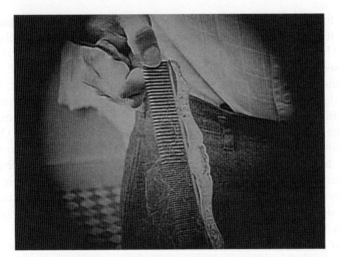

Figure 7   including a clogged comb

Lawrence's other divorce-drama, *Lady Chatterley's Lover*, written and rewritten in the period between October 1926 and February 1928, published in 1928, makes intelligent use of the idea of a woman combing to mediate extreme desire's encounter with extreme phobia. Like Siegfried, Connie Chatterley and Mellors are prone to allegorize. Speaking as one, they blame the world's brokenness on someone, or something, else. They regard modernization as a collective moral failure. The greatest threat to their necessary illusion – the intense sexual fulfilment they experience together – is the intensity of the hatred they feel for modern bourgeois life. The novel is at its most profound, I would argue, when it asks whether they will ever take responsibility for the bitterness of their own disillusionment.

In order to answer this question, Lawrence had to modernize himself. Like Degas and Woolf, he revised the *toilette de Venus* tradition, not isolating comb from mirror, as Degas did, but setting these elements in a new relation to each other, as Woolf did. It wasn't easy. The second version of the novel, which he probably began to write in December 1926, incorporates a new scene in which Connie Chatterley, having for the first time spent the night in the gamekeeper's cottage, washes herself in an 'ugly basin' in the bedroom, and wonders about his wife, Bertha Coutts. 'And as she combed her hair with the little black comb he had laid on the bare dressing-table, she thought how many times the swivel mirror had reflected the face of the other woman.' There is something a bit complacent about this, in its scrupulous attention to detail. Lawrence's exclusive emphasis on what Connie sees (or imagines seeing) in the mirror represents her to us in thoroughly traditional terms. She is jealous – and still prone to allegory, blaming what has happened to Parkin (as he is in this version) on Bertha's violence and 'coarse egoism'.[44]

When Lawrence re-wrote this scene in the novel's third and final version, he stripped out the detail, as Degas had stripped out the documentary context from his earlier representations of *toilette*, relying instead on the expressive capacities of dialogue. The morning after their first night together in the cottage, Connie gets out of bed to find nothing at all in the bare little room except a chest of drawers and a bookshelf.

> She came downstairs, down the steep, narrow wooden stairs. Still she would be content with this little house – if only it were in a world of its own.
> He was washed and fresh, and the fire was burning.
> 'Will you eat anything?' he said.
> 'No! Only lend me a comb.'
> She followed him into the scullery, and combed her hair before the handbreadth of mirror by the back door. Then she was ready to go.
> She stood in the little front garden, looking at the dewy flowers, the grey bed of pinks in bud already.
> 'I would like to have all the rest of the world disappear, she said, 'and live with you here.'
> 'It won't disappear,' he said.[45]

What is new in the revised version is Connie's explicit awareness both of the power of illusion and of its vulnerability. She would like to live in the little house, 'if only it were in a world of its own', which it clearly isn't. *Toilette* is the rite of passage which re-absorbs her back into the 'rest of the world' and its manifold imperfections. In representing it, Lawrence has beautifully re-adjusted the customary proportion of comb to mirror. To comb your hair while inspecting yourself fully in a mirror is to create an illusion. To comb your hair before a *handbreadth* of mirror, on the other hand, a mirror so small that you cannot see in it as much of yourself as you need to see, is to reckon with both illusion and disillusionment: to know that you will never be seen exactly as you might wish to be seen. Connie has left her inner Venus behind her in the bedroom. For Lawrence's second major revision relocates her *toilette* to the scullery. Combing her hair in the scullery, in a handbreadth of mirror, she must acknowledge that the 'rest of the world' starts inside the little house, inside arcadia. The mirror's insufficiency has stopped her from expecting too much of sexual tenderness. It permits repair-work, but not performance, not illusion. As far as we can tell, Mellors remains oblivious, or indifferent, to what she has done with her hair. Where his response might have been, Lawrence instead proposes her admiration of the flowers in the little front garden: a bit more arcadia, held most firmly as it is about to be relinquished. His third major revision is to foreground the ensuing brief conversation about the likelihood (or not) of the rest of the world's imminent disappearance. The fact that dialogue now concludes the scene, and with it the whole overwrought episode, is as expressive as anything the two lovers find to say to each other. For dialogue is a way not to resolve the tension between necessary illusion and necessary disillusionment built into all meaningful and valuable experience. The attention Lawrence pays to Connie's exercise of aptitude and energy to uncertain (by no means wholly purgative) effect has wonderfully complicated his understanding of the nature and scope of redemption.

Notes

1   *BLAST 1*, facsimile edition (Santa Barbara: Black Sparrow Press, 1981), 50.
2   Eliot's contributions to the genre include 'Paysage Triste' and 'In the Department Store': *Inventions of the March Hare: Poems 1909–1917*, ed. Christopher Ricks (London: Faber and Faber, 1996), 52, 56. Pound's include 'The Garden', 'The Encounter', and 'The Tea Shop': *Collected Shorter Poems* (London: Faber and Faber, 1952), 93, 120, 127. Kasia Boddy named the 'as if' poem, and my thinking about it has been shaped by conversations with her.
3   For reasons of economy, this essay will concern itself with female *toilette* only. Male *toilette* was a topic of great, though not *as* great, interest during the period. The notion of *toilette* includes the process of dressing as well as that of washing and grooming, but it is attention to the latter which could be said to distinguish Modernist literature from what went before. Danielle Dupuis has shown how crucial attention to the former was to Balzac's project, for example: 'La Poésie de la toilette féminine chez Balzac', *L'Année Balzacienne*, 5, 1985, 173–95; 'Toilette féminine et réalisme balzacienne', *L'Année Balzacienne*, 7, 1986, 115–38; Toilette féminine et structure Romanesque', *L'Année Balzacienne*, 10, 1989, 289–99. As Dupuis points out, Balzac was strikingly reticent, by contrast, on the subject of washing and grooming: 'Poésie', 188.
4   *The Annotated Waste Land*, ed. Lawrence Rainey (New Haven: Yale University Press, 2005), 59–60.
5   *The Waste Land: A Facsimile and Transcript of the Original Drafts*, ed. Valerie Eliot (London: Faber and Faber, 1971), 23.
6   'Introspection', *Poetry: A Magazine of Verse*, 15.6, 1919–1920, 298–9, p. 299.
7   'Sudden Death', *Coterie*, 3, December 1919, 55–7, p. 56.
8   'Imaginary Conversation', ibid., 42–9, p. 43.
9   'Of Modern Poetry', *Collected Poems* (London: Faber and Faber, 1955), 239–40, p. 240.
10   On these programmes, see Suzanne Raitt, 'The Rhetoric of Efficiency in Early Modernism', *Modernism/Modernity*, 13.1, 2006, 89–106.
11   *BLAST 1*, 25; *Rhythm*, 7, August 1912: iv.
12   David Trotter, *Cooking with Mud: The Idea of Mess in Nineteenth-Century Art and Fiction* (Oxford: Oxford University Press, 2000).
13   The significance of hair in nineteenth-century literature has received a good deal of attention. See, for example, Taylor Hagood, 'Hair, Feet, Body, and Connectedness in *Song of Myself'*, *Walt Whitman Quarterly Review*, 21.1, 2003, 25–34; Carol Rifelj, 'The Language of Hair in the Nineteenth-Century Novel', *Nineteenth-Century French Studies*, 32. 1&2, 2003–2004, 83–96; and Galia Ofek, 'Sensational hair: gender, genre, and fetishism in the sensational decade', in Kimberly Harrison and Richard Fantina, eds., *Victorian Sensations: Essays on a Scandalous Genre* (Columbus: Ohio State University Press, 2006), 102–14.
14   *The Pre-Raphaelite Body: Fear and Desire in Painting, Poetry, and Criticism* (Oxford: Clarendon Press, 1998), 136.

15 'Body's Beauty', no. 78 in *The House of Life: A Sonnet Sequence*, in *Collected Writings*, ed. Jan Marsh (London: J.M. Dent, 1999), 275–325, p. 314.

16 *Adam Bede*, ed. Stephen Gill (Harmondsworth: Penguin Books, 1980), 149.

17 'Facturing Femininity: Manet's *Before the Mirror*', October, 74, 1995, 74–104, pp. 79, 89–90.

18 My discussion of this painting relies heavily on Patricia Phillippy, *Painting Women: Cosmetics, Canvases, and Early Modern Culture* (2006), 165–71.

19 'The "Makeup" of the Marquise: Boucher's Portrait of Pompadour at Her Toilette', *Art Bulletin*, 82.3, 2000, 453–75, pp. 453, 464, 468.

20 Tamar Garb, *Bodies of Modernity: Figure and Flesh in Fin-de-Siècle France* (1998), 131–6.

21 *Ulysses*, ed. Jeri Johnson (Oxford: Oxford University Press, 1993), 256.

22 *Bid Me to Live* (London: Virago, 1984): 40.

23 *Degas beyond Impressionism* (London: National Gallery Publications Limited, 1996), 143–9, 155–7.

24 Ibid., 218.

25 Ibid., 166–8.

26 'A Discipline of Distortions', *New Age*, 11.6, 6 June 1912, 138–9, p. 139.

27 *Degas beyond Impressionism*, 168.

28 *John Sloan's New York Scene: From the Diaries, Notes, and Correspondence, 1906–1913*, ed. Bruce St. John (New York: Harper and Row, 1965), entries for 13 August 1910 and 6 December 1910.

29 'Mesopotamia-Cézanne', *New Age*, 5 March 1914, reprinted in *Walter Sickert: The Complete Writings on Art*, ed. Anna Gruetzner Robins (Oxford: Oxford University Press, 2000), 338–42, p. 342.

30 *Burlington Magazine*, 31, 1917, 183–91.

31 *Degas beyond Impressionism*, 218–19.

32 *Paterson* (Harmondsworth: Penguin Books, 1983), 145.

33 Letter of May 1918, reprinted by Denys Sutton, 'The Degas Sales and England', *Burlington Magazine*, 131, 1989, 266–72, p. 271. Sutton gives a full account of the intricate and ultimately frustrating negotiations that ensued. See also Fry, 'Degas', in *Characteristics of French Art* (London: Chatto and Windus, 1932), 130–8, p. 136.

34 Letter of 15 April to Nicholas Bagenal, *Collected Letters*, ed. Nigel Nicolson, 6 vols., (London: Hogarth Press, 1975–80), 2. 230.

35 Letter of 16 February 1919 to Vanessa Bell, *Collected Letters*, 2. 331. Woolf's most substantial essay on the visual arts took the form of *Walter Sickert: A Conversation* (London: Hogarth Press, 1934).

36 Letter of 22 April 1918 to Vanessa Bell, *Collected Letters*, 2. 230.

37 'A Sketch of the Past', in *Moments of Being: Unpublished Autobiographical Writings*, ed. Jeanne Schulkind (London: Triad/Granada, 1978), 71–159, pp. 81–2.

38 *Night and Day*, ed. Suzanne Raitt (Oxford: Oxford University Press, 1992), 359–60, 362–3.

39 For Marcel Proust, however, whose interest lay above all in the power of illusion, the mirror continued to count for more than the comb: *Remembrance of Things Past*, tr. C.K. Scott Moncrieff and Terence Martin, 3 volumes (Harmondsworth: Penguin Books, 1983), 1. 343, 384–5.

40 *Certains* (Paris: Librarie Plon, 1925), 25.

41 *Oeuvres completes*, ed. Lucien Descaves (Paris: G. Crès, 1928–34), 3. 53.

42   *The Trespasser*, ed. Elizabeth Mansfield (Cambridge: Cambridge University Press, 1981), 51.

43   Cited in translation by Susan Buck-Morss, *The Dialectics of Seeing: Walter Benjamin and the Arcades Project* (Cambridge, MA: MIT Press, 1989), 161.

44   *The First and Second Lady Chatterley Novels*, ed. Dieter Mehl and Christa Jansohn (Cambridge: Cambridge University Press, 1999), 444.

45   *Lady Chatterley's Lover*, ed. Michael Squires (Cambridge: Cambridge University Press, 1993), 213.

6

British First World War Combat Fiction

In James Hanley's *The German Prisoner* (1930), two defiantly proletarian British soldiers, O'Garra and Elston, lose contact with their unit during an assault on the German lines. The 'fog of war' has had the effect, it seems, of putting them once and for all beyond authority's reach. They capture a young German soldier called Otto Reiburg whose fair hair and fine clear eyes represent to them a provocatively bourgeois 'grace of body'. The buried 'rottenness' in O'Garra shoots up like filth from a sewer in a deathly premature ejaculation. O'Garra and Elston begin to beat Reiburg unconscious. Elston urinates on him. O'Garra drives a bayonet into his anus. 'Elston laughed and said: "I'd like to back-scuttle the bugger."' And that appears to be that. The worst obscenity, in a performance obscene from beginning to end, is that Reiburg remains unraped. The Sadean utopia O'Garra and Elston have built for themselves inside war's thickening excremental fog is dedicated to the pursuit of death alone. A shell duly puts an end to them both.[1]

Gunn, the veteran protagonist of Liam O'Flaherty's *Return of the Brute* (1929), is another man subject to deathly ejaculations. The object of Gunn's desire is a raw recruit feminised by cowardice, whose timidity becomes to him a 'seductive temptation'. He at once gives in to and overcomes temptation by murdering a sadistic corporal, as it were on his friend's behalf, while they are out on a raid. 'Now he was really an animal, brutish, with dilated eyes, with his face bloody.'[2] Gunn has joined O'Garra and Elston inside war's excremental fog.

Such brutishness is not absolutely unprecedented in fiction, of course. But there is nothing else quite like it in British First World War combat fiction. Indeed, it is from the scarcity of such scenes that an account of such fiction must begin. The most obvious explanation for the scarcity turns on class. Hanley and O'Flaherty were of proletarian origin; both served in the ranks during the war, and both fully intended to do justice to the brute's point of view. Most British war novels were written by middle-class writers who fully intended to do justice to the point of view either of the officer and gentleman, or of the gentleman-ranker (that is, the un-brutish private soldier whose superior education made him worthy of, though not necessarily ambitious for, a commission). The implicit investment these novels all make, with or without enthusiasm, is in the durability of the class-system. The class-system goes to war, and survives, even if its individual representatives do not (they often do not). What gets lost in the excremental fog conjured up by Hanley and O'Flaherty is not just desire, but the class-system.

Not having to worry about the class-system's survival enables Hanley and O'Flaherty to conceive protagonists whose existence is in action. O'Garra, Elston, and Gunn act on their impulses. They get to do things they might not otherwise have done. They kill people intentionally. Middle-class writers, by contrast, seem to have convinced themselves that the price of collective durability was the individual's painful and sometimes profoundly damaging adaptation to a new and hostile environment. Adaptation is in essence reactive. It often entails, or is realized by, suffering; at the very least, it requires one not to do things one might otherwise have done. On the whole, British combat novels, like British combat memoirs, have a lot to say about physical and mental suffering. Reading these novels and memoirs, one wonders why the Germans ever lost the war, since little meaningful action is ever taken against them. What requires explanation, in the paradigmatic British combat novel, is the belief it articulates that a maximum of individual adaptability will ensure a minimum of collective change.

The Nature of Damage

According to Samuel Hynes, the figure of the 'damaged man' began to receive sympathetic attention during the middle years of the war. Hynes has shown that after the war's conclusion this figure became a 'dominant character' in literature, radically altering the 'whole idea of literary war.'[3] His main example of the figure of the damaged man is Harry Penrose, the protagonist of A.P. Herbert's *The Secret Battle* (1919), a sensitive and idealistic young man who endures the ordeal of Gallipoli – an ordeal to which the laziness and spite of some of his fellow-officers is a major contributing factor – and is then sent to France. In France, his superiors start, at first with little justification, to doubt his courage. Obliged to undertake ever more dangerous tasks in order to prove himself, Penrose is wounded, and evacuated to England. His nerve has gone. However, he insists on returning to the Front, where he breaks down under fire, and turns tail. He is court-martialled, and shot.

In his vivid fantasy of participation in a 'Greeklike struggle', as in his susceptibility to the macabre tales savouringly told by veterans, Harry Penrose greatly resembles Henry Fleming, the protagonist of Stephen Crane's *The Red Badge of Courage* (1895), who also turns tail, but gets his red badge anyway, from a random blow to the head, and honourably resumes combat.[4] *The Red Badge of Courage* is the archetypal 'secret battle' novel, the first modern war book. In September 1916, somewhere in the Ypres salient, Ford Madox Ford found that Crane's 'visualization' of an army encampment had 'superimposed' itself on the 'concrete objects' in the world around him.[5] He was, for a moment, living the book.

There is, however, a crucial difference between Crane's version of the secret battle and Herbert's. Penrose, unlike Fleming, but like the vast majority of the protagonists of British First World War fiction, including those who serve in the ranks, is middle-class, and conscious of it. He is every inch – in his basic decency, in his Oxford education, in the crush he develops on a 'young Apollo' among his fellow-officers – the English gentleman. The performance at issue in this fantasy of status (this classed and gendered fantasy) constitutes the British combat novel. The protagonist must perform, or be branded a coward; so must the novel. If one fails, the other may yet succeed, by readjusting expectations.

The novel's readjustment involves a description of the battlefield: the environment in which the protagonist has been required to perform. The plain-speaking narrator of *The Secret Battle*, a fellow-officer (Herbert had served at Gallipoli and in France) insists that the explanation for Penrose's conduct is to be found among the 'dreary commonplaces of all war-chronicles'.[6] These commonplaces might be thought dreary because they turn neither on exhilaration nor on terror, but on disgust. There is no escaping disgust, in First World War combat narratives. Disgust might be thought the inevitable (that is, 'natural') response to many of the scenes witnessed during battle and its long-drawn-out aftermath. But it is more than that. It is the feeling above (or below) all others which these war-chronicles intend to provoke in their readers. Oddly, given its pervasive-ness, little account has been taken of the nature and uses of this feeling. Here, I shall concentrate on disgust's relation to fear.

As a response, disgust lies somewhere between fight and flight. The nineteenth-century French psychiatrist Théodule Ribot concluded that disgust takes over when flight is impossible: 'the organism cannot escape by movement in space from the repugnant body which it has taken into itself, and goes through a movement of expulsion instead.'[7] In the trenches, of course, flight *was*, indeed, impossible. Precisely because it sets in when one is immobile, however, disgust can sometimes produce a phenomenol-ogy: a description of being-in-the-world, of what existence still means, if anything, once the customary methods of conceiving it (political, moral, theological) have been suspended. British combat novels and memoirs achieve a quite astonishing purchase on the texture of event.

Trench warfare instigated a carnival of all the faculties. 'Everything visible or audible or tangible to the sense – to touch, smell and perception – is ugly beyond imagination,' wrote W. Beach Thomas, who had witnessed five months of fighting on the Somme in 1916.[8] Returning from leave, in May 1916, Lieutenant Wyn Griffith realized that he now had more to lose, 'for the deadening power of months of trench habit had been lifted from my mind leaving my fibre bare to the weakest blast of war'. The medium of war's weakest (but still toxic) blast was disgust. 'Sound, sight and smell were all challenged at once, and they must in concert submit to the degrading slavery of war.'[9] The ugliness, then, was complex. But the complexity, as articulated by the novels and memoirs, reveals a high degree of organisation, a *history*.

Steven Connor has suggested that modernity should be understood not in terms of the subordination of the proximity senses, as typified by the ear, to the hegemony of the eye, but rather in terms of a fraught and continually renewed argument between the powers of ear and eye. Ear and eye offer different versions of what being-in-the-world is like. Sight has often been understood as a principle of integration, sound as disintegrative. Although we can only see one thing at a time, we can hear several sounds simultaneously. Furthermore, sound often carries menace unless we can trace it back to a specific source, or visualize its origin. Noise, especially loud noise, is always 'agonistic': it involves the maximum at once of arousal and of passivity.[10] The sound of the guns, composite and sourceless, was a primary terror for the soldier in the trenches. And not just enemy guns. Chronicle after chronicle describes a journey to or from the front line during which concealed British artillery abruptly looses off.

In the hierarchy of the senses, sight belongs at the top, largely because the distance at which it acts makes possible an array of measures of precaution and control. The proximity senses traditionally rank lower. Lowest of all is smell. That there are bad sounds need not diminish the glory of hearing. That there are delightful fragrances has done little to elevate smell: traditionally, the best odour is not a good odour, but no odour at all.[11] The combat novels and memoirs describe smell as the most disintegrative principle of all, the most damaging to moral and perceptual fibre. Everywhere it undermines vision. The eyes can usually be averted from a bad sight (though it may well return as a mental image). But a bad smell is inside you before you can do anything about it. It takes possession.

The difference is semantic as well as cognitive. Smells are hard to define. 'Even though the human sense of smell can distinguish hundreds of thousands of smells and in this regard is comparable to sight or hearing,' Dan Sperber has observed, 'in none of the world's languages does there seem to be a classification of smells comparable, for example, to colour classification.' There is no taxonomy of smells, no semantic field. When we define smells, we do so in terms either of their causes (the smell of incense, the smell of excrement) or of their effects (a heady perfume, an appetising smell). In the domain of smell, 'metonymy remains active and infallibly evokes cause or effect'.[12] Whereas the unpleasantly tactile possesses its own rich and versatile idiom (oozy, squishy, gummy, dank, and so on), an idiom richly at work in combat-novels and combat-memoirs, the unpleasantly odorous does not. The tactile is a stimulus to literary invention.[13] By contrast, it is the *lack* of an appropriate semantic field which renders the mere allusion to a bad smell in narrative profoundly unsettling. It produces either a helpless metonymic proliferation, or an abrupt halt, a lapse into no-meaning. A bad smell always returns from elsewhere, from beyond conscious recollection.

The Secret Battle chronicles Harry Penrose's education in disgust, which connects with, but is not quite the same thing as, his education in fear. On his way to war, Penrose amply betrays his infatuation with an heroic ideal, as Stephen Fleming had done before him. On their first night in the front line, the narrator introduces him to reality in the shape of the stench emanating from a dead Turk. For the narrator, it is enough to know that the stench exists. Penrose needs to define it minutely by tracing it back to a source. 'Forthwith he swarmed over the parapet, full of life again, nosed about till he found the reeking thing, and gazed on it with undisguised interest' (*SB* 40). He shows, as yet, no sign of horror or disgust. War will destroy that immunity. It will train him in horror and disgust. A 'complex irritation' made of sounds, smells, animosities, slights, and the 'disgustful torment' of disease corrodes his 'young system' (89). The enemy plays a part in all this, but only a small part. The final stage in the destruction of Penrose's young system occurs when the company takes over a trench seized from the Turks. Surveying the corpses sprawled in the 'corrupt aftermath' of battle, the narrator adopts the position of a generalized observer. Such corrupt aftermaths, we are to understand, were drearily commonplace.

> But there was a hideous fascination about the things, so that after a few hours a man came to know the bodies in his bay with a sickening intimacy, and could have told you many details about each of them – their regiment, and how they lay, and how they had died, and little things about their uniforms, a missing button, or some papers, or an old photograph sticking out of a pocket ... All of them were alive with flies, and at noon when we took out our bread and began to eat, these flies rose in a great black swarm and fell upon the food in our hands. After that no-one could eat. All day men were being sent away by the doctor, stricken with sheer nausea by the flies and the stench and the things they saw, and went retching down the trench.

The phenomenology is in the enforced intimate attention, in the nausea. The narrator remembers that first evening when Penrose had jumped over the parapet to look at the dead Turk. 'He had seen enough now' (104–6).

The best solution to nausea was to remain uneducated in it; or, more precisely, to fall back on a different kind of training, a training in ignorance of the body. Fortunately for the British army such training had been amply provided by the public schools. Penrose knows, and is able convincingly to enact, paternalism. He is a good officer because he performs concern for his men, and nonchalance. He cheerfully undertakes the 'melancholy rite' of demonstrating to a reluctant sentry how safe it is to raise one's head above the parapet by doing so himself, without fuss. 'He had a keen dramatic instinct, and I think in these little scenes rather enjoyed the part of the unperturbed hero calming the timorous herd' (*SB* 51). It is no coincidence that the scene involves a reassertion of the ascendancy of sight. When he volunteers to act as scouting officer, Penrose makes himself into the very epitome of the powers of the eye. His task is not just to see, but to see without being seen. The scout performs invisibility. If a flare goes up, he freezes, because 'to keep still in any posture is better than to move'. Penrose's performance of seeing-without-being-seen is a way to exorcise the body on all other occasions in the trenches brought so fully into play, by sound, smell, touch, and taste. When one of his men panics, and the scouting party is caught out in the open, the exposure destroys his ability to perform in general (123–4). Thereafter, he has no defence against disgust, and the phenomenology it generates.

It may be that the British public was not ready, in 1919, for Herbert's account of the incapacitating effects of an education in disgust. The book did not sell. It was re-issued, however, in 1924, with an admiring preface by Winston Churchill; and then again in 1928, as the demand for chronicles of damaged men and women took off, ten years after the end of the war which had done the damage. Britain in the late 1920s was of course not quite the same place. Much has been made, for example, of the fact that the 'classic' memoirs and novels were written in the aftermath not of the war itself, but of the General Strike, 'war's echo in society', which began on 4 May 1926.[14] Eric Leed even suggests that it was not until the Depression had 'closed the gap' between civilian and ex-soldier, by reducing both to powerlessness, that the combat novels and memoirs began to appear in larger numbers.[15] Another significant difference, and one to which I shall return, lay in the development in the early 1920s of a particular psychiatric vocabulary. In their depiction of mental suffering, the memoirs and novels were to some extent the product of a new traumatology, a 'culture of trauma'.[16] Broadly speaking, however, there was a fair amount of consistency between the war literature published before traumatology and the Great Strike and the war literature published after it. With some notable exceptions, as we have seen, they had the same story to tell: the story of damage, of middle-class suffering.

The power of the paradigm is evident even, or especially, in those novels which sought to modify it from within. John Hardcastle, the hero of James Lansdale Hodson's *Grey Dawn – Red Night* (1929), is of working-class origin. Like Paul Morel, in D.H. Lawrence's *Sons and Lovers* (1913), whom he closely resembles, Hardcastle has raised himself above both physical labour and a drunken father by employment in white-collar jobs, first as a solicitor's clerk, then as a journalist. On the boat to France, he reads two stories about running away, Crane's *The Red Badge of Courage* and Conrad's *Lord Jim*.[17] He could become Stephen Fleming, the canny proletarian survivor; or Lord Jim, who owns up, like the gentleman he is, and takes his punishment.

Work matters, in this novel: it is one of the few to describe in detail the working-practices, as the British Army conceived them, of warfare.

Hardcastle, a lance-corporal in the Twentieth Royal Fusiliers, believes that he will win his secret battle against fear and disgust by a commitment to work. For him, as for the gentlemanly Harry Penrose, the real test lies the corrupt aftermath of ground taken from the enemy. 'It affected him more than all else, and now that they had passed through the dread spot, from time to time the stench again came and dwelt in his nostrils' (GD 248). He escapes the stench, as before the war he had escaped his drunken father, by employment in a 'white-collar' job: as an orderly at Company headquarters. He might have become an upwardly mobile Henry Fleming. But Hodson cannot leave it there. He seems to have felt that his novel had to be a story about middle-class suffering, even though the hero is not (or not yet) middle-class. Conrad eclipses both Crane and Lawrence. Hardcastle is killed while on his way back from Company headquarters to take up the offer of a commission. The novel itself has left him out in the open. It does not know how to tell a story about combat which would include social mobility (or a story about social mobility which would include combat).

If the prospect of social mobility sets one limit to the story of middle-class suffering, then the prospect of cowardice unpunished, or punished lightly, sets another: we need to ask (the combat novel needs to ask) how far adaptation can go. A.D. Gristwood's The Somme (1927), a story of middle-class suffering, begins with a description of ground just taken from the enemy. As in The Secret Battle, the flies settling on bloated corpses form the pièce de résistance, the ultimate provocation to nausea. In his preface, H.G. Wells characterized The Somme as an antidote to the 'high enthusiastic survey' of the war which had been undertaken by Herbert's admirer, Winston Churchill. Low, and unenthusiastic, it most certainly is. Gristwood seems to want to ask how low and unenthusiastic one can get, as a combatant and a writer, without ceasing to be a gentleman.

Everitt, Gristwood's protagonist, doesn't run away. But he doesn't *not* run away, either. The Somme is the story of his survival, after being wounded in a futile 'advance', and of the long journey back from no-man's-land to No. 5 General Hospital at Rouen. Everitt fails to perform. He abandons his part in the assault on the enemy trenches and flops into a shell-hole. 'Perhaps after all they could *not* see him. Above all he must lie still, for it seemed that shots answered his slightest movement.' But he cannot perform immobility, either. He is hit in the leg and the arm. Everitt is a bit of a brute. Like Hanley's O'Garra and Elston, like O'Flaherty's Gunn, he comes into his own in no-man's-land, in war's excremental fog. Unlike them, he will not act, but suffer. What he suffers is an immobilization in and by disgust more complete than that suffered by any other protagonist in British combat fiction. The novel's concluding section describes his near-entombment in a hammock slung two feet from the roof of a carriage on a hospital train full of the dead and dying. He realizes that his wounds have gone septic. 'The stench seemed more offensive whenever in his twistings and turnings he raised the folds of the blanket on his cot. The sickening sweetish odour filled him with a shuddering disgust, and appetite fled.'[18] Everitt's shuddering disgust is an adaptation of a kind; but a great deal too close to brutishness for comfort.

Soldiering as Philanthropy

There are no British war novels about colonels (let alone brigadiers or field-marshals). As far as literature is concerned, this was indeed, as the title of Charles Carrington's memoir has it, *A Subaltern's War*.[19] The novels, like most of the memoirs, have a lot to say about the trials and tribulations of leadership, and of being led: but not much about the enemy, who are a nuisance, and frequently the cause of spectacular random destruction, but do not figure in the defining psychomachia. The term 'strafe', ubiquitous in both, has reference rather more often to reprimands delivered by unsympathetic senior officers than it does to incoming artillery fire. The class-position specific to a subaltern in the Kitchener battalions raised at the beginning of war was an ambiguous one. The power of the novels and memoirs some of them subsequently wrote stems from that ambiguity.

John Keegan has described the difficulties an embryonic officer in this largely non-professional army might expect to face in 'adopting a personal style to match the rank which chance had thrust upon him'. The difficulties were eased somewhat by the army's decision to recruit the first temporary officers as far as possible from the public schools. Keegan points out that the eighteen-year-old who went on to the Royal Military College could be treated on arrival as someone 'already formed' in character and attitude, someone whose only deficiency was in tactical training.[20] These eighteen-year-olds achieved a certain style merely by being themselves. Like the relationship between classes in civilian society, the relationship between officers and men in the British Army was based on the exchange of deference for paternalism. Junior officers enjoyed all the privileges of rank, on condition that they did not shirk the dangers and hardships to which the men under their command were exposed and made a genuine effort to protect them from the excesses of military discipline.[21] Most combat novels include at least one officer who constitutes the epitome of New Army paternalism. Captain Mottram, in Hodson's *Grey Dawn – Red Night*, 'was gentle, almost womanly, with wounded or exhausted men, and would walk behind you and offer to share your load of rations' (GD 204). The generalizing 'you' and 'your' indicate that such officers, although exceptional, were by no means a rarity. O'Flaherty's brutes speak fondly of an officer who looks after them 'with the same enthusiasm that a man would show towards expensive and cherished horses on hunting days'.[22]

The enthusiastic or almost womanly concern, the pride taken in service: that was what being oneself meant. There was, of course, an abundant moral earnestness in the subaltern's paternalism. But it also had a psychological or even psychiatric dimension. Paternalism entailed, inexorably, a literal and figurative *self-lowering*. The subaltern knelt at his men's feet. 'Their feet were the most important part of them, I thought, as I made my sympathetic inspection of sores and blisters.'[23] If there was a precedent for self-lowering, in British middle-class culture, it is to be found in that combination of evangelical or reforming fervour with an insatiable curiosity about how the other half lives which constituted the philanthropic movement. There was sacred glamour to be won by such renunciations. On the whole, however, the privileges of birth survived intact. The philanthropist did not, for example, marry into or encourage political organization within the working-class. He or she remained recognizably middle-class, and proud of it, whatever the environment. Philanthropy combined a maximum of individual adaptability with a minimum of collective change.

Some of the best-known war-writers were brought up philanthropically. Robert Graves's mother, for example, had wanted to go to India, after training as a medical missionary; but marriage to a widower with five children suggested to her that she 'could do as good work on the home-mission field'.[24] Others, like Siegfried Sassoon, developed an interest in social reform as a result of what they had seen during the war.[25] The combat novel also witnessed one or two such transformations. Peter Currage, the protagonist of Christopher Stone's *The Valley of Indecision* (1920), falls under the sway of a visionary General who believes that the war has reinvigorated the 'officer class' by obliging its members to attend, for the first time, to the needs of those over whom they exercise authority. Currage, like the hero of a nineteenth-century Condition of England novel, resolves to lead a crusade against materialism and complacency.[26] The General's political prescription (strong leaders, discipline, comradeship) sounds a lot like fascism, and it would be possible to think of one or two British combat novels in those terms. On the whole, however, the subaltern philanthropists did not do fascism. Stone's later novel, *Flying Buttresses* (1927), is an account of Currage's emergence from this 'religious phase, or craze,' to play a more productive role as a traditional village squire.[27] The belief that the war had created a classless brotherhood of suffering and sacrifice was by no means widespread but it found an echo in some rather unexpected places. In *The Well of Loneliness* (1928), for example, Radclyffe Hall allows Stephen Gordon to convince herself that the service she and other 'inverts' have given during the war will be the means of their subsequent integration into society.[28]

The part played in nineteenth-century philanthropy and social reform by the slum was taken over, in the British combat novel and memoir, by the labyrinthine trench-system. Graves spent much of his first spell as officer of the watch in the trenches acquainting himself with their deceptive 'geography': he repeatedly got lost among 'culs-de-sacs and disused alleys'.[29] The war correspondent Philip Gibbs, whose work took him backwards and forwards between GHQ and the trenches, reported that the former had indeed heard of the latter, but only in the way that the fashionable West End of London had heard of the sordid East End, as a 'nasty place' full of 'common people'.[30] Edmund Blunden remembered a stint as Field Works Officer during which the trenches in his sector 'began to look extremely neat'. An itinerant General with a mania for chloride of lime complimented the Field Works Officer on his achievement of a truly dazzling level of whiteness; 'but actually it was powdered chalk that had enabled us to satisfy his sanitary imagination'.[31] Here, as so often in the combat novels and memoirs, the subaltern acts as the West End's representative in the East. Sharing the condition of his men – mud, vermin, shell-fire, exhaustion – he looks after them, and polices them, in the name of a distant authority. Trench-warfare, one might say, was Victorian philanthropy's last hurrah (or last gasp).

One novelist who experienced the war as Philip Gibbs had was R.H. Mottram. Mottram saw combat, but his fluency in French got him transferred to the Claims Commission, whose task it was to settle disputes between the British Army and its civilian hosts and suppliers. Although not a Staff Officer, he was attached to Divisional Headquarters, and thus saw life, as he put it, from a level slightly above the trenches, but slightly below officialdom.[32] Mottram's admirable *The Spanish Farm Trilogy* (1924–6) is much concerned with points of view, including that of its main British protagonist, Geoffrey Skene, an architect in civilian life, now serving in France as a liaison officer. Like Gibbs, Mottram was in no doubt about the rigidity of the class-system which regulated life in the army. 'If the trenches were the slums of that great city of two million English-speaking men, stretching across eighty miles of France,' the narrator observes, then the roads travelled by a liaison officer like Skene were a 'residential suburb', while Corps Head-quarters had 'the atmosphere of a London Club': 'tea, cigarettes, conversation all belonged to people used to the very best, who were not going to alter their habits for a mere war.' Fortunately, Skene possesses the philanthropist's talent for self-revision. The 'endless adaptability' required of the New Army officer encourages him to put his skills as an architect to use, not because he has been told to, but because the work interests him. It is grimly appropriate that he should finish the war conducting sanitary inspections from a base in the cellar of a model house destroyed by shell-fire: 'social reform murdered'.[33] Mottram's development of a narrative method attuned to the intensities and limitations of point of view enables him to render effectively the fluidity of the subaltern-philanthropist's positioning at or just above the level of the slum.

The adjustment downwards undertaken by philanthropist and subaltern alike was at once a de-classing (a wilful abandonment of the privileges of birth) and a de-classifying: the loss of the set of distinctions, between inside and outside, self and world, which had hitherto made identity conceivable. Disgust, which is the ultimate act of de-classifying, the body's acknowledgement that the distinction between self and world has collapsed (that the bad sound or bad smell is already inside), configures the philanthropic encounter. That is what the slum feels like, or the trenches, to those who

cannot altogether forget the bourgeois drawing-room they chose honourably to abandon. Disgust brings one down to the level of things which have
been brought down by an exposure of their materiality, their formlessness:
the pile of excrement in the centre of a courtyard, the rotting corpse on the
parapet. The rhetorical function this disgust serves, in the slum- or trench-
chronicle, is to establish a certain singularity. The nausea felt by the
philanthropist sets him or her apart both from the lower-class men and
women whose behaviour or circumstances have induced it, and from the
upper-class men and women who have never known anything like it.

Even more comprehensively brought down by nausea than the
subalterns were the gentleman-rankers who had honourably abandoned
the privileges of birth in order to serve as private soldiers. In Hodson's *Grey
Dawn – Red Night*, John Hardcastle, who is working-class, but a journalist by
profession, enlists as a private. So evident are the marks of a superior
education (the marks which will eventually single him out for middle-class
suffering) that he is immediately put in charge of 'four or five youths and
men, who were without collars, who smelt, and who were more or less
tipsy' (*GD* 97). These he conducts to a camp near Liverpool. 'Hardcastle lay
there feeling as if he had been dropped from the sky into a filthy slum from
which there was no escape.' Procuring a pass, he catches the train to
Liverpool, and gratefully blends into a crowd of staff officers drinking
whisky and soda at the Midland Adelphi Hotel. The Lawrence Hodson
seems closest to here is the Lawrence whose disgust at the spectacle of mass
conscription was to form the basis of the 'Nightmare' chapter of *Kangaroo*
(1923).[34]

The most celebrated gentleman-rankers in British First World War fiction
are Bourne, in Frederic Manning's *The Middle Parts of Fortune* (1929), and
Winterbourne, in Richard Aldington's *Death of a Hero* (1929): the coincidence in naming indicates that both these men are at a social and psychic
limit, a 'bourne' of some kind. Winterbourne is bullied by the N.C.O.s of his
training battalion, who are all Old Army regulars, and take revenge on what
remains of his gentility by forcing him to remove the accumulated filth from
the Officers' Mess Kitchen. The memory of this degradation haunts him
nauseously; he attributes to it the anxiety and depression he feels in combat.
'He suffered at feeling that his body had become worthless, condemned to a
sort of kept tramp's standard of living.' But, ever the philanthropist, indeed,
all the more the philanthropist after his reduction to kept tramp, he remains
unwilling to apply for a commission: 'it was contrary to his notion that he
ought to stay in the ranks and in the line, take the worst and humblest jobs,
share the common fate of the common men.'[35] Staying in the ranks costs
him his life.

At one point in *The Middle Parts of Fortune* an officer called Mr Rhys tries
to 'get into touch' with the men, and to learn their thoughts, 'without
putting aside anything of his prestige and authority over them'. 'Only a
great man,' the narrator concludes, as the narrators of so many Condition of

England novels had concluded before him, 'can talk on equal terms with those in the lower ranks of life.' Mr Rhys, it seems, is 'neither sufficiently imaginative, nor sufficiently flexible in character, to succeed'.[36] Much the same could be said of someone like Walter Egremont, in George Gissing's *Thyrza* (1887), who tries to bring 'spiritual education' to the 'upper artisan and mechanic classes' (there is no point, he reckons, in disturbing the 'mud' at the bottom of the social order).[37] Bourne, by contrast, does possess flexibility of character.

Bourne is, as far as I know, the only fictional trench-philanthropist who succeeds in developing, as a way not to be himself, an effective working-class style. Bourne improvises brilliantly. He can conjure a meal, or a bottle of whiskey, or some sympathetic advice, out of nothing. His abilities as a scrounger earn him a kind of celebrity. These exploits establish *bricolage* as the working-class alternative to the middle-class show put on by Captain Malet, who likes to anticipate the launch of an attack by climbing out of the trench and strolling up and down on the parapet.[38] Malet performs nonchalance. Bourne puts things (anything and everything) to use. Bourne's style seems to work as well, in its way, as Malet's. But it is only a style. For all his scrounging, Bourne remains indisputably a gentleman in the eyes both of his companions and of his superiors. Acknowledging this – acknowledging the falseness of his hesitation between styles – he decides, reluctantly, to apply for a commission. Like Gissing's Walter Egremont, he will retreat from his slum. He is killed, like Hodson's John Hardcastle, on the point of setting off to train as an officer. Manning, like Hodson and Aldington, can see no way out for the gentleman-ranker. The gentleman-ranker cannot be allowed to cross that threshold within the class-system whose preservation is the only reason for his existence.

Trauma (or the Uses of Nausea)

In H.M. Tomlinson's *All Our Yesterdays* (1930), the narrator, an Intelligence Officer, visits a front-line unit in trenches somewhere beyond Ypres. 'I was led through roofless houses and by broken walls, traversed a back-kitchen and yard where there was nothing but old bottles and a perambulator without wheels, passed a dead horse, and then met an aerial torpedo.' Aerial torpedo apart, this could be a passage taken from any number of nineteenth-century accounts of the social reformer's or sensation-seeking journalist's entry into an urban slum. As, indeed, could the description which follows it of the descent into a damp, cluttered, foul-smelling dugout (for dugout, read slum-cellar). The occupants regale their visitor with the story of a fellow-officer who has been blown up by a shell, but will not get a wound stripe, because he was 'only' driven head-first into the belly of a corpse. 'And after that Mac never sang. He wouldn't eat. He only wanted to wash out his mouth with neat whisky.' Disgust not only marks those who have been lowered, perhaps beyond redemption; it has become their uniform, their style, their element.[39]

It is quite likely that the story of the man driven head-first into a corpse derives from the psychiatric literature on 'shell shock'. In 'Repression of War Experience', printed in the *Lancet* on 2 February 1918, and then in *Instinct and the Unconscious* (1920), W.H.R. Rivers had written about an officer 'flung down' by an explosion in such a way that his face struck and penetrated the belly of a German soldier several days dead. 'Before he lost consciousness the patient had clearly realised his situation, and knew that the substance which filled his mouth and produced the most horrible sensations of taste and smell was derived from the decomposed entrails of an enemy.' Haunted thereafter by 'persistent images of taste and smell', like Mac in *All Our Yesterdays*, the man had to leave the army.[40] One point which Rivers tactfully does not make about his patient is that for him nausea evidently had its uses: it got him honourably out of the war, wound stripe or no. Rivers seems to have thought that so intense a disgust had left no room for fear. In another context, he described more explicitly the way in which horror and disgust sometimes took the place of fear in war-neurosis.

> In those who suffer thus from the effect of war-experience, one party in the original conflict is usually the re-awakened danger-instinct in some form or other with its accompanying affect of fear, but this is often wholly displaced by the affect of horror associated with some peculiarly painful incident of war, or by the affect of shame following some situation which the sufferer fears that he has failed to meet in a proper manner.[41]

What traumatology seems to be saying, in this instance, is that war-experience, which we might consider absolute in its extremity, is in fact relative. The feelings which constitute it derive their force not only from the horrific event which first provoked them, but also from their relation to each other. Experience at the human limit is not something one has, or succumbs to, but something one tries, often unsuccessfully, to put to use. Being disgusted is better than being afraid. It serves that purpose, at least. To grasp the relativity of traumatic experience is to create some space beyond it, so that one is no longer right up against the void.

The narrator of *The Secret Battle* develops a 'theory of the favourite fear'. The favourite fear both disables and enables. It disables because it identifies a particular situation as intolerable. It enables because the panic induced by that situation in particular makes the panic induced by other situations seem trivial by comparison. 'One man feels safe in the open, but in the strongest dug-out has a horror that it may be blown in upon him' (*SB*, 132–3). In *Instinct and the Unconscious*, Rivers returned frequently to the case of an officer in the Royal Army Medical Corp who suffered acutely from claustrophobia.[42] A phobia is always a 'favourite' (that is, highly specific) fear. The enclosed spaces intolerable to the claustrophobe are a haven to the agoraphobe, who fears open terrain above all; and vice versa. On 9 January

1918, James Dunn, a medical officer in the Royal Welch Fusiliers, noted in his diary that he had always found confinement in an enclosed space 'hateful'. He was subsequently awarded the MC and Bar and the DSO for his exploits in attending to the wounded in the open under heavy fire.[43]

Was it possible to nurture favourite disgusts, as well as favourite fears? I have already described the revulsion provoked in Harry Penrose and John Hardcastle by a highly specific battlefield horror: the 'corrupt aftermath' of ground taken from the enemy. Similarly Edmund Blunden's 'unwelcome but persistent retrospect' of a place called Stuff Trench was of a shell-hole which had been put to use as a latrine, 'with those two flattened German bodies in it, tallow-faced and dirty-stubbled'.[44] It is the first time we've met the bodies, in *Undertones of War*; no story attaches to them. But to Blunden they are none the less utterly specific ('*those* two flattened German bodies'). The act of specification, performed at the time or in retrospect, seems to have been a way to consolidate a favourite disgust. Robert Graves devoted a poem and a vivid passage in *Goodbye to All That* to an 'unforgettable' corpse he had come across in Mametz Wood.[45] Specification puts these corpses to use. It converts them from something to be frightened by, as evidence of death's near-certainty, into an object of disgust: an object of disgust *like no other*. So acute was the disgust provoked in him by one corpse in particular that Edwin Vaughan, returning to headquarters for instructions, felt unable to pass by it, and chose instead the shell-swept road. He took back with him to the front line an old oilsheet, which he spread over the offending corpse. It was from this point, with its horror outshining all other horrors, that he next led his platoon into action. It may be that he could not have done so from any other point.[46]

A combat novel does not have to be psychiatric to be effective. But the most effective First World War combat novels, I would suggest, are those which recognize that, for many of those who served in it, fear and disgust were a resource rather than an affliction. In *The Middle Parts of Fortune*, Bourne devises for himself a kind of battlefield phenomenology. He begins with the thought that 'it is infinitely more horrible and revolting to see a man shattered and eviscerated, than to see him shot.' But such burdens fall on the eye, whose distance from the horrible and revolting sight is also a guarantee of safety. 'The mind is averted as well as the eyes ... And one moves on, leaving the mauled and bloody thing behind.' The favourite disgust – a disgust powerful enough to supervene on all other disgusts – may require a further self-lowering, from sight to touch, or smell. Suddenly he remembers the 'festering, fly-blown corruption' of the intermingled British and German dead in Trones Wood. 'Out of one bloody misery into another, until we break. One must not break.' The sheer relativity of horror is its saving grace. Later in the novel, Bourne, knowing that his nerve has almost gone, uses his awareness of the location of a particularly loathsome corpse to force himself out into and through an artillery barrage. Manning, however, has set a limit to Bourne's phenomenology, and to his bricolage:

he is shot while returning from a raid designed to exploit and develop powers of improvization.[47] The most effective British combat novel of them all, Ford Madox Ford's *Parade's End* (1924–8), is the subject of my next chapter.

Notes

1   *The German Prisoner* (London: privately printed, 1930), 25, 32–3, 35–6.
2   *The Return of the Brute* (London: Mandrake Press, 1929), 186.
3   *A War Imagined: The First World War and English Culture* (London: Bodley Head, 1990), 304.
4   *The Red Badge of Courage*, ed. Pascal Covici (Harmdonsworth: Penguin, 1983), 46.
5   Max Saunders, *Ford Madox Ford: A Dual Life*, 2 vols. (Oxford: Oxford University Press, 1996), 2. 21.
6   *The Secret Battle*, 4th edition (London: Methuen, 1929), 1. Henceforth *SB*.
7   *The Psychology of the Emotions* (London: Walter Scott, 1897), 213–14.
8   *With the British on the Somme* (London: Methuen, 1917), 275.
9   *Up to Mametz* (London: Severn House, 1981), 111–13. First published in 1931.
10 'The Modern Auditory I', in Roy Porter, ed., *Rewriting the Self: Histories from the Renaissance to the Present* (London: Routledge, 1997), 203–23.
11 William Miller, *The Anatomy of Disgust* (Cambridge, Mass.: Harvard University Press, 1997), 75.
12 *Rethinking Symbolism*, trans. Alice L. Morton (Cambridge: Cambridge University Press, 1975), 115–16.
13 Santanu Das, '"Kiss Me, Hardy": Intimacy, Gender, and Gesture in World War I Trench Literature', *Modernism/Modernity*, 9, 2002, 51–74.
14 Hynes, *War Imagined*, 420.
15 *No Man's Land: Combat and Identity in World War I* (Cambridge: Cambridge University Press, 1981), 191–2.
16 Ben Shephard, *A War of Nerves: Soldiers and Psychiatrists, 1914–1994* (London: Pimlico, 2002).
17 *Grey Dawn – Red Night* (London: Victor Gollancz, 1929), 151. Henceforth *GD*.
18 *The Somme* (London: Jonathan Cape, 1927), 57, 112.
19 *A Subaltern's War* (London: Peter Davies, 1929).
20 *The Face of Battle* (Harmondsworth: Penguin, 1978), 278–80.
21 G.D. Sheffield, *Leadership in the Trenches: Officer-Man Relations, Morale and Discipline in the British Army in the Era of the First World War* (Basingstoke: Macmillan, 2000), 72.
22 *Return of the Brute*, 38.
23 Siegfried Sassoon, *Memoirs of an Infantry Officer* (London: Faber and Faber, 1997), 130.
24 *Goodbye to All That* (Harmondsworth: Penguin, 1960), 13.
25 *Siegfried's Journey 1916–1920* (London: Faber and Faber, 1945), 114–15.
26 *The Valley of Indecision* (London: Collins, 1920), 189–90.
27 *Flying Buttresses* (London: A.M. Philpot, 1927), 27.
28 Claire Buck, '"Still Some Obstinate Emotion Remains": Radclyffe Hall and the Meanings of Service', in Suzanne Raitt and Trudi Tate, eds., *Women's Fiction and the Great War* (Oxford: Oxford University Press, 1997), 174–96.

29   *Goodbye*, 88.
30   *Now It Can Be Told* (1920), quoted by Paul Fussell, *The Great War and Modern Memory* (Oxford: Oxford University Press, 1975), 83.
31   *Undertones of War* (Oxford: Oxford University Press, 1956), 90, 128–9, 132.
32   'A Personal Record', in R.H. Mottram, John Easton, and Eric Partridge, *Three Personal Records of the War* (London: Scholartis Press, 1929), 4–5.
33   *The Spanish Farm Trilogy* (London: Chatto & Windus, 1927), 376–7, 465.
34   Mark Kinkead-Weekes, *D.H. Lawrence: Triumph to Exile* (Cambridge: Cambridge University Press, 1996), 332, 382–4.
35   *Death of a Hero* (London: Chatto and Windus, 1929) 273–4, 276, 333–8, 388.
36   *The Middle Parts of Fortune* (Harmondsworth: Penguin, 1990), 149.
37   *Thyrza*, ed. Jacob Korg (Hassocks: Harvester, 1974), 14.
38   *Middle Parts*, 22.
39   *All Our Yesterdays* (London: Heinemann, 1930), 412–13, 416, 423–6.
40   'Repression of War Experience', in *Instinct and the Unconscious: A Contribution to a Biological Theory of the Psycho-Neuroses*, 2nd edn. (Cambridge: Cambridge University Press, 1922), 185–204, pp. 192. 'It was peculiarly horrible,' Gristwood observed in *The Somme*, 'to fall face downwards on a dead man' (37).
41   *Instinct*, 123.
42   Ibid., 170–84.
43   Keith Simpson, 'Dr James Dunn and Shell-shock', in Peter Liddle and Hugh Cecil, eds., *Facing Armageddon: The First World War Experienced* (London: Leo Cooper, 1996), 502–19, p. 512.
44   *Undertones*, 157.
45   *Goodbye*, 175.
46   *Some Desperate Glory* (Basingstoke: Macmillan, 1994), 218–21.
47   *Middle Parts*, 11, 173–6, 235.

7

Ford Against Joyce and Lewis

The focus of this essay is *Parade's End* (1924–8); or, to be precise, the second volume in the tetralogy, *No More Parades* (1925); or, to be more precise still, the novel's opening chapter, and the coincidence in and around that chapter of two kinds of high anxiety, one explicit, the other implicit. *No More Parades*: the book's title echoes, or predicts, the title of the tetralogy. The *idea* of the parade is at issue, for the first time, perhaps, at the moment when there are to be no more of them. What are parades *for*? Their failure, in *No More Parades*, and indeed in *Parade's End* understood as a whole, exposes to view in the starkest manner imaginable the anxieties which both necessitate and justify them. 'It seemed to me,' Ford subsequently explained, 'that, if I could present, not merely fear, not merely horror, not merely death, not merely even self-sacrifice . . . but just worry; that might strike a note of which the world would not so readily tire.'[1] Worry is indeed the note struck, to memorable effect, in the opening chapter of *No More Parades*. It is a chapter full of anxious people. Anxious people scarcely come as a surprise, of course, in a war-novel. What is surprising, perhaps, is the extent to which the author of this one seems to have found anxieties other than the fear of death – indeed, anxieties other than the anxieties customarily displaced by the fear of death – richly to preoccupy him.

Fear and horror, as opposed to anxiety, had played a significant part in Ford's own experience of war. The severe concussion caused when he was blown into the air by a high-explosive shell in July 1916, during the Battle of the Somme, brought on a breakdown of some kind. Lying in the Casualty Clearing Station at Corbie, he struggled to recover his memory, and to ward off a horrific 'day-nightmare' involving immense shapes in grey-white cagoules or shrouds. Ford connected this 'Corbie-phobia' with childhood dreads. Corbie-phobia continued to haunt him well into the 1920s. Ford, then, knew about horror. He suffered from shell-shock, or what we would call Post-Traumatic Stress Disorder. His writing from 1916 onwards bears the 'impress' of Corbie-phobia, as Max Saunders has amply demonstrated.[2] But Corbie-phobia, to judge by Ford's description of it, was not a phobia at all (phobia would have been classified, at the time, and ever since, as an anxiety neurosis, rather than as trauma). It is interesting, none the less, that the term phobia became attached to it. Ford knew all about phobia, too. If we want to understand why he chose to write a war-novel about worry, and why he wrote so well about it, we need to ask exactly what it was that he knew about phobia.

Agoraphobia

In July 1904, Olive Garnett spent ten days in Salisbury with Ford and his wife Elsie, at her request: Ford, it seemed, was suffering some kind of nervous breakdown. 'I think I had never heard of neurasthenia,' Garnett was to recall in a memoir based on the journal she had kept at the time,

> & for a few days all went well; but it was a hot July, & on leaving Lake House ... to walk over the Plain to Amesbury, Ford had an attack of agoraphobia, & said if I didn't take his arm he would fall down. I held on in all the blaze for miles, it seemed to me, but the town reached, he walked off briskly to get tobacco and a shave; and when I pointed this out to Elsie she said 'nerves'. He can't cross wide open spaces.

Garnett's arm was not the only support Ford had needed. He got himself across Salisbury Plain by surviving from bench to bench; at each one, restored for the time being to a physical limit, an enclave, he would sit down and rest. All the while he chewed lozenges as a prophylactic against the wide open spaces.[3] When he got back to London at the end of the month, a specialist recommended rest and travel, and he left for Germany, to visit Hüffer relatives, and to undergo further treatment. 'There's such a lot of breakdown in the land,' Ford was able to report contentedly. 'They've a regular name for lack of walking power here: Platz Angst.'[4] *Platzangst* was one of a number of terms which had been in circulation in German psychiatry since the mid-1860s for the newly-acknowledged, spatial pathology Carl Otto Westphal was to christen 'agoraphobia' (above, p. 30).

Phobia particularizes anxiety, to the point at which it can be felt and known *in its particularity*, and thus counteracted or got around. The particularity remains: the cavalry officer in uniform or on horseback has not conquered his fear of open spaces, merely gotten around it. However, the counteracting or circumventing manoeuvre, which exploits the known asymmetry between stimulus and response, could be said at the same time to take a critical distance from itself. The manoeuvre can be understood, for the first time, *as* a manoeuvre.

Of some interest, from this point of view, is the panic attack Christopher Tietjens suffers, in *Some Do Not ...*, during the visit he and Vincent Macmaster make to the Duchemins, in Kent. It is during the visit, of course, that he first encounters Valentine Wannop, on the golf course, and then again at Mrs Duchemin's breakfast-party. After breakfast, Tietjens and Valentine Wannop go for a walk down a country path. The path down which they have wandered ends at a stile, with a road beyond. Tietjens reveals that he doesn't like walking on roads. Exposure unsettles him. When told that the next stile lies fifty yards away, he panics, and breaks into a run, pursued indulgently by Valentine. The panic clearly precedes the rational anxiety soon incorporated into it, that someone will see them together, and suspect the worst. As they scuttle down the road, they are overtaken by a horse and cart containing Mrs Wannop and an aged retainer. Tietjens's panic subsides in a display of practical knowledge concerning horses and carts so profound that the aged retainer immediately acknowledges him as 'Quality'. Like the cavalry officer who could only cross open spaces when in uniform or on horseback, Tietjens has found a performance which will control his anxiety. Mrs Wannop, her horse, cart, and handy-man thus set resolutely in order, drives off.

> He was aware that, all this while, from the road-side, the girl had been watching him with shining eyes, intently, even with fascination.
> 'I suppose you think that a mighty fine performance,' she said.
> 'I didn't make a very good job of the girth,' he said. 'Let's get off this road.'
> 'Setting poor, weak women in their places,' Miss Wannop continued. 'Soothing the horse like a man with a charm. I suppose you soothe women like that too. I pity your wife . . . The English country male! And making a devoted vassal at sight of the handy-man. The feudal system all complete . . .'
> Tietjens said:
> 'Well, you know, it'll make him all the better servant to you if he thinks you've friends in the know. The lower classes are like that. Let's get off this road.'
> She said:
> 'You're in a mighty hurry to get behind the hedge. Are the police after us or aren't they? Perhaps you were lying at breakfast: to calm the hysterical nerves of a weak woman.'
> 'I wasn't lying,' he said, 'but I hate roads when there are field-paths . . .'
> 'That's a phobia, like any woman's,' she exclaimed.[5]

This is the first time that Tietjens's substance, or Quality, has been characterized as performative through and through: an enactment of gender and class difference. Valentine's subsequent identification of his hatred of roads as phobic seems merely to supplement, or decorate with scorn, this new understanding. But it may be its prerequisite. Only from the point of view of phobia's irredeemable triviality, which Valentine has wilfully feminized for sharper effect, can the manoeuvre that temporarily disables it (donning the uniform of patriarchy, of the 'feudal system all complete') be understood *as* a manoeuvre, as a kind of parade.

War Phobia, War Performance

While on active service, Ford, as we know, often found 'private troubles' a useful distraction. 'I have gone down to the front line at night, worried, worried, worried beyond belief about happenings at home in a Blighty that I did not much expect to see again – so worried that all sense of personal danger disappeared and I forgot to duck when shells went close overhead.'[6] Tietjens, in *No More Parades*, appears similarly afflicted, during his more or less successful management of a transit camp behind the lines. The strain put upon him by the erratic arrival and departure of drafts, by perpetual strafing from superior officers and enemy airplanes, and above all by his wife's continuing machinations, is set against the more clearly defined insanity of a fellow officer, McKechnie, whom Tietjens for some reason knows as Mackenzie. McKechnie, we might say, is beyond phobia's help. By his own account, he suffers from claustrophobia: a fear that he will be hit by splinters of stone or metal from buildings which pen him in. He needs to persuade himself that the hut he shares with Tietjens is in its flimsiness to all intents and purposes an 'open space' (*PE* 305). But he cannot act upon his claustrophobia, or put it to use.

In the opening chapter of *No More Parades*, a bomb does indeed land nearby, killing a man (0 Nine Morgan, a battalion runner), who lurches into the hut and collapses. Tietjens, moving towards the body to raise it, becomes engrossed in particularity. 'He hoped he would not get his hands all over blood, because blood is very sticky. It makes your fingers stick together impotently.' All over blood is exactly what he does get:

> Tietjens let the trunk of the body sink slowly to the floor. He was more gentle than if the man had been alive. All hell in the way of noise burst about the world. Tietjens's thoughts seemed to have to shout to him between earthquake shocks. He was thinking it was absurd of that fellow Mackenzie to imagine that he could know any uncle of his. He saw very vividly also the face of his girl who was a pacifist. It worried him not to know what expression her face would have if she heard of his occupation, now. Disgust? ... He was standing with his greasy, sticky hands held out from the flaps of his tunic ... Perhaps disgust! It was impossible to think in this row ... His very thick soles moved gluily and came up after suction ... (*PE* 308)

Tietjens picks his way through shock and the possibility of trauma by means of a pseudophobia: a fixation on the tactile qualities of blood, and the nausea they induce. The disgust so sharply rendered is clearly his before it is Valentine's. 'His very thick soles moved gluily and came *up* after *su*ction.' The double dose of assonance makes this a sentence in which the syllables have as hard a time extracting themselves from each other as Tietjens does his thick-soled boots from the blood spread on the floor. Tietjens's engrossment in the particularity of a sticky sensation has engrossed him away from the 'all hell' let loose around him.

Later, standing on the spot where 0 Nine Morgan collapsed, Tietjens realizes that the engrossment in stickiness has become a 'complex' (*PE* 473). It is, however, a saving complex. For it unlocks something in him. The effort to imagine how Valentine's face would express disgust is an acknowledgement of his love for her. Perhaps it is the memory of her original diagnosis of phobia in him which enables him to diagnose in her a pseudophobia which is in fact his own. Tietjens, we learn shortly, 'had a rule: *Never think on the subject of a shock at the moment of a shock.* The mind was then too sensitized. Subjects of shock require to be thought all round' (*PE* 315). In this case, the subject of the shock has been thought all round through pseudophobia. Shortly after his realization that he has acquired a 'complex', Tietjens hears that he is to return to the front line. As the news sinks in, he begins to wonder what his mind will 'pick out' as its 'main terror'. 'The mud, the noise, dread always at the back of the mind? Or the worry? The worry! Your eye-brows always had a slight tension on them . . . Like eye-strain!' (*PE* 477). Like the protagonists of so many combat novels and memoirs, he, too, will need to consolidate a favourite fear or disgust.

Ford and Lewis

There is another kind of disturbance at work in this opening section of *No More Parades*: a *literary* disturbance, on Ford's own part. Its origin, I think, was a celebrated encounter with Wyndham Lewis, during which Lewis poured scorn on him and his associates. I quote from the version in *Mightier than the Sword* (1938). 'You and Mr Conrad and Mr James and all those old fellows are done,' Lewis insisted. 'Exploded! . . . *Fichus!* . . . *Vieux jeu!* . . . No good! . . . Finished!' Lewis's beef was with literary 'impressionism'. 'You fellows try to efface yourselves; to make people think that there isn't any author and that they're living in the affairs you . . . adumbrate, isn't that your word? . . . What balls!' Adumbration was rather ostentatiously the method of Ford's *The Good Soldier*, whose opening chapters were shortly to appear in *BLAST*. Lewis thought that people had had enough of all that. They did not want self-effacement. They wanted brilliant fellows like him performing stunts and letting off fireworks. 'What's the good of being an author if you don't get any fun out of it?'[7] Max Saunders has quite rightly pointed out that Ford had in fact got plenty of fun out of being an author: his impressionism was every bit as much of a performance as Lewis's stunts, albeit of an implosive rather than an explosive kind.[8] By the time of *Mightier than the Sword* he had in any case rather evidently outlasted the stunts. But it would be wrong, I think, to overlook the note of apprehension that remains. Lewis's bristling attitude may have continued to seem to Ford, for some time, like one of those subjects of shock which need to be thought all round. Ford's thinking all round it is evident, I believe, in the opening of *No More Parades*: a description of the hut in which Tietjens and McKechnie sit, in the transit camp.

> When you came in the space was desultory, rectangular, warm after the drip of the winter night, and transfused with a brown-orange dust that was light. It was shaped like the house a child draws. Three groups of brown limbs spotted with brass took dim high-lights from shafts that came from a bucket pierced with holes, filled with incandescent coke and covered in with a sheet of iron in the shape of a funnel. Two men, as if hierarchically smaller, crouched on the floor beside the brazier; four, two at each end of the hut, drooped over tables in attitudes of extreme indifference. From the eaves above the parallelogram of black that was the doorway fell intermittent drippings of collected moisture, persistent, with glass-like intervals of musical sound. (*PE* 291)

The description of this space contrasts starkly with the description of the perfectly appointed railway-carriage conveying Tietjens and Macmaster down into Kent which opens *Some Do Not . . .* . That description is as scrupulously placid as the world described, in its catalogue of fixtures and fittings, and in its assumption that there is no need to specify a point of view: the scene is always already intelligible. The hut in the transit camp, by contrast, has to be brought before us by means of a random observer summoned for the purpose ('When you came in . . .'). The scene, then, is there *for* someone. But for whom, exactly?

It might conceivably be there, I think, for the reader with some faint recollection of the first issue of *BLAST*, and in particular of Lewis's unperformable 'play' and/or Gnostic meditation, *Enemy of the Stars*, which had featured in it side by side with the extract from *The Good Soldier*. In *Enemy of the Stars*, the action (a death-grapple between ex-student Arghol and his truculent disciple, Hanp) takes place in a wheelwright's yard somewhere to the north of Berlin. The yard is a 'Vorticist arena,' as Paul Edwards puts it, 'rather than a plausible spot in nature'.[9]

> A canal at one side, the night pouring into it like blood from a butcher's pail. Rouge mask in alluminum mirror, sunset's grimace through the night.[10]

Ford, I think, has tried to emulate Lewis in converting his plausible spot into an arena. For him, as for Lewis, abstraction comes first (vehicle precedes tenor). In Lewis, the sunset is a rouge mask in a mirror before it is a sunset. In Ford, the light is a brown-orange dust before it is light, the doorway a parallelogram of black before it is a doorway.

Abstraction, however, would by no means be adequate as an account of Lewis's writing, in *Enemy* (I'm not altogether sure what *would* be adequate). The blood in a butcher's pail and the rouge mask in an aluminium mirror are a good deal more concrete than the late-Romantic platitudes they have supplanted. Despite (or because of) its debt to philosophies of asceticism, *Enemy of the Stars* is a text dedicated to the exposition of base matter. It looks forward to Bataille as well as back to Schopenhauer. As both Hanp and Arghol discover, all thought leads 'back to physical parallel'. All thought, we might say, is phobic. Hanp's hatred of Arghol 'would have been faint without physical repulsion to fascinate him, make him murderous and sick.'[11] *Enemy of the Stars* announces a phobic Modernism.

There is something else about Ford's description that we need to take account of: the arrangement of the men in the hut into three groups of brown limbs, one group (crouched by the brazier) 'hierarchically smaller' (*PE* 291). That arrangement would have been familiar to Ford from some of Lewis's war-art. I'm thinking of some of the drawings and watercolours Lewis exhibited at the Goupil Gallery in London in February 1919 under the general heading of 'Guns'. In this work, Lewis often grouped figures into pairs or trios; and he returned again and again to the spectacle of men under fire.[12] The grouping into pairs and trios is even more evident, as an element of composition, in his war commissions: most notably in *A Battery Shelled* (1919), in which three enigmatic figures loom large in the left foreground, while in the middle ground further groups dive for cover. These latter could be said to be in some sense 'hierarchically smaller', as Ford's are, diminished by more than perspective. Ford, then, may have been alluding to Lewis's Vorticist war-effort. He perhaps made use of Lewis, or of the apprehension Lewis provoked in him, in order to start his novel (an anxious novel, a novel about anxiety) differently. The relatively direct allusion announces that he has started as he does not mean to go on, abstractly, by literary fire-works. The work of writers other than Lewis certainly informs his going on, but not through direct allusion.

Ford and Joyce

Lewis, of course, was not the only younger rival around. In an essay on 'The Realistic Novel' first published in the *Piccadilly Review* in 1919, Ford remarked that the fields that lay open to the novel as a form were now 'illimitable'.[13] The publication of *Ulysses* in 1922 confirmed his view that Joyce was the one contemporary writer to have grasped that opportunity:

> *Ulysses* contains the undiscovered mind of man; it is human consciousness ana-
> lysed as it has never before been analysed. Certain books change the world. This,
> success or failure, *Ulysses* does: for no novelist with serious aims can henceforth
> set out upon the task of writing before he has at least formed his own private
> estimate as to the rightness or wrongness of the methods of the author of *Ulysses*.[14]

In *No More Parades*, the episode of the bombing concludes with what I take to be Ford's own estimate of the rightness or wrongness of the methods of the author of *Ulysses*:

> Two men were carrying the remains of 0 Nine Morgan, the trunk wrapped in a
> ground sheet. They carried him in a bandy chair out of the hut. His arms over
> his shoulders waved a jocular farewell. There would be an ambulance
> stretcher on bicycle wheels outside. (*PE* 311)

This reversion to exteriority, to the impersonal annotation of gesture and motion, is a salient feature of the so-called 'initial style' in *Ulysses*. I am thinking of 'Wandering Rocks', in particular, where the initial style is tested to destruction, before the onset of experiment in 'Sirens'. This is Blazes Boylan, not saluting the Viceroy:

> His hands in his jacket pocket forgot to salute but he offered to the three ladies
> the bold admiration of his eyes and the red flower between his lips.[15]

Ford's third sentence ('His arms over his shoulders waved a jocular farewell') could only have been written by a writer who was hearing Joyce in his head as he wrote. There is an echo, here, but no allusion: remembering Blazes Boylan doesn't help us to understand what Ford might want us to think about the demise of 0 Nine Morgan. The echo is a way to get something done. Ford, in short, seems to have internalized Joyce's method in a way he could never have internalized Lewis's. He deliberately performs Joyce. He puts a Joycean lozenge in his mouth, as it were, in order to get himself across empty literary space: across the illimitable fields which lay open to the novel as a form. It's worth noting that the qualities he associated most closely with Joyce's achievement in *Ulysses* were composure and serenity.[16]

The episode concerning the death of 0 Nine Morgan has been brought to a conclusion by another kind of performance: by Tietjens's performance of the role of officer (of paternalism, of hierarchical largeness). Despite Morgan's death, which Tietjens could in theory have prevented, his men still regard him as an excellent officer. Their understanding and admiration is the uniform he needs to get himself across empty space. A single maxim, Ford wrote, in a 1924 essay in the *transatlantic review*, had been drummed into the junior officer: 'The comfort and equanimity of the Men come before every exigency save those of actual warfare!'[17] Throughout *No Mores Parades*, Tietjens consistently behaves in accordance with that maxim. The apology he makes to a Staff Officer whom he has kept waiting is a declaration of pride. There were, he explains, some men to see to. 'And, you know ... "The comfort" and – what is it? – of the men comes before every – is it "consideration"? – except the exigencies of actual warfare' (*PE* 340). Tietjens is still performing 'Quality', still performing class-difference.

No More Parades in fact concludes with a parade, a last, triumphant performance, as Tietjens conducts the general who has just had him transferred to the front around a cathedral-like cook-house. There's quite a bit of Joyce here, too: for example, when the general approaches one of the cooks standing stiffly to attention:

> The general tapped the sergeant's Good Conduct ribbon with the heel of his crop. All stretched ears heard him say:
> 'How's your sister, Case? ...'
> Gazing away, the sergeant said:
> 'I'm thinking of making her Mrs Case ...' (*PE* 500)

The formula for the audience's attentiveness ('All stretched ears heard him say') is one Joyce frequently used in *Ulysses* to indicate uniform movement, for example among the congregation in All Hallows, in 'Lotus Eaters' – 'All crossed themselves and stood up' (*U* 79), or among the guests at Mat Dillon's on the night when Bloom, as he recalls in 'Sirens', first met Molly: 'All looked. Halt. Down she sat. All ousted looked' (264). These are all examples of collective, even communal, activity. Internalizing Joyce's initial style, Ford has reinstated the idea or principle of the parade. This is how *No More Parades* concludes:

> With his light step the shining general went swiftly to the varnished panels in the eastern aisle of the cathedral. The white figure beside them became instantly tubular, motionless, and global-eyed. On the panels were painted: TEA! SUGAR! SALT! CURRY PDR! FLOUR! PEPPER!
> The general tapped with the heel of his crop on the locker-panel labelled PEPPER: the top, right-hand locker-panel. He said to the tubular, global-eyed white figure beside it: 'Open that, will you, my man? . . .'
> To Tietjens this was like the sudden bursting out of the regimental quick-step, as after a funeral with military honours the band and drums march away, back to barracks. (*PE* 500)

In that 'went swiftly', I sort of hear Leopold Bloom on his way to Westland Row, in 'Lotus Eaters':

> By lorries along sir John Rogerson's quay Mr Bloom walked soberly, past Windmill lane, Leask's the linseed crusher's, the postal telegraph office. (*U* 68)

What Ford has taken from Joyce is a syntax and a cadence. Joycean lozenge in mouth, he gets himself across the space on the page between paragraphs, across a literary landscape otherwise devoid of appropriate method, to that 'sudden bursting out of the regimental quick-step'. The parade has come to an end. It has been a vindication. Now the anxious writer can return to barracks, to prepare for further parades.

In a 1923 essay on Conrad, Ford distinguished between style and writing. 'Style implies a man in parade uniform; writing, the same man in working dress.' Style was a matter of tonality and cadence, writing a matter of 'the getting in of "things"' (or leaving them out).[18] One of the ways Ford hoped to get across the illimitable fields open to the novel was, I think, by putting on the parade uniform of someone else's style (of someone else's composure and serenity). War, however, had a habit of catching a person off-parade, in working dress, in a dirty, blood-stained tunic. On those occasions, Ford, like Tietjens, seems to have dogged it out, by the cultivation of a favourite fear or phobia, a nausea gripping enough to take the mind off danger. Lewis may well have helped him to shape that favourite phobia.

Joyce enabled Ford to make something out of phobia: to describe war as no other writer has described it. Lewis *was* the phobia. He gave phobia shape, in his person, as in his writing. I feel confident in describing what Ford thought he was doing with Joyce. Where Lewis is concerned, I'm not so sure. But then neither was Ford.

Notes

1   *It Was the Nightingale* (London: Heinemann, 1934), 206.
2   *Ford Madox Ford: A Dual Life*, 2 vols. (Oxford: Oxford University Press, 1996), 2. 228–41.

3   The memoir, now at Northwestern University, is quoted by Saunders, *Ford Madox Ford*, 1. 171, 537.

4   Quoted by Arthur Mizener, *The Saddest Story: A Biography of Ford Madox Ford* (London: Bodley Head, 1972), 95–9.

5   *Parade's End* (Harmondsworth: Penguin, 1982), 112–13. Henceforth *PE*.

6   'A Day of Battle', essay not published in Ford's lifetime, dated 15 September 1916; quoted by Saunders, *Ford Madox Ford*, 2. 197.

7   *Mightier than the Sword* (London: Allen & Unwin, 1938), 282–3.

8   *Ford Madox Ford*, 2. 189.

9   *Wyndham Lewis: Painter and Writer* (New Haven: Yale University Press, 2000), 142.

10 *Enemy of the Stars*, in *Blast 1*, facsimile edition (Santa Barbara: Black Sparrow Press, 1981), 62.

11 Ibid., 71.

12 The catalogue is reprinted in *Wyndham Lewis: Paintings and Drawings*, ed. Walter Michel (London: Thames and Hudson, 1971), 433–6.

13 'The Realistic Novel', in *Critical Essays*, ed. Max Saunders and Richard Stang (Manchester: Carcanet, 2002), 190–2, p. 190.

14 'A Haughty and Proud Generation', in *Critical Essays*, 208–17, p. 217.

15 *Ulysses*, ed. Jeri Johnson (Oxford: Oxford University Press, 1993), 243. Henceforth *U*.

16 'Haughty and Proud Generation'. 215; and '*Ulysses* and the Handling of Indecency', in *Critical Essays*, 218–27, p. 225.

17 'Chroniques I: Editorial', *Transatlantic Review*, 2, 1924, 94–8.

18 'Mr Conrad's Writing', in *Critical Essays*, 228–31, pp. 228–9.

8

Hitchcock's Modernism

Alfred Hitchcock has been mentioned with increasing frequency in Modernist despatches. For the most part, this interest has taken the form of the elaboration of intellectual and cultural contexts for a particular film. *The Lodger* (1926), for example, has quite often been described as the one British film of the period to absorb fully the consequences of experiment in cinema in France and Germany, of which Hitchcock was certainly aware by that time, and even in Russia, of which he may well not have been aware. Much has been made of the part played by the London Film Society, and by one of its members in particular, Ivor Montagu, who was brought in to help complete the film, in spreading the word about German and possibly Russian cinema. 'The London Film Society's most significant outcome,' Peter Wollen has written, 'was its impact on Alfred Hitchcock, a habitual and doubtless punctual attender at screenings. There Hitchcock not only mingled with the cultural elite but also absorbed modernist aesthetic ideas, which he later attempted to nurture within narrative film.'[1] A second line of enquiry concerns Hitchcock's adaptation of Joseph Conrad's *The Secret Agent* (1907) as *Sabotage* (1936). Much has been made of a shared interest in urban experience, or manipulation and mastery, or the politics of sabotage.[2] But the general picture remains far from clear. We simply don't know enough yet about the range and intensity of Hitchcock's interests and friendships during this period. For example, while his debt to German cinema has been explored to admirable effect, there is much yet to discover about his French and American connections.[3] My aim here is not to find Modernism in Hitchcock, but Hitchcock in Modernism. I shall try to define a particular aesthetic, literary in origin, which so informed popular film-making in the 1920s and 1930s that one might want to think of some of his films as in some respects Modernist.

When *was* Modernism, in cinema? After the Second World War, would be one answer. 'Around 1960,' David Bordwell has proposed, 'European directors launched what came to be recognized as a modernist cinema.' At that moment, the realism of the 1940s and 1950s gave way both to a 'new stylization' in cinema and to a new understanding of the history of the medium. Critics such as Noël Burch set out to define an 'oppositional tradition' which had consistently 'denaturalized' the techniques, and thus the ideologies, of mainstream cinema.[4] Burch's view has become something of an orthodoxy.[5] However, the consistency of this oppositional tradition stretching from experiment in the 1920s through to experiment in the 1960s has rather more often been asserted than proven. As Bordwell himself puts it, commenting on Burch, there is as yet no clear understanding of the 'historical dynamic' shaping the tradition of the new in cinema. And one might add that there's a similar vagueness to his own brief account of the 'accessible art' and 'didactic realism' the post-war New Waves were supposedly reacting against.[6] The argument for a post-war cinematic Modernism remains as hard to ignore as it is to adopt.

It is one which has considerable consequences for our understanding of Hitchcock, a film-maker operative in both eras. In a 1979 essay on 'The Art Cinema as a Mode of Film Practice', Bordwell describes a 'modernist cinema', exemplified by films ranging from Eisenstein's *October* (1928) to Bresson's *Lancelot du Lac* (1974), which always involves a 'radical split of narrative structure from cinematic style'. This was the Modernism renewed, and made safe, by post-war art cinema. According to Bordwell, Hitchcock should be understood not as a Modernist, but as the classical film-maker who had the most art cinema about him, as demonstrated by the way in which films like *Psycho* 'foreground the narrational process'.[7] Others have proved less circumspect. Joe McElhaney, for example, regards *Marnie* (1964) as an attempt to 'incorporate' into mainstream film-making the innovations of European 'modernist cinema' of the early 1960s, particularly Antonioni.[8] For Slavoj Žižek, by contrast, it is the films of the Selznick period, from *Rebecca* (1940) to *Under Capricorn* (1949), with their elaborate tracking-shots and traumatized heroines, which are most fully Modernist;[9] while Fredric Jameson finds in the episodic narrativization of the 1960s films – most notably the 'adventures of space' undertaken in *North by Northwest* and the 'autonomy of physical detail' these permit – a Modernism distinct from classical cinema, and yet not wholly compatible with 'other forms of modernist film, let alone the other arts'.[10] Valuable though these accounts are, there doesn't seem to be much consistency to them. There have been few attempts to establish how the Modernism apparent in the films Hitchcock made in Britain before the Second World War might have some bearing on the films he made in America after it. John Orr's illuminating formal analysis of *The Birds* (1963) might be reckoned the exception which proves the rule.[11]

We need also to reckon with the deconstructive turn in Hitchcock scholarship, which has sought to remove him altogether from Modernism's orbit. Tom Cohen has argued forcefully that the 'cryptonomic networks' and 'secret writing systems' which traverse Hitchcock's work from beginning to end – spectres, blackouts, hieroglyphs, puns, postal relays, trace chains, markings and marrings of all kinds, in short the whole 'matter' of notation in, on, and around film – constitute a 'graphematics' requiring us to conceive cinema as other than a primarily visual medium. Such *différance* is the epistemo-political premise of what we think we see when we go to the movies. It is the matrix or surplus of signification out of which arises each and every prosthetic representational order, making

Figure 8   Hitchcock as editor

believe that the world can be apprehended once and for all from an identifiable (individual or collective) point of view. The men and women in Hitchcock's films who find themselves occupying that matrix or surplus – who know altogether 'too much' about *différance* – thereby lay bare and negate the long association of knowledge with sight in the West. What they cannot see is what they know: that cinema does not represent, or re-represent, so much as absent itself systematically in and through writing. As will be evident, Cohen has drawn heavily and to compelling effect on Nietzsche, Benjamin, and Derrida. For him, the spectrographic knowing too much inscribed in Hitchcock's films amounts to a 'cognition' of death, not life.[12]

Cohen also wants to claim for those films an 'accelerating role' in a 'teletechnic revolution'. *The Lodger* emerges in this account as the crucial early film, seeming to announce by its preoccupation at once with mass-media and with serial violence the coming 'era of techno-genocides and globalization in which life systems would be precipitously made extinct and democracies overtake and then recede, falling to their own mediatric trances.' Hitchcock's inaugural cameo in *The Lodger* shows him as an editor seated in a glass booth, his back to us, in front of him the array of 'telemachines' (radio and print) which will spread the news of serial killing (fig. 8). He has installed himself, Cohen argues, 'at the core of a telemedial empire'. That makes him, of course, postmodern: a connoisseur of the estrangements built into circuit, switch, and relay. For Cohen, Hitchcock is nowhere more the teletechnic revolutionary than in *Sabotage*, which sacrifices representation as such, with its ever more desperate conjurings of human presence, 'in and toward a post-Enlightenment and amodernist logic'.[13] The problem with this account is that cinema is not a tele-machine or tele-medium of any kind. It is not a method (*technē*) for communicating at a distance (*tele*). It is a method of storage and representation. We need to distinguish in a rough and ready fashion between media (telegraph, telephone, television, radio, fax) governed by the principle of simultaneity, or increasingly, wherever possible, the principle of *interactive* simultaneity; and media (photography, cinema, gramophony) governed by the principle of representation through time-delay. In the latter, the image, whether visual or sonic, has always been captured in another place at another time; it reaches us most often, after some delay, in stored and storied form, and our experience of it is the experience of re-presentation. The axiom of telecommunication media might be two places at one time; that of representational media, two places at two times. There can be no question that the ever-increasing technological mediation of human experience became a matter of great concern to writers and film-makers alike during the first decades of the twentieth century. But the literature and cinema of the period do not simply represent the use and abuse of telecommunication media. They represent that use and abuse from the point of view of representation itself: from the point of view of the meaning and value attributed, both then and now, to the storage of a record of some kind for the purposes of subsequent reflection upon it elsewhere.[14] I shall argue, against Cohen, that Hitchcock's films continued to represent human experience from the point of view of representation; while acknowledging, in a manner we might call Modernist, that the nature and scope of representation's 'point of view' had become, more urgently than ever before, the issue.[15] It seems to me that their murderousness has been greatly exaggerated, and not just by Cohen.[16] They have, I think, a way of living up to death which ought not to remain beneath our attention.

Modernism's way of living up to death stems from its 'commitment to the ordinary'.[17] Of course, many Modernist writers and film-makers took little or no interest in the ordinary. Among those who did, however, *over-commitment* was if anything the norm. Their excessive zeal produced a new and vital understanding of the ordinariness of ordinary existence. Some film-makers of the period shared with some writers of the period a conviction both that the instrumentality of the new recording media had made it possible for the first time to represent (as well as to record) *existence as such*; and that the superabundant generative power of this instrumentality (the ever-imminent autonomy of the forms and techniques it gave rise to) put in doubt the very idea of existence as such.[18] The ordinariness exposed in and through the representation of existence as such is a *radical* ordinariness, at once particular and universal. It goes to the root of lived experience, to that which is and must always remain fundamental to it. To attempt to enlist Hitchcock in such a project is of course to raise doubts about the general view of the narrative structure of his films, a view articulated with commendable clarity by Peter Wollen in 1966, and since then heard more or less everywhere in the criticism. According to Wollen,

Hitchcock consistently took care to place his protagonists in an environment habitual both to them and to the spectator. 'Then by a trick of fate, a chance meeting or an arbitrary choice, they are plunged into an anti-world of chaos and disorder, a monstrous world in which normal categories shift abruptly and disconcertingly, in which the hero is cut off from all sustaining social relations and flung, unprepared and solitary, into a world of constant physical and psychological trauma.'[19] I shall argue here that there is in fact no such absolute separation, in Hitchcock's British films, at any rate, between world and anti-world; and that his primary concern as a film-maker during this period lay with what is disclosed neither by habit nor by trauma.

Sensationalism

If Hollywood cinema did indeed become, during the 1920s, the 'first global vernacular', it did so, as Miriam Hansen has put it, by developing a 'reflexive relation' to modernity articulated primarily through 'sensory experience' and 'sensational affect'[20] Sensational affect is of course an old story – or an old modern story – having to do with melodrama and the forms it had decisively taken by the beginning of the twentieth century. 'Those who have lived before such terms as "high-brow fiction", "thrillers" and "detective fiction" were invented,' T.S. Eliot wrote in 1927, 'realize that melodrama is perennial and that the craving for it is perennial and must be satisfied.' Literary fiction had become a fiction without thrills. 'If we cannot get this satisfaction out of what the publishers present as "literature",' Eliot concluded, 'then we will read – with less and less pretence of concealment – what we call "thrillers".'[21] And not only read, as Alfred Hitchcock, author of 'Why "Thrillers" Thrive', first published in the *Picturegoer* on 18 January 1936, would no doubt have been happy to point out.[22]

What defined the first global vernacular was its dependence not only on low genres such as the thriller, but on genres which made a point and indeed a spectacle of lowness itself. Foremost among these was Naturalist fiction, plotting decline. These were stories not just of social lowness, but of social lowness lowered yet further both physically and morally. And they had, for all their apparent incompatibility with the classical Hollywood narrative's purposeful protagonists and rising curve of action, a not inconsiderable influence on a wide range of film-makers, as Lea Jacobs has amply demonstrated.[23] They did after all manage to combine a great deal of 'elemental' sex and violence with ribald commentary on the intoxicating transformation of Western societies by consumer capitalism. Naturalist fiction provided a steady supply of what an embryonic narrative cinema was most badly in need of: sensation. Zola's novels have been adapted over and over again. 'Naturalism,' as Dudley Andrew remarks in his study of French cinema of the 1920s and 1930s, 'sits rather comfortably within the secure circle of middlebrow entertainment, even as it provocatively raises the banner of the scandalous.'[24] The German cinema with which Hitchcock became acquainted during the mid-1920s did not consist entirely of Gothic asylums. Of equal importance was the *Kammerspielfilm*: 'filmed chamber plays emphasizing in often meticulous detail the life – and more often than not, the decay – of individuals living in claustrophobic environments.'[25] Hitchcock made his name with films which *almost* deliver on the promise of sensational decline lapsing into even more sensational decay.

As Jacobs has shown, D.W. Griffith did as much as anyone to incorporate 'reduced or dilatory' plotting into an emergent narrative cinema, from the Biograph two-reeler *The Country Doctor* (1909) through to features like *A Romance of Happy Valley* and *True Heart Susie* (both 1919).[26] Griffith, we know, was a director Hitchcock thought very highly of indeed: 'A Columbus of the Screen', he called him, in a 1931 article for *Film Weekly*.[27] 1919 was also the year of *Broken Blossoms*, one of Griffith's most ambitious films, not least in the technical virtuosity it brings to bear on the spectacle of decline's lapse into decay.

Broken Blossoms, set in the Limehouse district of London during the First World War, is a sympathetic portrayal of the love that develops between an idealistic young Chinese immigrant who has lost his way in the opium dens and the brutalized daughter of Battling Burrows, a degenerate cockney prize-fighter. Adapted from 'The Chink and the Child', a short story by Thomas Burke, a writer whose specialism was East End slum picturesque (or, rather, East Asian East End slum picturesque), it certainly does not lack for sensation.[28] Griffith did his best to sanitize Burke's slumming. In the story, for example, the heroine Lucy, is 12; in the film, a marginally more respectable 15. Griffith's aim, at this point in his career, was the gentrification of cinema. The energetic publicity campaign for the film characterized it as high art with serious political and philosophical ambitions.[29] Griffith's most influential film in France, and possibly the first major film explicitly to aspire to poetic realism, as Dudley Andrew puts it, *Broken Blossoms* 'sublimated its crude masochism into delicate figures of lighting and acting that lift it effortlessly into the realm of art.' The Chinese hero's exquisite suicide enabled that sublimation into art to be understood as the '(spiritual) refining of lower instincts'.[30] Hitchcock remembered the film for its use of soft focus.[31]

All the more striking, then, that it should also investigate with a startling lack of sentiment the spectacle of social lowness lowered yet further, both physically and morally. I am thinking, in particular, of the sequence which introduces us to the heroine, Lucy, and to the life she has led since one of her father's ex-girlfriends casually deposited her on his doorstep. 'When not serving as a punching bag to relieve the Battler's feelings,' an intertitle notes, 'the bruised little body may be seen creeping around the docks of Limehouse.' That is indeed what we then see. David Bordwell has pointed out that the narrative strategies of classical Hollywood cinema work to '*personalize* space'. Environments achieve significance through their ability to 'dramatize individuality'.[32] A close shot shows us Lucy seated on a coil of rope beside a dock, hunched in reverie. The reverie takes the form of a flashback: a Naturalist play in two scenes whose topic is the choices open to her if she is to escape from her abusive father; namely, marriage, or prostitution. The first scene, an example of deft but entirely orthodox analytical editing, exposes the misery of married life in a squalid tenement room. Worse is to come. Lucy, we learn, has been 'Warned as strongly by the ladies of the street against their profession'.

The second scene marks an abrupt departure from the continuity system. An establishing shot shows two prostitutes standing on the pavement at the corner of a building, somewhere in Limehouse. One of them glances briefly to her right (off-screen left), and drops the mirror in which she has been examining herself. Lucy, who has entered the shot from the opposite direction, filling the space beside the two women so that the group forms a triptych, stoops to pick it up. Griffith alternates between shots of the two women, as they warm to their theme, and of Lucy's response. This alternation remains within the diegesis already established. We know exactly where Lucy is even when she is not in shot. The classical continuity system, Bordwell notes, does not allow for holes in 'scenographic space'.[33] During the second two-shot, however, the woman who had previously glanced to her right (off-screen left), does so once again, at greater length this time, while her companion continues to admonish Lucy. The look unbalances the diegesis by bringing into play an unknown or unmapped scenographic space: somewhere along the other sidewalk, the one Lucy did not arrive by, loiters a potential client. As Lucy turns to leave, Griffith stays with the two women, and with the look. The story has already moved on: we will soon return to Lucy hunched in reverie on the coil of rope, at which point these retrospective scenes cease to have any meaning other than as an enduring influence upon her character. But we remain aware that the diegesis has for a moment somehow lost its balance, or its bearings. The hole created in scenographic space remains, as an absolute limit to the continuity system's capacity to draw us into individual tragedy. What the camera has 'seen' is prostitution as a social and economic practice stripped of the lustre which human curiosity and censoriousness invariably endow it with. By staying with the look, Griffith abandons, for a moment, high art and its civilizing mission. He comes out as a Naturalist.

In Naturalist fiction, there is a further formal lowering, which may also have had some consequences for cinema, from narrative of any kind into (excess) description. In *Nana* (1880), Zola, developing a hint from Manet, who had himself developed a hint from *L'Assommoir* (1887), made elaborate and influential use of a variant of Naturalism's enduring preoccupation with female *toilette*: the actress in her dressing-room getting ready to go on stage. In adapting the novel for the screen, Renoir, as we've seen (above, pp. 53–5), went to considerable lengths to preserve (and indeed improve upon) the devil in the scene's descriptive detail. Hitchcock, I think, was from the outset of his career by no means averse to such lowerings. His first film, *The Pleasure Garden* (1925), opens at the theatre, where an elderly admirer singles the heroine out from the chorus-line and approaches her by way of the manager, exactly as Muffat had approached Nana in Zola's novel and was soon to approach her again in Renoir's film. 'I had to meet you,' he says, 'because I was charmed by that lovely curl of hair.' She promptly detaches it and hands it to him. Stretching it out, he realizes its artificiality. He returns it with a look of vivid disgust. This is a Muffat whose desire is not strong enough to carry him across the phobic limit. Hitchcock, we can say, like Renoir, began in Naturalism. It's most unlikely that he stayed up late reading Zola. But Zola and his followers had by their descriptive zeal and their choice of subject-matter made certain kinds of sensory experience available to those with up-to-date representational technologies at their disposal, and enough of the will-to-invention to put them to productive use. Ordinariness now appeared in a new light – or a new, phobic darkness – radically. The first global vernacular could claim to be Modernist as and when renderings of sensory experience could be said to outweigh renderings of sensational affect in the reflexive relation it proposed to modernity.

Hitchcock's Phobic Picturesque

In his 1936 essay on thrillers, Hitchcock observed that a director's style takes shape slowly, and often, as in his case, by means of a good deal of 'dabbling about'. 'Then I began to get more and more interested in developing a suspense technique.' By the time he made *Secret Agent*, *Sabotage*, and *The 39 Steps*, he had found his niche.[34] It seems to me that the dabbling about undertaken in early films such as *The Lodger* contributed significantly to the articulation of Hitchcock's suspense technique in ways which could be understood as Modernist, and which furthermore do little to reinforce the view that his plots have it as their aim to fling the protagonist, 'unprepared and solitary, into a world of constant physical and psychological trauma.'[35] Hitchcock, as is well known, consistently favoured suspense, which requires that the audience knows what the protagonist does not know, over surprise, shock, and terror, which happens without warning. He insisted again and again on the need to inform: to give the audience something to be afraid of, but not too much, or not all at once.[36] He was against trauma in art. Or at least he was in 1936, when he objected strongly to the sort of horror film which delivers the necessary 'emotional jolt' to its audience by provoking 'extreme aversion'.[37] My argument will be that in films like *The Lodger* and *Sabotage*, it is the moderate and manageable aversion provoked by Hitchcock's phobic picturesque which keeps us on the edge of our seats (but not off them, or under them). What interests him, in these films, and should interest us, is domesticity's radical ordinariness. To move an audience by phobia rather than shock is radically to inform.

In *The Lodger*, narrative is a malevolent force. It is the instrument of sensation, of rogue affect, of paranoia. The investigation which constitutes it is conducted not only by Joe Betts (Malcolm Keen), the policeman who is in love with Daisy Bunting (June), but by the camera, by the way in which

Hitchcock has shot and edited the film. Its predetermined outcome, which Hitchcock both wants and does not want, is the (false) identification of Jonathan Drew (Ivor Novello), the lodger, as the serial killer, the Avenger. What stands in the way of that outcome, and is the film's method of reflecting on its own overdetermination, is a phenomenology (for lack of a better term): familiarity with an inhabited domestic space, an even sense of likelihood and unlikelihood. For despite rumours to the contrary, there is little or no uncanniness in this film. All is canny, that is, *knowing*. But it is a particular kind of canniness, which should not be confused with complacency. Domestic feeling, in early Hitchcock, as in Griffith's *Broken Blossoms*, is, and needs to be, robust. It sustains both necessary illusion and necessary disillusionment. Phobia crops up every now and then in these films as that disillusionment with the world which need not be absolutely fatal to illusions concerning it. In *The Lodger*, Hitchcock makes brief but brutally effective use of Naturalism's phobic picturesque immediately before he introduces the first of his main characters, Daisy Bunting. He cuts from the dissemination by print and radio of the news about the Avenger's latest outrage to the dressing-room allocated to the chorus of the 'Golden Curls' revue. The dancers rush in, shedding blonde wigs, to discover the dresser immersed in the evening paper. The camera picks out one of them, a natural blonde who sits combing her curly hair in the mirror, while chatting with her friend, a natural brunette. The news troubles her, though she submits willingly enough to her friend's teasing. Hitchcock frames her closely as she wipes off the thick layer of cold-cream she has applied to her make-up (fig. 9). She touches her hair and laughs nervously. A prankster masquerading as the Avenger looms suddenly behind her,

Figure 9   as she wipes off the thick layer of cold-cream

stabbing at her with a comb for a knife. The scene subtly links the Avenger's predations to the insidious but less harmful manoeuvres at a phobic limit described by Manet, Zola, Renoir, and Hitchcock himself, in *The Pleasure Garden*. It posits a relation between phobia and psychosis. The blonde with curly hair will be the Avenger's next victim.

The lodging-house where most of the action in the film takes place is a complex space, but one we learn our way around. Hitchcock made sure that he at least knew which way was up by having it built as a single set in the studio.[38] Continuous movement up and down the stairs, reinforced by a relay of gazes, establishes the relation of one room to another on its four floors. The famous shot 'through' the ceiling of the ground-floor living-room, as Jonathan Drew paces to and fro in his apartment above, merely confirms the transparency of the space Hitchcock has constructed. Charles Barr has remarked on the subtlety of the 'permutations' Graham Cutts, Hitchcock's colleague at Gainsborough Pictures, was able to develop in *The Prude's Fall*, a melodrama shot in 1923, out of a 'limited number of static set-ups, within a three-dimensional spatial system'.[39] The permutations Hitchcock developed in *The Lodger* were subtler still, but no less dependent for their effect on the rapidly established coherence of a comparable 'spatial system'. So familiar do we become with the space inhabited by a family in transition that events taking place within it can acquire a significance which exceeds (or indeed resists) their narrative function. Inside these four walls, description rules, keeping us well enough informed about our familiars to feel anxious on their behalf. Outside them, in the London fog, narrative rules. When ambiguously vengeful Jonathan Drew looms at the front door, or detective Joe Betts comes bustling down the steps into the basement kitchen, they bring story with them. Inside, the phobic picturesque, strengthening domesticity by its penetration down into radical ordinariness; outside, trauma, the boredom of Gothic psychosis.

Mr and Mrs Bunting (Arthur Chesney and Marie Ault) discuss the latest murder, in the basement kitchen, while Daisy takes the Lodger's breakfast up to his room. Joe arrives to fill in the gruesome details: Mrs Bunting seems transfixed, as the men talk eagerly. Then Hitchcock cuts to a shot of what might be catastrophe: stuff tumbles off a table, a mess forms on the floor. The cut opens a gap in the spatial system Hitchcock has so carefully pieced together. Where exactly does the catastrophe occur? Does it occur in the 'space' of paranoid fantasy which the narrative has relentlessly defined by identifying Jonathan Drew, from his first appearance on the doorstep, with the Avenger? That is what Joe has been programmed to think, by jealousy as much as detective fiction. Hearing the crash, he hurtles up the stairs, followed closely by the Buntings. This movement has already begun to reorientate us in familiar space, a space before paranoid fantasy, a space in which catastrophes occur which are not necessarily beyond repair. We witnessed Daisy bringing Drew his breakfast on a previous occasion, and we know that the fearsome Avenger does not customarily strike while taking tea with a boiled egg and toast. Joe throws open the door to the Lodger's room. We see Daisy and the Lodger in each other's arms, framed by a window on one side and a stretch of bare wall on the other. Joe moves forward. The next shot, from his point of view, tracks in as much on the window as on the couple beside it, then swerves at the last second to encompass them exclusively. The camera doesn't often move, in *The Lodger*, or indeed in Hitchcock's films before *The Farmer's Wife* (1928). Here, the movement has, initially, a curious automatism. The camera announces its presence by rushing to judgement. There's a blind impetuosity to its hermeneutic lunge forward, an impetuosity without a subject. The lunge expresses the principle of narrative itself: or of that (more or less anyhow) structured narrative which constitutes plot. Any explanation will do. Only at the last second does the camera recall, acting once again on Joe's behalf, as though he'd brought it into the house with him, that its job is to find guilt not just anyhow, at random, but in the Lodger's face (and Daisy's). A confrontation ensues between Joe and the Lodger, with the Buntings looking on. Daisy calmly informs them that she had been scared by a mouse: the catastrophe was an accident. Mess is contingency's signature, and its description proof that bad things often happen which don't in happening annihilate the symbolic order. As she bends down to clear it up, she seems to tell her two admirers not to fight over a dropped tray. Absorbed in paranoia, in the identifications the plot of a thriller might be thought to demand, they ignore her.

It's a beautifully realized scene, and a powerful statement to the effect that the lower-middle-class domesticity understood in and through manageable aversion is more than just a bit of bourgeois ideology awaiting 'subversion' by Gothic eruptions from beyond or beneath the symbolic order. The niche thrillers of the 1930s do of course flatten out that idea of domestic life by reconfiguring it as a national heritage to be preserved through romance and heroic bonhomie against the dastardly foreign menace. Hitchcock was to say in 1950 that he had 'derived' more from novelists like John Buchan, J.B. Priestley, John Galsworthy, and Marie Belloc Lowndes than from the movies. 'I like them because they use multiple chases and a lot of psychology.'[40] So far, so classical Hollywood narrative, even if made in Elstree. But these films were never more suspenseful, I would argue, than when they kept their audiences informed in and through manageable aversion. Why else would Hitchcock have remained so keen to adapt Joseph Conrad's *The Secret Agent*, in appearance a detective story involving anarchists, but in fact a quasi-Naturalist drama of lower-middle-class domestic life: of social lowness lowered yet further both physically and morally. 'Winnie Verloc's story,' Conrad called it in his 'Author's Note'.[41] Avrom Fleishman has pointed out that while Hitchcock's adaptation 'misses out on Conrad's political wisdom', it improves upon the original in its depiction through 'low mimetic detail' of a distinctive shabby-genteel London milieu. 'Hitchcock's honesty in displaying his familiarity with – indeed, indulgence in – this level of social reality not only exceeds Conrad's, but is one of his strongest assets in this film and throughout his English career.'[42]

Sabotage begins with the lights going out all over London. In Battersea power-station, engineers and bureaucrats gather anxiously round what looks like the cause of the problem: a handful of sand in a sump. They chorus their concern:

> A: Sand.
> B: Sabotage.
> C: Wreckage.
> D: Deliberate.
> B: What's at the back of it?
> C: Who did it?

This circular, rhythmic exchange defines the event as political. But we might also say that it defines political event as theatre. For the staging of the scene is nothing if not theatrical. Indeed, it may even allude to a particular form of contemporary political theatre: that of the Auden gang. Auden's *The Dance of Death*, an allegorical masque describing the terminal decline of the English middle-classes, first produced for Group Theatre members in 1934, and then for the wider public the next year, incorporates a variety of comparable exchanges. For example:

> CHORUS: What shall we do
>   To pull us through?
> A: Furl the sails.
> B: Jettison the cargo.
> C: Cast anchor.
> A: This way.
> B: This way.
> C: This way.[43]

And so on. In each case, the impersonal, ritualized voicing by representative figures of an attitude to crisis indicates that the conventions of political discourse apply. Not for long, though, where *Sabotage* is concerned. Hitchcock cuts directly to the ominous figure of Verloc (Oscar Homolka), in close-up, with the power-station chimneys visible in the distance behind him. No question, then, as to who's at the front of it, if not the back. A montage of blackout chaos follows. But it's Verloc we want to find out about, and we find out about him domestically. Back home, in the apartment behind the Bijou Cinema, he washes the grit off his hands in a basin (a sludgy swirl, in close-up). Hitchcock's polluted basin is hardly a match for Renoir's. But the phobic picturesque has made its point. This particular terrorist outrage has taken effect extraordinarily, in an outbreak of political discourse among the experts, and cheerful stoicism among citizens in general; and ordinarily, in the reiteration of those familiar and familial displacements of waste-matter which draw attention to its materiality. Low mimetic detail, rather than Audenesque allegory, will continue to characterize Hitchcock's representation of the crises engendered by sabotage. Sensory experience outweighs sensational affect, for a while at least.

Sabotage was the film Hitchcock most often used to explain the distinction between suspense and shock, largely because he came to believe that in it he had broken the contract with the audience which establishes that those on whose behalf we have been induced to endure suspense will remain shock-free. Specifically, he felt that he had been wrong to send Stevie (Desmond Tester), a small boy 'with whom the audience was encouraged to fall in love', out into the streets of London with some cans of film and a parcel containing a bomb under his arm. Our knowledge of him should have kept him safe. 'I blew him up anyway.'[44] Stevie's death is indeed shocking. It shocks because the film has hitherto invested so much phobic picturesque in its description of him. *Sabotage*'s Stevie is not *The Secret Agent*'s idiot, but an ordinary – that is to say, messy – small boy. We are introduced to him as he precipitately removes the dinner from the oven, in the process ripping the outsize apron he wears and smashing a plate (he shoves the pieces into the nearest drawer). Mess, or contingency, remains his element. Once granted his errands, he takes forever to get out through the door, driving Verloc to distraction. He tosses a coin. Heads he'll wash before leaving, tails he won't. It's tails, of course. So instead he rearranges disorder laboriously, tugging at his socks, pulling a broken comb through his tousled hair. This is Naturalism lite. Out in the streets, we discover, he has taken mess with him. A salesman waylays him, slathering his teeth with sample toothpaste and his hair with sample hair-oil. Stevie rinses, spits, and wipes his mouth with his tie, in a further rearrangement rather than disposal of waste-matter. When Hitchcock blew up this walking embodiment of mess, he blew up a film style. He blew up the phobic picturesque.

I want in concluding to emphasize just how effective that style was by touching briefly on two scenes. The first demonstrates the extent to which Hitchcock's 'permutations' still relied, in 1936, on the underlying coherence of a spatial system. In *Sabotage*, as in *The Lodger*, it is the agents of genre fiction who bring narrative into a domestic space made familiar to us by description; here, furthermore, the living-quarters adjoin a cinema, so that an avid response to genre fiction pulses against the curtains shrouding the inner sanctum. On the evening of the first explosion, Verloc, pretending to have been roused from an afternoon nap, awaits his dinner in the dining-room. Domesticity has re-absorbed the saboteur who pares his nails while the cat licks itself in counterpoint. Dinner arrives, and he complains about the burnt cabbage. Detective Ted Spencer (John Loder), who has been keeping an eye on the place from the greengrocer's next door, brings a choice of lettuce; and a bit more genre fiction, by way of a gentle enquiry about what Verloc has been up to. Suddenly a small high window opening on to the area behind the cinema-screen flips inward as if propelled by a scream. Like the sound of the dropped tray in *The Lodger*, the scream opens a gap in the spatial system Hitchcock has established with such care. Where does it emanate from? Ted assumes that it has taken place in the paranoid police fantasy which has made of the apartment behind the cinema an anarchist chamber of horrors. 'I thought someone was committing a murder,' he says. Verloc knows better. He knows that genre fiction is already domestic. 'Someone probably is, on the screen there.'

Hitchcock also used the phobic picturesque to work out how much privacy a lower-middle-class person might be able to construct in public, in London in the mid-1930s. Ted takes Mrs Verloc, played by the American actress Sylvia Sidney, and Stevie to lunch at Simpson's-in-the-Strand. 'Have you ever been here before?' Mrs Verloc asks Ted, as they stand at the entrance of the dining-room as though on the verge of a precipice. 'No, never,' he replies. There's no mistaking the agoraphobic dismay she feels when confronted by a milieu apparently without limits. How does one behave, in this famous (and famously English) eatery? Hitchcock accompanies them to their table with a circuitous and rapidly accelerating dolly-shot, whose momentum so precipitously deposits Stevie in his chair that he takes most of the tablecloth with him. The shot beautifully describes both the bold performance required to manage and so overcome agoraphobia, and its all too likely outcome in a spillage provoking further (diminished) phobia of a different kind. The tablecloth's unprovoked attack on Stevie is of course consistent with what we already know of his susceptibility to mess. Ted, in fact, *has* been here before. The waiter recognizes him. Indeed, he is here now in his capacity as detective rather than aspiring husband. But who cares? This fake 'happy little family', sitting down to a hearty roast lunch, having heartily understood and overcome an easily identifiable phobia, is about as genuine as it gets in Hitchcock. We want it to live up to its messy description as a family rather more powerfully than we want the carefully plotted disclosure of criminal conspiracy.

The aim of this essay has been to develop the idea that films like *The Lodger* and *Sabotage* can usefully be approached with Modernism in mind. I have sought to connect them to an aesthetic derived from literary Naturalism which made possible the representation in an emerging global vernacular of sensory experience as well as sensational affect. For Hitchcock, I believe, the method constituted a value. The radical ordinariness laid bare by spillage, greasiness, and fracture – by the phobic feeling they provoke – was in his view what made the home a home: a laboratory for those disillusionments not wholly destructive of illusion. In so far as his English films put the emphasis on sensory experience rather than sensational affect, in their enquiries into existence as such, they count as Modernist. It doesn't surprise me at all that the critic who has come closest to grasping that emphasis should be Penelope Gilliatt, in discussing a retrospective of English Hitchcock from *The Lodger* to *Sabotage* held at the Museum of Modern Art in New York in September 1971. In the later films, Gilliatt remarks, Hitchcock's 'appetite for what it is to be morally non-plussed' can seem 'gluttonous'. The early films, by contrast, reveal a different kind of intensity. There, Hitchcock is 'the calligrapher of off-centre worry, showing us people quarrelling and interrupted by a char-woman, or a man in emergency with hiccups, or a crisis spun out because a dentist is taking his time; in the English films, where he was working in a social context that he must have had deep feelings about, the characteristic seems not a device but a true and stirring piece of observation.' Interviewing the director in his Bel Air home, Gilliatt had been overcome momentarily by claustrophobia when invited to inspect the walk-in freezer. Hitchcock immediately 'recalled a story about his childhood when his father sent him, aged four or five, to the police station with a note asking the sergeant to lock him into a cell for five or ten minutes.' That child's claustrophobia, Gilliatt concludes, is 'very much present' in the English films.[45]

Could the argument be extended to that other 'Modernism' of the American films of the 1950s and 1960s? I doubt it. There remains a consensus, recently restated in emphatic terms by John Orr, to the effect that Hitchcock's departure for Hollywood in 1939 should be seen both as a 'watershed' and as the 'start of something profound'. 'In the American phase,' Orr argues, 'he gets serious. Suspense modulates into psychodrama.'[46] Phobic feeling, crucial to the creation of suspense, tends not to make itself felt in full-blown psychodrama. There is, rather remarkably under the circumstances, no bird-shit in *The Birds*.

Notes

1 'The Last New Wave', in *Paris Hollywood: Writings on Film* (London: Verso, 2002), 164–82, p. 170. Wollen develops this view in '*Rope*: Three Hypotheses', in Richard Allen and S. Ishii-Gonzalès, eds., *Alfred Hitchcock: Centenary Essays* (London: BFI Publishing, 1999), 75–85, pp. 78–9. See also Tom Ryall, *Alfred Hitchcock and the British Cinema*, (London: Athlone, 1996), 25–6; Richard Allen, '*The Lodger* and the Origins of Hitchcock's Aesthetic', *Hitchcock Annual*, 2001–2, 36–78; and by way of cautionary note, Charles Barr, *English Hitchcock* (Moffat: Cameron & Hollis, 1999), 31.

2 Sidney Gottlieb, 'Early Hitchcock: The German Influence', in Gottlieb and Christopher Brookhouse, eds., *Framing Hitchcock* (Detroit, MI: Wayne State University Press, 2002), 35–58; Joseph Garncarz, 'German Hitchcock', ibid., 59–81; Bettina Rosenbladt, 'Doubles and Doubts in Hitchcock: The German Connection', in Richard Allen and S. Ishii-Gonzalès, eds., *Hitchcock: Past and Future* (London: Routledge, 2004), 37–61.

3 Respectively, Roger Webster, 'The Aesthetics of Walking: Literary and Filmic Representations of London in Joseph Conrad's *The Secret Agent*', in Gail Cunningham and Stephen Barber, eds., *London Eyes: Reflections in Text and Image* (New York: Berghahn Books, 2007), 91–116; Mark Wollaeger, *Modernism, Media, and Propaganda: British Narrative from 1900 to 1945* (Princeton, NJ: Princeton University Press, 2006), 38–70; and Christopher GoGwilt, 'The Geopolitical Screenplay: Sabotage from Joseph Conrad to Alfred Hitchcock', in *The Fiction of*

Geopolitics: After-Images of Culture, from Wilkie Collins to Alfred Hitchcock (Stanford, CA: Stanford University Press, 2000), 160–98.

4   *On the History of Film Style* (Cambridge, MA: Harvard University Press, 1997), 83–4, 101.

5   See, for example, Timothy Corrigan and Patricia White, *The Film Experience: An Introduction* (New York: Bedford/St Martin's, 2004), 154; and Kristin Thompson and David Bordwell, *Film History: An Introduction*, 2nd edn. (Boston: McGraw Hill, 2003), 357–9.

6   *Film Style*, 115, 84.

7   'The Art Cinema as a Mode of Film Practice', in *Poetics of Cinema* (London: Routledge, 2008), 151–69, p. 157.

8   'Touching the Surface: *Marnie*, Melodrama, Modernism', in *Centenary Essays*, 87–105, pp. 88–9.

9   'Alfred Hitchcock, or, The Form and its Historical Mediation', in Žižek, ed., *Everything You Always Wanted to Know about Lacan (But Were Afraid to Ask Hitchcock)* (London: Verso, 1992), 1–12, p. 4.

10   'Spatial Systems in *North by Northwest*', ibid., 47–72, pp. 51, 58–60, 65.

11   *Hitchcock and Twentieth-Century Cinema* (London: Wallflower Press, 2005), 18–25.

12   *Hitchcock's Cryptonomies*, 2 vols. (Minneapolis, MI: Minnesota University Press, 2005), 1. xi, xx, 169, 172.

13   Ibid., 1. 2, 20–4, 160.

14   An argument I develop more fully in 'e-Modernism: Telephony in British Fiction 1925–1940', *Critical Quarterly*, 51.1, 2009, 1–32. Cohen would probably argue that storage technologies such as writing and cinema are teletechnical in the sense that they store the memories we regard as constitutive of consciousness outside (at a distance from) consciousness. If so, he would be following a Derridean line of enquiry exemplified by Bernard Stiegler, *Technics and Time, 1: The Fault of Epithemus*, trans. Richard Beardsworth and George Collins (Stanford, CA: Stanford University Press, 1998). My objection to this line of enquiry is that it risks conflating literal with metaphoric distance. It is the physical extent or reach of telecommunication media which made them, and still makes them, remarkable.

15   For a deconstructive approach to cinema which understands the 'photogrammatic track' as an incentive to Modernism, and which Cohen does not engage with, see Garrett Stewart, *Between Film and Screen: Modernism's Photo Synthesis* (Chicago: University of Chicago Press, 1999). Preferable to both, I think, is Julian Murphet's account of Modernism as a 'structural adjustment within a given social and historical media ecology, or media system,' in *Multimedia Modernism: Literature and the Anglo-American Avant-garde* (Cambridge: Cambridge University Press, 2009).

16   E.g., William Rothman, *Hitchcock: The Murderous Gaze* (Cambridge, MA: Harvard University Press, 1982); Peter Conrad, *The Hitchcock Murders* (London: Faber and Faber, 2000).

17   Liesl Olson, *Modernism and the Ordinary* (Oxford: Oxford University Press, 2009), 4. Olson's focus is on Joyce, Woolf, Stein, and Stevens.

18   This claim is the basis of my *Cinema and Modernism* (Oxford: Blackwell, 2007).

19   'Alfred Hitchcock', in *Signs and Meaning in the Cinema*, expanded edn. (London: BFI Publishing, 1998), 140–3, p. 141.

20   'The Mass Production of the Senses: Classical Cinema as Vernacular Modernism', *Modernism/Modernity*, 6.2, 1999, 59–77, pp. 68–70. See also her 'Fallen

Women, Rising Stars, New Horizons: Shanghai Silent Films as Vernacular Modernism', *Film Quarterly*, 54.1, 2000, 10–22.

21 'Wilkie Collins and Dickens', in *Selected Essays*, 3rd edn. (London: Faber and Faber, 1951), 409–18, p. 409. See David E. Chinitz, *T.S. Eliot and the Cultural Divide* (Chicago: University of Chicago Press, 2003).

22 'Why "Thrillers" Thrive', in *Hitchcock on Hitchcock: Selected Writings and Interviews*, ed. Sidney Gottlieb (London: Faber and Faber, 1995), 109–12.

23 *The Decline of Sentiment: American Film in the 1920s* (Berkeley: University of California Press, 2008), ch. 2.

24 *Mists of Regret: Culture and Sensibility in Classic French Film* (Princeton: Princeton University Press, 1995), 303.

25 Gottlieb, 'Early Hitchcock', 39.

26 *Decline of Sentiment*, 27–33.

27 Reprinted in Sidney Gottlieb and Richard Allen, eds., *The Hitchcock Annual Anthology* (London: Wallflower Press, 2009), 79–81.

28 First published in *Limehouse Nights: Tales of Chinatown* (London: Grant Richards, 1917).

29 Vance Kepley, 'Griffith's *Broken Blossoms* and the Problem of Historical Specificity', in James Naremore, ed., *Quarterly Review of Film Studies* (New York: Redgrave Publishing Co., 1978), 37–48; Dudley Andrew, '*Broken Blossoms*: The Vulnerable Text and the Marketing of Masochism', in *Film in the Aura of Art* (Princeton: Princeton University Press, 1984), 16–27; Lary May, 'Apocalyptic Cinema: D.W. Griffith and the Aesthetics of Reform', in John Belton, ed., *Movies and Mass Culture* (London: Athlone, 1996), 25–58.

30 *Mists of Regret*, 36.

31 'Columbus of the Screen', 81.

32 'Space in the Classical Film', in *Classical Hollywood Cinema*, 50–9, p. 54.

33 Ibid., 58.

34 'Why "Thrillers" Thrive', 115.

35 Wollen, 'Alfred Hitchcock', 141.

36 E.g. 'The Enjoyment of Fear', in *Hitchcock on Hitchcock*, 116–21. Originally published in *Good Housekeeping*, in February 1949.

37 'Why "Thrillers" Thrive', 111.

38 Donald Spoto, *The Dark Side of Genius: The Life of Alfred Hitchcock* (New York: Ballantine Books, 1983), 95.

39 *English Hitchcock*, 21. For more on Cutts, see Christine Gledhill, *Reframing British Cinema 1918–1928* (London: BFI Publishing, 2003), 111–19.

40 'Core of the Movie – The Chase', in *Hitchcock on Hitchcock*, 125–32, p. 131.

41 *The Secret Agent*, ed. John Lyon (Oxford: Oxford University Press, 2004), 228–33, p. 233.

42 '*The Secret Agent* Sabotaged?', in Gene M. Moore, ed., *Conrad on Film* (Cambridge: Cambridge University Press, 1997), 48–60, pp. 58, 53.

43 *The Dance of Death*, in *Plays and Other Dramatic Writings*, ed. Edward Mendelson (Princeton, NJ: Princeton University Press, 1988), 80–107, p. 93.

44 'Enjoyment of Fear', 120–1.

45 'Of Hitchcock', in *Three-Quarter Face: Reports & Reflections* (London: Secker & Warburg, 1980), 43–60, pp. 45–8.

46 Orr, *Hitchcock and Twentieth-Century Cinema*, 11.

9

Phoning It In

Anyone old enough to have made use of public phone-booths on a regular basis will know that they were more often than not damp, cold, filthy, and foul-smelling, and while amply supplied with the phone numbers of prostitutes, practically impossible to make any sort of call from. So folk memory insists, at any rate. So literature insists. A quick online search or waft through the bulkier paperbacks at the airport bookstall will confirm that urban phone-booths in particular have become indelibly associated in the literary imagination with urine. What invariably greets the protagonists of genre fiction as they open the door of a booth to make some life-or-death call is the stickiness left behind by a previous user. Expecting to speak and to listen, they instead inhale the anonymous yet fiercely intimate odour of population itself. They have seen and smelt, and may still touch or even taste, the fact of the crowd, the fact of the city.

The protagonist of Howard R. Simpson's Vietnam spy-novel *Someone Else's War* (2003) has information to gather. He makes a call. 'The phone booth smelled of urine; someone had spat generously on the floor and a loud argument in Cantonese was going on at the stamp counter.'[1] Booths should keep sound both out and in. They should be secretive. But Simpson, like many other novelists, has felt it necessary to compound secrets with secretions; not just urine, but phlegm, too, for good measure. A spilt body has preceded, and maybe prefigured, espionage's spilling of minds. Simpson wants us to understand that all the spilling in spying is a dirty business. The implication he draws on, the implication of the folk memory endlessly re-cycled in genre fiction, is that we don't fully recognize a phone-booth as a phone-booth until we've felt just a little bit sick at the sight and smell of it. The disgust *is* the recognition. But what exactly has it recognized?

Of course, better things do happen to patrons of public telephone systems, at least in fiction. Clark Kent and Dr Who regularly disappear into booths maintained to high standards of hygiene in order to pick up where they left off as extra-terrestrials. The time-travelling booth which launched *Bill and Ted's Excellent Adventure* (1989), and as a result Keanu Reeves's even more excellent career, had a curious retractable tripod fizzing with static on top, but no sign of insanitary behaviour below. Phone-booths have continued to provide Reeves with lift-off, most notably in *The Matrix* (1999), where he plays Thomas Anderson, a.k.a. Neo, a company man turned hacker turned messiah. At the film's conclusion, Neo phones in a final proclamation of defiance from a booth on a busy street in the virtual world into which the bulk of the human species has been absorbed, before stepping outside, donning dark glasses, and ascending into heaven, while Rage Against the Machine break out their heavy-metal anthem 'Wake Up'. But it isn't all CGI, yet, at reality's interface with illusion. Harry Potter, for example, nips into a sanctuary of rather more traditional design to place a call to the Ministry of Magic. J.K. Rowling has enough respect for folk memory to register his surprise that the phone actually works.[2]

A lot depends on genre. Don't go there, would be sound advice to characters in most kinds of Hollywood movie. They invariably do. Why, when Hitchcock's homicidal birds swoop down in earnest on the main drag in Bodega Bay, does Melanie Daniels (Tippi Hedren) rush out of the diner from which she's witnessed the onset of the attack and headlong into what is about to become the most famous phone-booth in the history of cinema? If she had wanted to make a call, there's a perfectly good phone inside, which she's just used to tell her father about an earlier attack on the local school, and then to summon her boyfriend and the police. Hitchcock, of course, knows why. What he gets from Melanie's mistake is an image of isolation and exposure, as she twists and turns in torment in her transparent cubicle, and the glass shatters (fig. 10). Generations of commentary have led one to suppose that the danger stems from inside rather than outside the psyche. The Bodega Bay cubicle was the first to serve as a lightning-conductor for the unconscious. After that, it was only a matter of time before someone made *Phone Booth* (2002), in which a sniper armed with a high velocity rifle traps publicist Stu Shepard (Colin Farrell) behind glass on

Figure 10 and the glass shatters

a street in New York, forbidding him to put the receiver down until he has agreed to confess his sins (that is, his desire); or *Run Lola Run* (1998), in which Man communicates despair and self-hatred from the Berlin equivalent, while Woman does something about it, in postmodern fashion, three times over.

As these examples demonstrate, phone-boxes have led an exciting imaginary life, and not always in big cities. A good deal of folklore attaches to the booth which once stood on the Aiken Mine Road in the Mojave Desert, in California, about 15 miles from the nearest highway. It even earned a cameo in an *X-Files* episode.[3] Technology's far-flung outposts in the wilderness have fulfilled a variety of tasks, up to and including the reconfiguration of traditional communities by international capital.[4] In Bill Forsyth's comic-utopian *Local Hero* (1983), the young executive sent to Scotland to buy a fishing village on behalf of Knox Oil and Gas has no other means of communication with his boss in Houston, Texas, than a public phone-box on the quayside across the road from the hotel. The locals have a whip-round to supply him with 10p coins, and thereafter attend assiduously on each visit to the box, wiping the receiver for him (folk memory dies hard), or supplying a glass of whisky. On one occasion, the outside of the cubicle is repainted while he frets inside; on another, a previous user, who has fallen asleep *in situ*, bolt upright, emerges to relay an important message. The phone-box is the point at which traditional community forms and re-forms in mildly carnivalesque fashion around the connection to modernity, which once made will never be un-made. At the end of the film, as the executive gazes out at Houston from the penthouse apartment to which he has reluctantly returned, Forsyth cuts to a long shot of the quayside portal, in which the phone rings.

In cities, by contrast, we enter phone-boxes off the street in order to be private in public. That is, we once did, before we all had mobiles. Nowadays you don't go somewhere special to phone in unless your mobile's broken, or you've left it at home. The new urban spectacle consists of people apparently in earnest conversation with themselves, whom we might once have crossed the road to avoid, or broadcasting the gory details of personal fiasco to a railway-carriage full of strangers. It is in fact the prospect of the phone-box's imminent complete supersession by the mobile which has most effectively laid bare its original purpose (fig. 11). For each of these mobile-users is engaged, as we once were when we stepped into a phone-box, in constructing privacy in public. The difference is that they rely upon an understanding of the distance between themselves and the next person whose expression is social and cultural, rather than physical. That understanding has not yet quite become a consensus. But it is already powerful enough to have altered urban experience. The history of the urban phone-box, which is also the history of the city since electrification, is the history of the construction of privacy in public by physical as well as social and cultural means.

Figure 11   Ex-phone booth. Philadelphia. September 2009. Photograph: Kasia Boddy

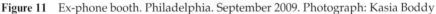

The history is a complicated one, and its complication reveals that public privacy – call it living in a city – is always under construction. In a phone-box, we are impersonally personal, in that we communicate with someone we know well or at least can identify, but not in person; and personally impersonal, in that previous users, whom we do not know and cannot identify, have indeed been there in person, have left us themselves to touch, taste, smell, while those yet to come gaze at us from outside.[5] Where, exactly, is the intimacy in all this, the being private in private? And where is that consensual acknowledgement of common purpose, that being public in public, forever built into the city's other communicative and regulatory systems, into postbox, bus-stop, and road-sign, into traffic-lights, and speed and security cameras, into all those items of street furniture which, unlike the phone-box, we have agreed not to vandalize? For vandalism there has always been, where phone-boxes are concerned. Many have left their mark on one who would not look twice at a No Entry sign. It's hard, for example, to see Martin Amis's prose-style (never mind his more pathologically-inclined protagonists) passing up on an opportunity for booth-rage. In *Money* (1984), John Self duly lets rip. 'I had been wanting to smash a telephone for a long time. The bakelite split obligingly, then retaliated with an electric shock. I got to my feet and left the hot receiver dangling from its mauled base.'[6] In Britain, there is a further complication to this long history, in the fact that ownership of the booths in which we once learnt to be personally impersonal and impersonally personal has passed during the last hundred years from private into public hands and back again.

My aim here is to examine the uses made in literature and film of the feelings aroused by the (once) commonplace phone-box, -booth, or –kiosk. These include rage, and terror, of course. But descriptions of privacy constructed in public are often at their most subtle, inventive, and compelling when in a minor key. The two feelings I shall have most to say about here are disgust and tenderness. We need to ask what disgust and tenderness might know about living in a city that could not otherwise be known. The examples I have chosen from literature and film concern London, for the most part, but not only London.

Bacteriological Boxes

The telephone was invented in March 1876, by Alexander Graham Bell. Queen Victoria witnessed a demonstration of the new device on 14 January 1878. On 7 April 1882, the *Aberdeen Weekly Journal* reported that the establishment of a rudimentary telephone system in London had 'justified the most sanguine expectations of its proprietors'. The commercial development of such systems encountered a variety of obstacles, but by the turn of the century the telephone had none the less become a necessary basis for the proper organization of middle-class social, economic, and cultural life in major cities around the world. Using the device was one way to be modern, in public and in private. 'In Berlin, Zurich and Hamburg, telephonic kiosks have been established, so that anyone walking along and desirous of sending a communication by telephone, or asking a question, or giving an order, or making a correction overlooked in recent conversation, may do so, and the charge is twopence halfpenny.' The Directors of the London Telephone Company were hoping to make a similar provision.[7] The term 'kiosk' drew at once on a faint association with the Turkish pavilion or summerhouse, and on a rather more palpable one with the familiar outdoor stands offering newspapers, or tea and buns.

'Today,' trumpeted the *Daily News* on 1 April 1891, 'the new Telephone line between London and Paris is open to the public.' A person with eight shillings to spare could gossip with anyone in Paris she or he could find to gossip with for a period of three minutes. What most preoccupied the *News*, however, was not the science behind this latest technological triumph, but the material construction of the 'chamber' in which calls were to be made.

The marvel lay as much in the raising of a social and cultural barrier between one person and another in London as in the lowering of the physical barrier between one person in London and another in Paris. For the person in London wishing to call Paris 'steps into a little sort of padded sentry-box, the door of which is edged with india-rubber.'

> When this closes upon him he is hermetically sealed, and might rave himself hoarse without conveying the faintest sound to anyone outside. There is a pane of glass in the door, so that the officer in charge could see the inmate of the box, though unable to hear him. On stepping in, the interior of the little cupboard is in darkness, but the telephoner by sitting down on the seat establishes connection, and an arc light instantly blazes out until he again rises, when it goes out till the next comer takes his seat. The telephone box is a wonderfully compact and all but perfect little institution, the only drawback being that it is entirely unventilated, and the person sitting in it is literally hermetically sealed up.[8]

As the repetition of the phrase 'hermetically sealed' makes clear, the emphasis in this early assessment of this new method of telecommunication was on enclosure. The guarantees offered concerning privacy had literally to be iron-clad. From the outset, there was a certain excess in the construction of privacy in public by physical as well as social and cultural means. The box had to be sealed, yes. But *hermetically* sealed, so that one could scarcely breathe inside it?

On 1 January 1912, the General Post Office, a government department, became to all intents and purposes the monopoly supplier of telephone services in the United Kingdom, and was to remain so until the creation of British Telecom in 1981. In 1912, phone-boxes entered public service. They had thereafter to be ubiquitous, and uniform in design. The first kiosk satisfactorily to combine form and function, the K2, built out of cast iron to a neoclassical design by Sir Giles Gilbert Scott and painted a glossy Post Office red all over, came into service in 1927. It was as much emblem as shelter: ventilation came from holes pierced through the top fascia in the shape of a crown. The smaller and more durable K6, also designed by Scott, and set up in villages across Britain to celebrate George V's Jubilee in 1935, acquired the status of an institution. In August 1986, a K2 kiosk in London Zoo's Parrot House became the first phone-box ever to receive listed building status. By that time, British Telecom had become British Telecom PLC, flagship of the Thatcher government's ambitious privatization programme. In 1987, BT's phone-box monopoly was broken up. So began the conversion, memorably described by Patrick Wright, of the only remaining 'public' element of a now otherwise privately-owned service into a (privately-owned) heritage industry. Boxes began to come in different shapes and sizes. Respectable neighbourhoods could hope for a bit of roof, and two or three walls. 'The new and growing underclass, meanwhile, would have to settle for a sawn-off metal stump with an armoured cardphone bolted onto it.'[9] Scott's totemic cubicles disappeared from the streets. Many of them have since found their way to the United States, where they do duty as interior or exterior decoration. One now resides in a room at Twitter HQ in San Francisco, its sole contents a plastic chair.[10]

The K6 was supposed to be an amenity as well as an emblem and shelter. According to the *Post Office Electrical Engineers' Journal*, a 'modernistic touch' had been supplied by the 'horizontal glazing scheme', which 'furnishes a remarkably free view from the inside of the kiosk'.[11] The interior surfaces were of bakelite-faced plywood, and the stainless steel fittings included a pipe- or cigarette-rack and a hook for umbrellas.[12] By converting the original hermetically-sealed sentry-boxes into a middle-class room with a view, the Post Office designers had built a supplementary layer of social and cultural distance into the physical construction of privacy in public. It was a futile gesture (albeit one that today's mobile-users have unknowingly taken to heart). What people wanted in a phone-box was a box, even if they didn't always much like some of the consequences.

However lavishly furnished, the phone-booth was at once an enclosure and a facility accessible to all and sundry; that is, a health hazard. In August 1906, a 'call office attendant' wrote to the *Lancet* to complain about 'the growing danger arising from the use of the common mouthpiece by promiscuous callers at public telephones'. Cleaning up after a caller with a particularly violent cough, the hapless attendant had found the instrument still damp with 'congealed breath'.[13] A year later, the journal returned to the theme, remarking that the telephone call station should rather be described as 'a bacteriological box in which pathogenic and other organisms are carefully nourished.'[14] In March 1908, a correspondent reported on a wide variety of London booths in which 'the condition of the apparatus was unsatisfactory, the vulcanite mouthpieces frequently containing debris with a more or less bad odour.'[15] In June, Dr Frances J. Allan, Medical Officer of Health of the City of Westminster, reported the results of tests done on swabs taken from the mouthpieces of transmitters in public call boxes. One had attached to it a 'mass of whitish-grey viscid substance'. The viscid substance was injected into two guinea-pigs. One died after 23 days, the other after 27.[16] Nor did the transfer into public ownership altogether solve the problem. In February 1924, the *Lancet* reported on a series of further tests carried out in February 1912 by the aptly-named Dr H.R.D. Spitta at St George's Hospital in London, which had shown that the transmission of tuberculosis by means of the telephone mouthpiece was 'practically impossible'.[17]

The phone-box is the place where one kind of communication – one way to be in contact – intersects another. Tuberculosis may no longer have been a worry. But the disgust provoked by the debris, odour, and viscid substance previous users had promiscuously left in and around the mouthpiece did not diminish. Indeed, it strengthened. It took shape as a common perception of the phone-box as phobic object or site. Penelope Gilliatt's plague-novel, *One by One* (1965), begins with an abortive call from a public booth so hot that the caller's hand leaves a mark on the receiver 'as though he were covered in mutton grease'.[18]

Few things give greater pause for thought to the amnesiac ex-commando in John Lodwick's ambitiously daft *Peal of Ordnance* (1947), who has been laying explosive charges on monuments across central London, than the state of the box from which he rings the BBC to tell them there's a bomb in one of their studios.

> The booth smelt of urine and spittle gouts. He opened the directory; obsolete, tatty and well thumbed ... signatures into the bargain (Jack H. Rossbach; U.S.N. Yonkers, N.Y.), and here and there addresses underlined with words of advice: 'Call her up any time. She'll be there.'[19]

The nausea anchors and provides some kind of justification for a free-floating anxiety which also includes sex and foreigners. Phone-boxes have always been 'obscene'. One of the accusations leveled against Leopold Bloom in the Nighttown episode of James Joyce's *Ulysses* (1922) is that 'Unspeakable messages he telephoned mentally to Miss Dunn at an address in d'Olier Street while he presented himself indecently to the instrument in the callbox'.[20] In so far as he 'presented himself' to the instrument, rather than to the more or less oblivious Miss Dunn, Bloom, too, might be thought to have left a viscid substance behind him. In Christopher Isherwood's *Mr Norris Changes Trains* (1935), the homosexual Baron Kuno von Pregnitz, pursued by the police on charges of political corruption, locks himself in panic into a cubicle in a public lavatory. Next day, the newspapers uniformly report him as having finally been run to ground in a telephone-box.[21] By the end of the 1990s, it was costing Westminster City Council's Street Enforcement Department around £250,000 a month to remove prostitutes' cards from booths in central London. On 1 September 2001, Sections 46 and 47 of the Criminal Justice and Police Act came into force, making it an offence to place such advertisements in, or in the immediate vicinity of, a phone-booth.[22] According to Jonathan Glancey, what's wrong with the new deregulated London is too much instant availability. 'Unprotected sex with eastern Europeans on the make for a few quid just a piss-streaked telephone-kiosk's call away.'[23] It certainly doesn't help that the sex on offer is from some of those east Europeans who have been invading England imaginarily ever since Count Dracula first landed his coffins at Whitby. Like Howard Simpson, and many others, Glancey feels the need to be absolutely precise about the location and extent of the traces of piss (at least the punters in his part of London aim high).

It is possible, however, for disgust to express a sense if not of community, then of a construction of privacy in public which includes rather than excludes the acknowledgement of strangers. Tony Harrison's 'Changing at York' takes place in a phone-booth in York railway station, where he has gone to inform his son that his train has been delayed. The booth is replete with phobic objects and sensations: a vandalized directory, the smell of alcohol and dossers' pee, and (a touch the *Lancet* would have appreciated) 'saliva in the mouthpiece'. Harrison thinks himself away from phobia into a sorrowing account of the deceptions interactivity at a distance has enabled him to inflict on those he loves. He concludes the poem by returning to the son he now has to call, and remembering him

> in this same kiosk with the stale, sour breath
> of queuing callers, drunk, cajoling, lying,
> consoling his grampa for his granny's death,
> how I heard him, for the first time ever, crying.[24]

To bring the material remnant back in is to think with phobia, rather than away from it. Phobia replaces Harrison in the company of strangers. For the chronicle of the activities undertaken by previous callers – cajoling, lying – carries straight over the line-break into the son's tearful consolation, which has been bound further into them by rhyme (crying/lying) and half-rhyme (cajoling/consoling). The consolation the poem itself finds could be said to lie in phobia's bitter-sweet acknowledgement of our intimacy with people unknown to us who do as we do.

The key to these experiences was inadvertency. You went into a booth in search of one kind of privacy in public and ended up with another; and the experience made you think.[25] For smell, touch, and taste were not the only kinds of inadvertency you might find yourself shut in with. During the public payphone's *belle époque* you would after all have been as likely to witness somebody else using one as you would have been to use one yourself. Shutting themselves in in order to speak and listen, these people were also there to be seen, if you wished to see them. A view of a person in a phone-booth works wonders, in literature and film; and because sight, unlike taste, touch, and smell, has distance built into it, the sensations provoked are often gentler. The experience has to do with stimulation by fellow-feeling rather than with stimulation by threat.

Aquarium

George Harvey Bone, the protagonist of Patrick Hamilton's *Hangover Square* (1941), suffers from psychotic episodes, begun and concluded with a curious click, which separate him off from ordinary existence, and eventually induce him to murder Netta, the woman of his obsessions. The closest he gets to understanding the nature and scope of these episodes is when he calls Netta from a public payphone in Earl's Court station.

> In the line of telephone booths there were a few other people locked and lit up in glass, like waxed fruit, or Crown jewels, or footballers in a slot machine on a pier, and he went in and became like them – a different sort of person in a

different sort of world – a muffled, urgent, anxious, private, ghostly world, composed not of human beings but of voices, disembodied communications – a world not unlike, so far as he could remember, the one he entered when he had one of his 'dead' moods.[26]

The 'ghostly world' Bone inspects, of people 'locked and lit up in glass', is like his dead moods in its separation from ordinary existence, but unlike them in that its inhabitants enter it and leave it at will. What he in fact sees, perhaps, is an alternative version of those moods, in which his own anxiety, though scarcely diminished, at least resembles everyone else's. Entry into the booth is the only occasion in his adult life on which he can be said to have *become like* a 'few other people'. The likeness is too fleeting to mature into liking. But Bone's awareness of a shared experience of spectatorship – he could be a tourist in the Tower of London, or a slot machine addict – has drawn him momentarily out of obsession. He has been touched into that awareness by the pathos of strangers.

Buchi Emecheta's *Second-Class Citizen* (1974) is a novel about the early phases of London's gradual, uneven, and incomplete post-war transition to a multi-ethnic metropolis. Adah joins her husband Francis in London, where he has taken and continues to take interminable accountancy exams, from Lagos. She works as a librarian, gives birth, is beaten up, and humiliated, and keeps going. The crucial narrative development concerns her exchange of the status and function of second-class citizen as a wife under Ibo patriarchy for the status and function of second-class citizen as an immigrant under institutionalized racism. Emecheta manages this development indirectly, by telling the story of Adah's friend Janet, a white girl married to another Nigerian student, Babalola. Babalola had first met Janet while standing outside a phone-booth waiting for her to finish a call. 'It started to drizzle and he was getting soaked to the skin, so he banged on the kiosk door, and shook his fist at the girl to frighten her. Then he looked closer, and saw that the girl was not phoning anybody, she was asleep, standing up.'[27] Janet had at that time been sixteen, and pregnant. Babalola had taken her home, lent her to his friends, then fallen in love with her, and married her. Janet does not in fact feature extensively in Adah's story; she is there primarily as an image of a person in a phone-box. Her introduction into it opens that story out: to new dangers, but also to the potential for change, in Adah herself and in others.

Such images seem in an obvious sense cinematic, and there are indeed phone-booth virtuosos among directors: Hitchcock, undoubtedly, for example, and Margarethe von Trotta, who learnt much from him. Von Trotta's controversial films about the politics of the person offer an incisive and deeply-felt analysis of the gendering of public and private spheres in post-war middle-class German society. Her uncompromising activism of the intellect requires that middle-class women not only cross over from a private sphere understood as feminine into a public sphere understood as masculine, but feminize the latter in the process. They must *speak out*, as women, on the hustings, and in law-court, lecture-theatre, and television studio. But crossing over also involves the occupation of civic as well as political and cultural space. The domestic interiors which immobilize the more anxious among her protagonists have often been described as labyrinthine. Recessive might be a better term: frame within frame within frame, a vista narrowed down at its far end to a boxy cell or incubator of depression. In these films, enforced privacy kills (or provokes to murder) by absorption into an unfathomable interior depth or black hole. A phone-booth is, of course, a recess of a kind. But it is a recess projected into the world, a recess with an apprehensible outside to it – a place you go in order to be private *in public*.

Von Trotta dramatizes inadvertency. Her protagonists are at their wits' end when they seek refuge in the booth. They lift the receiver and dial. The person they wish to speak to cannot be reached. There is no-one, friend or functionary, to speak out *to*. In the meantime, like it or not, they see and are seen. They find themselves, in more than one sense, in public. And finding themselves in public, flee – if they get the chance. In *Sheer Madness* (1982), Ruth (Angela Winkler), an artist smothered by a protective, bullying husband, finally overcomes her fear of other people to the extent of leaving the house on her own to call her closest friend from a public payphone in a post-office. The payphones nestle in spacious booths transparent from three sides. Ruth lifts the receiver. She stops listening, and looks: down the row of occupied booths to her left, then across at the bank of post-boxes on the wall opposite, then down the row of booths to her right. In the booth next to hers, a face looms grotesquely. This is her George Harvey Bone moment. Bone had become like these strangers locked and lit up in glass. Ruth, knowing that she will never become like them, flees, as Christa (Tina Engel) had, in *The Second Awakening of Christa Klages* (1979), when spotted by someone she knows. Carla (Carla Aldrovandi), in *The Long Silence* (1993), trailed by a mafia assassin, does not even get the chance to flee. For Von Trotta, the phone-booth *is* the public sphere in its civic dimension: a dangerous place for women who have been taught to invest all they have in staying private.[28]

Phone-booths encourage us to think about one city in relation to another, one film in relation to another. André Bazin once chose a scene in William Wyler's *The Best Years of Our Lives* (1946) to exemplify the long-take deep-focus style he regarded as a 'liberal and democratic' alternative to the standard manipulation of point of view through rapid-fire editing. The scene, set in a bar in Boone City, involves three variously damaged ex-servicemen who have become friends on the flight home. Homer (Harold Russell) plays piano in the near foreground, while Al (Fredric March) looks on, and Fred (Dana Andrews) makes a call he would rather not make from a booth in the distant background. Wyler filmed the scene in long shot, with both planes of action in sharp focus. Homer's playing (he has hooks for hands) absorbs our interest and admiration, and Al's. But the 'true drama', Bazin suggests, may be that which is taking place in the 'little aquarium' at the far end of the room, where Fred renounces his love for Al's daughter, who has offered him a way out of a miserable marriage.[29] Wyler cut in two close-ups of Al looking over towards the booth. The final look Al gives Fred, as he stands rigid in the booth after putting the phone down, could easily be construed as tenderness. It is indeed a look *given*.

One person who may have noticed it was a young Japanese director, Akira Kurosawa. Kurosawa's tenth film as director, *Stray Dog* (1949), is a Simenon-like thriller about a young detective, Murukami (Toshiro Mifune), whose gun goes missing. With some help from the older and wiser Sato (Takashi Shimura), Murukami eventually tracks the culprit down in Tokyo's seamy criminal underworld. Towards the end of the film, Sato, arriving at the hotel where the culprit has holed up, calls Murukami from a booth in the lobby. There is confusion and delay at the other end. Kurosawa almost literally suspends Sato in the booth, in a long shot held for twenty-five seconds, while the hotel manager flirts clumsily with the receptionist in the foreground. The thief escapes. As Sato leaves the booth in pursuit, the receiver dangles. He is shot down outside. Kurosawa, unlike Wyler, does not provide an intermediary gaze. But we don't need help to feel for the haunted Sato. We know that the balance of power and responsibility between veteran and novice, such an important theme in Kurosawa, has just tilted towards the novice, as the veteran's vulnerability is laid bare.

Such is the hauntedness of telephone-booths that they can distract attention from foreground drama even when empty. Towards the end of Carol Reed's *The Third Man* (1949), Anna (Alida Valli) and Holly Martins (Joseph Cotton) wait for Harry Lime (Orson Welles) in the Café Marc Aurel. An empty booth glows faintly behind Anna, in the depth of the shot, as she paces restlessly up and down. In Martin Scorsese's *The King of Comedy* (1982), fantasist Rupert Pupkin (Robert De Niro), on a first date with barmaid Rita (Diahnne Abbott), hopes to impress her by leafing through his autograph album. It's not long before our attention has been drawn away from his dismal performance to the area of the restaurant behind him, where two illuminated booths stand empty. This is not someone we want to feel sorry for. Another patron, who has witnessed the performance at close range, withdraws into the nearest booth, apparently to report on it in amazement. A waiter enters the booth behind him. Pupkin has been out-magnetized by less than zero. Scorsese has said that his aim was to make *The King of Comedy* in '1903 style', without close-ups and virtuoso camera-movements.[30] Here, the phone-booths, a featureless feature in the depth of the shot, enabled him to isolate his anti-hero without moving his camera an inch. Usually, though, in cinema, it's people we know who make the calls, and in so doing appear to us in a different light.

In a scene in Pedro Almodóvar's *Women on the Verge of a Nervous Breakdown* (1988), Pepa (Carmen Maura), who spends most of the film trying to get in touch with her faithless lover Iván (Ricardo Gullón), and realizes in the process that she can perfectly well do without him, has established herself across the road from the building in which Iván's ex-wife Lucía (Julieta Serrano) lives. In homage to *Rear Window*, the camera passes from one illuminated window to another, revealing as it does Madrid's answer to Miss Torso, and Lucía's son Carlos (Antonio Banderas) packing his suitcase for departure, to her considerable distress. Pepa crosses the road to the phone-booth in front of the building. A poster on which a grinning young girl holds a grinning young boy upside down by the ankles partly screens her from us. This is a harmless enough aquarium, as aquariums go. Pepa rings home. The only message on the machine is from her hapless friend Candela (María Barranco), who's got mixed up with terrorists. There's a violent thud, and the booth begins to shake. Like Melanie in *The Birds*, Pepa is under attack. Almodóvar shoots her from above as she twists and turns, as Hitchcock had shot Melanie; and then at knee level, as the receiver she has dropped dangles, while Candela intones 'Pepa, I'm in big trouble'. But this is a film which diminishes trouble rather than aggravating it. The thud was Carlos's suitcase bouncing off the roof. Its contents spill out. Pepa, stepping out of the booth, picks up a framed photograph and inspects it. The photograph, of Iván and Carlos, carries the inscription 'From your dad, who doesn't deserve you'. Carlos and his girlfriend Marisa (Rossy de Palma) argue obliviously across Pepa (even Miss Torso is somehow his fault), while she gazes intently at him. Marisa bundles her back into the booth ('Weren't you making a call?'). Accident, and a little by-the-book urban discourtesy, have broken into her obsession with the truly undeserving Iván. In a later scene, Pepa marches resolutely back towards the building she lives in, having dumped Iván's belongings in a skip across the street. She occupies the foreground, in sharp focus; while Iván, a blur in the phone-booth in the middle distance, smooth-talks her answering machine. As she enters the building, Almodóvar pulls focus to capture Iván, still in the booth, still burbling, but also, in the far distance, Lucia on the warpath.[31]

In all the examples I have considered so far, the phone-box is understood as an object in space rather than in time. That this cannot long remain the case is amply demonstrated by the first series of the cult TV drama *The Wire* (2002), in which a public payphone on the end wall of one of the low-rises in and around which the bulk of the drug-dealing is done features prominently.[32] The dealers re-supply by means of a system involving pagers and public payphones which one of the detectives refers to as a 'throwback'. *The Wire* is insistently elegiac. It dreams of 'back in the day': the day of trades unions and investigative reporting, of policing before arrest statistics ('I love this job'), of gangsters who obey a code. No wonder it sometimes resembles a Western. And no wonder there's a phone-booth in there somewhere, in the first series. A middle-management gangster alerts his boss to the whereabouts of a rival scheduled for kidnap, torture, and elimination. The camera aligns one 'throwback' with another, conscience-stricken thug with public payphone: the booth glows coolly in the night, a blue-green aquarium against the warm red brick behind it.

So what is to be done with phone-boxes? Or, increasingly, without them? Some will no doubt survive, merged imperceptibly into the general urban information fuzz (fig. 12). Others may enjoy an afterlife as tourist attraction, temporary internet office, or excuse for performance art.[33] The rest will vanish. But the question these cubicles have posed for more than a century is as pertinent today as it ever was. How are we to go on being private in public? The lesson to be learnt from the history of the phone-box is that the construction of privacy in public by physical rather than social and cultural means always tends to excess. The physical structure (box, booth, or kiosk) brought about experiences which, although they did not concern telecommunication, became indelibly associated with it. The lesson to be learnt from the representation of the phone-box in folk memory, and in literature and film, is that we remember the piss and the phlegm, and the hauntedness. There is knowledge in that remembering, knowledge we wouldn't otherwise have, of what ordinary co-existence in dense populations might actually amount to. In short, we'll miss out on a lot of inadvertency, both good and bad, if we give up constructing privacy in public by physical means. We may find ourselves in a world in which the boundary between public and private is either non-existent or policed by surveillance and legal constraint. That doesn't sound to me like much of an improvement on those anxious, savoury minutes spent locked and lit up in the toxic aquarium.

Figure 12   Phone-booth. Venice. October 2009. Photograph: David Trotter

Notes

1 *Someone Else's War* (Dulles, VA: Brassey's Inc., 2003), 162.

2 The booth is first encountered in *Harry Potter and the Order of the Phoenix* (London: Bloomsbury, 2003), 115.

3 For its discovery as a venue for performance art, and eventual demise, see the account at http://www.deuceofclubs.com/moj/mojave.htm.

4 In Peter Riley's 1981 (unpaginated) Ferry Press book of verse and prose, *Lines on the Liver*, a phone-box on the edge of the Pennines in North Staffordshire becomes the site of an encounter with a neo-Wordsworthian vagrant who, glimpsed through the glass panes from a passing car, appears to articulate or perform 'the final pact between the person and his existence'.

5 Urban theory now pays considerable attention to the concrete physical relationships formed by sense-impression: Paul Rodaway, *Sensuous Geographies: Body, Sense, and Place* (London: Routledge, 1994); John Urry, 'City Life and the Senses', in Gary Bridge and Sophie Watson, eds., *A Companion to the City* (Oxford: Blackwell, 2000), 388–97.

6 *Money: A Suicide Note* (London: Jonathan Cape, 1984), 257.

7 'Latest London News', *Aberdeen Weekly Journal*, 7 April 1882, 5.

8 'The London-Paris Telephone Open Today', *Daily News*, 1 April 1891, 2.

9 'How the Red Telephone Box Became Part of Britain's National Heritage', in *A Journey through Ruins: The Last Days of London* (Oxford: Oxford University Press, 2009), 145–59, pp. 152–3.

10 Bobbie Johnson, 'In the Eye of the Storm', *Guardian*, G2, 15 July 2009, 6–9.

11 F.J. Judd, 'Kiosks', *Post Office Electrical Engineers' Journal*, 29.3, October 1936, 175–7, p. 175.

12 W.A. Collett, 'Call Offices', ibid., 178–87, pp. 178–9.

13 Letter to the Editors, *Lancet*, 11 August 1906, 416.

14 'Annotations', *Lancet*, 27 July 1907, 240–1.

15 'Notes, Short Comments, and Answers to Correspondents', *Lancet*, 14 March 1908, 829.

16 'The Public Telephone Call Office as a Factor in the Spread of Disease', *Lancet*, 27 June 1908, 1862–3.

17 'Annotations', *Lancet*, 23 February 1924, 402.

18 *One by One* (London: Secker & Warburg, 1965), 5.

19 *Peal of Ordnance* (London: Methuen, 1947), 98.

20 *Ulysses*, ed. Jeri Johnson (Oxford: Oxford University Press, 1998), 503.

21 *The Berlin Novels* (New York: Vintage, 1999), 232.

22 Alan Collins, *Cities of Pleasure: Sex and the Urban Social Landscape* (London: Routledge, 2005), 64.

23 *London: Bread and Circuses* (London: Verso, 2001), 12.

24 'Changing at York', in *Selected Poems*, 2nd edn. (Harmondsworth: Penguin, 1987), 154.

25 And not just in Britain. Saul Bellow's Mr Sammler, wishing to report a black pickpocket to the New York police, is put off by the only available facilities. 'This phone booth has a metal floor; smooth-hinged the folding green doors, but the floor is smarting with dry urine, the plastic telephone instrument is smashed, and a stump is hanging at the end of the cord.' *Mr Sammler's Planet* (London: Weidenfeld and Nicolson, 1970), 12.

26 *Hangover Square* (Harmondsworth: Penguin, 2001), 60–6.

27 *Second-Class Citizen* (London: Allison and Busby, 1974), 48–9.

28 Those of von Trotta's callers who do get through, like Juliane (Jutta Lampe) in *The German Sisters* (1981), rather wish they hadn't: it's always bad news.

29 'William Wyler, or the Jansenist of Directing', in *Bazin at Work: Major Essays & Reviews from the Forties & Fifties*, trans. Alan Pierre and Bert Cardullo, ed. Cardullo (London: Routledge, 1997), 1–22, pp. 5, 8–9, 14–15.

30 *Scorsese on Scorsese*, ed. Ian Christie and David Thompson (London: Faber and Faber, 2003), 88.

31 Paul Julian Smith notes the subtlety introduced by Almodóvar's 'assured exploitation of spatial depth' in this scene: *Desire Unlimited: The Cinema of Pedro Almodóvar* (London: Verso, 1994), 99.

32 The narrator of Iain Sinclair's *Downriver* reckons that the new vandal-proof payphones 'have been commandeered throughout the East End by heroin dealers. They supply the perfect excuse for hanging around, doing nothing: and nobody can put his foot against the door to trap you.' *Downriver* (London: Paladin, 1991), 167.

33 In September 1994, Sophie Calle, obeying Paul Auster's instructions to pick a spot in the city and take as much pride in it as she would in her own home, occupied a booth in Greenwich Village for a week, furnishing it with a couple of chairs, a bouquet of flowers, and a copy of *Glamour* magazine: *Double Game* (London: Violette Editions, 1999), 246–93.

10

Lynne Ramsay's *Ratcatcher*

Lynne Ramsay's short film *Gasman* (1997) opens with a familiar family scene. A pair of grown-ups gets a pair of children ready to go out for the evening. Ma gets the children ready, polishing her son's shoes, ironing her daughter's party-dress; Da settles for getting himself ready by way of a cup of tea and a last-gasp fag. The occasion is a Christmas party. Lynne, the daughter, is in a high state of excitement; Steven, the son, sulks.

The shots which compose this scene frame the various activities involved in getting ready in extreme close-up, so that the graphic organization of the screen as an aesthetic object obtrudes on, and indeed could be said actively to hinder, the construction of a diagetic narrative space. They isolate a body-part (a shoulder, a pair of hands held in the air), or an aspect of an item of clothing or furniture. Whenever there is any depth to a shot, consistent racking of focus separates out one plane from another. We take this world in one piece at a time. We never see it as a whole. Nothing is established. Texture prevails over perspective: a texture of sounds (the crinkling of the polythene which protects Da's suit) as well as sights.

The effect of this sequence of shots could be conceived as estrangement: a familiar scene made radically unfamiliar. But it feels, to me at any rate, like absorption. The scene is *so* familiar. Some of us are parents; we've all been children. And, yes, it was, and for some of us still is, exactly like that. But now, watching the film, we know a little better what familiarity is (what family is). Familiarity is the world taken in one piece at a time. Familiarity is life lived in extreme close-up, by means of a racking of focus which never allows one plane to settle into coherent relation with another. Familiarity is all texture.

Absorption is itself a theme, in this scene. Steven expresses his reluctance to go out with his father by creating a game for himself. Standing at the kitchen counter, he pours sugar into the cockpit of a toy sports-car. The sugar spills out in all directions, forming a terrain of drifts through which the car can be manoeuvred at high speed towards a catastrophic encounter with a glass jar. On the soundtrack, Andy Williams sings 'Let It Snow'. Steven's engrossment in his game is a further deepening of his engrossment in the familiar, in the idea of home, in the world immediately around him, whose substance has provided the game's material medium, rather than a withdrawal from it. He really does not want to go out.

Steven has made a game (a game of his own). He has also made a mess, which his mother will have to clear up once he has left the house. A mess is an excess of matter. It is matter out of place: matter revealed as matter by an abrupt confounding of the basic categories which enable us to tell one thing apart from another, and so make sense of experience. Sugar in a jar is a substance on tap: ready to be made useful, ready to release its sweetness as and when required. Sugar dumped on the kitchen counter is so much grit. The camera knows it, in close-up, as grit; even while successive shots of Steven's game construct, with some help from Andy Williams, a diagetic world-within-a-world. Familiarity, it may be, is an excess of matter over meaning. We speak of renewing our familiarity with someone or something we had lost sight of, or lost touch with. Mess exacerbates that renewal by enforcing upon us sight and touch, sight-as-touch. It shows us matter *radically*: that is, not for the first time, but again (and again) through the displacements worked by spillage, tearing, fragmentation, decay. Mess is always already in close-up. By the time we've noticed it (seen it, touched it, smelt it), it's too late to gain any perspective on it.

There would seem to be plenty in these images to recommend them to the sorts of 'sensuous theory' currently taking transformative shape in (or across) film studies. Consider, for example, the theory of 'haptic visuality' which Laura Marks has put forward in her deservedly influential enquiries into avant-garde and intercultural cinema.[1] In classical Greek, *haptein* means to fasten. The nineteenth-century art historian Aloïs Riegl borrowed the term from physiology in order to delineate a way of looking in which the eyes function to some extent like organs of touch. Optical visuality (vision as ordinarily understood) depends on a degree of separation between the viewing subject and the object viewed. Haptic looking, by contrast, tends by Marks's account to 'move over the surface of its object rather than to plunge into illusionistic depth'. It does not so much distinguish 'form' as discern 'texture' (*SF* 162). Haptic looking's object is the haptic image. 'The works I propose to call haptic,' Marks goes on, 'invite a look that moves on the surface plane of the screen for some time before the viewer realizes what she or he is beholding.' Haptic images 'resolve into figuration' only gradually, if at all. While optical perception relishes the 'representational power' of images, haptic perception relishes their 'material presence'. The distinction between optical and haptic visuality is one of degree. 'In most processes of seeing,' Marks concludes, 'both are involved, in a dialectical movement from far to near' (163).

Texture, I've argued, is very much at issue in the opening scene of *Gasman*. Our look moves on the surface plane of the screen. Furthermore, Steven's mess-making thematizes the lack of illusionistic depth in these images. An excess of matter over meaning (an excess of familiarity) is what the scene is about. To put it another way, the framing of the shots resists narrative. The children resist their mother's efforts to get them ready for the party, one through deliberate reluctance, the other through irrepressible high spirits. Only when they have finally been coaxed and prodded out of the house does the illusionistic depth usually considered necessary to narrative film-making prevail. A journey begins into the (relatively) unknown, a journey involving appropriate amounts of desolate terrain (a railway siding), and a brush with strangers. It begins in extreme long shot. But whose journey is it? Not Steven's. The story *Gasman* tells is the story of the struggle between two daughters born to different mothers for the affections of the father they share. The father's two sons remain peripheral throughout. Steven, initially the focus of haptic visuality – indeed its embodiment and emblem – has *thereby* been disabled in and for narrative. Mess is pretty much all there is to him, and mess provides little scope for the kinds of moral and emotional development journeys are said to encourage.

In the resistance it puts up to narrative, the opening scene of *Gasman* conforms to sensuous theory. According to Marks, the haptic image 'forces the viewer to contemplate the image itself, instead of being pulled into narrative' (*SF* 163). It was only when its 'language' became standardized, during the early decades of the twentieth century, she argues, that cinema began to appeal to narrative rather than bodily identification: to an optical visuality intent on the image's 'representational power', rather than a haptic visuality intent on its 'material significance' (170–1). We don't, by this account, fasten haptically on to the chain of causes and effects which constitutes narrative.

There is a problem, here. All feature films appeal in some measure (usually in very large measure) to narrative identification. Does that mean that they must abandon haptic visuality altogether? Or are there ways in which narrative cinema might incorporate haptic imagery, without ceasing to narrate? These are questions Marks herself has recently framed, in passing, with regard to contemporary popular cinema. She has in mind the 'haptic opening scene' of Steven Spielberg's *Saving Private Ryan*.[2] They are questions provoked, even more urgently, by Lynne Ramsay's first feature film, *Ratcatcher* (1999). *Ratcatcher* is the story of a serial mess-maker.

Mess-Making

Salt cascades from the spout of an upturned tin. A mound forms on the shiny surface of a kitchen table. The twelve-year-old boy whose handiwork this is leans forward intently. He presses a finger into the mound, etching a groove or channel. On the table stand a teapot, a strainer, and some mugs. In the background, a blurred figure manoeuvres an iron across a garment spread on an ironing-board. As James Gillespie (William Eadie) develops the initial groove into a pattern, so focus is pulled, and the figure becomes identifiable as his teenage sister Ellen (Michelle Stewart), who has just put the finishing touches to a blouse. We next see the mound, by now splayed into a salty star. James has made a mess in order to make a pattern; though not, like Steven in *Gasman*, a diagetic world-within-a-world. Ellen, mean-while, has extracted her mother's make-up kit from a drawer. She is on her way out for the evening. James glances up at her as she applies some lipstick. 'Whit ur you starin at, ya wee pervert?' Nothing, he claims. Ellen's parting shot, after a further brief exchange, is a stern injunction against impromptu domestic sculpture. 'Stoap makin a mess at that table.'

After Ellen has left the room, James tops up his pile, and starts to doodle in it again, then suddenly sweeps the whole lot on to the floor. He wanders to the window, and looks down into the back yard, where Ellen has collected a cardigan from the washing-line, to an accompaniment of wolf-whistles. 'Wher ur you gone?' he yells. She flashes him a V-sign. He aims a gob at her: a mess of a different kind, a mess intended for someone, as a gesture of hostility, or contempt, or disgust. He hurries through to the front room in time to see her cross the road to the bus. She has abandoned him and his material messes for that other existence, verging on adulthood, and no more than a bus-ride away, in which she will put the 'representational power' of social and sexual display to the test.

Ellen is the least of James's problems. He and his family live on a 1970s sink estate in Glasgow made next to uninhabitable by a dustmen's strike: the streets are strewn with rat-infested garbage. At the beginning of the film, James's friend Ryan Quinn drowns in the poisonous canal which is their playground. James could possibly have saved him. Unable either to acknowledge his own indirect responsibility for Ryan's death, or to participate fully in the various ceremonies of consolation and disavowal undertaken by those older and more powerful than him, he makes common cause with Margaret-Anne (Leanne Mullen), who trades sex for a minimum of respect, and dreams of a new life (like Ellen's adulthood, no more than a bus-ride away) in a house among fields of golden wheat. The dream lets him down. This is a story about over-familiarity. There is too much that is familiar (too much that is family) for James to cope with. He has nowhere in which to do his own growing-up. He drowns himself in the canal, his death, Ramsay says, 'the realisation of what's around him'.[3]

This is a story about over-familiarity, haptically told. We know James by the messes he makes. The most significant of these accrue in oblique relation to his drunken, womanizing father. Claire Monk has remarked on the extent to which 1990s British cinema was 'preoccupied with men and masculinity in crisis.'[4] Da (Tommy Flanagan) takes his crisis out on James, a boy who in his eyes is not and never will be enough of a man (enough of a man like him). For James, over-familiarity begins and ends in his intractable relationship with his father. His mess-making in some sense inhabits or makes room within the otherwise unbearable physical and moral closeness of that relationship. But mess-making lacks the distance from the surrounding world necessary for critical reflection, for emergent identity (for whatever it is that journeys encourage). It will not protect him from his father's violence, or his own.

Da's finest moment involves the rescue of yet another small boy who has fallen into the poisonous canal. James comes home to find him fast asleep, naked apart from his underpants and a rich top-dressing of canal mud. James scoops up some of the breakfast cereal scattered around a bowl on the bedroom carpet (in close shot), and dribbles it along the length of his father's prone body, as though he were sowing seed. He studiously inserts a final Rice Krispy into Da's left nostril like a coin into a slot. There's a loud rap at the door. Council inspectors have arrived to assess the condition of the property. James lets them in, and then rouses Da, who's not best pleased at having to answer their questions while hunting for his trousers, and retaliates with bluster. As soon as the inspectors have left, Da turns savagely on James, who struggles to understand what it is that he's done wrong. 'Ur we getting the new hoose, Da?' It'll be his fault, Da yells, if they don't. 'Now get out of my sight.' We catch up with James down in the yard, where, in blurry, slow-motion close-up, he stabs ferociously with a stick at a rat burrowing beneath a bag full of garbage.

Da's heroics earn him an award for bravery. After the award-ceremony, he goes out on the lash, while Ma organizes a small celebration at home: dance-music, party food. While Ma dances with his sisters in the living-room, James stands in the kitchen chewing a sandwich. He allows himself just one small mess. He drives a cocktail-stick loaded with pickled onions and pieces of cheese into the pink icing on a cream-bun. Enter Da, whose spree had ended in a fight, bleeding profusely. Da has bought James some football-boots (more manliness) which are way too large for him, and which he doesn't want anyway. When Ma appears, Da slaps her viciously, without warning. James slings the offending boots at him in fury, and leaves the room. We catch up with him running full tilt along the canal bank.

Messes of the kind James so persistently makes play a part comparable to that played by D.W. Winnicott's 'transitional' objects in the dialectic of illusion and disillusionment which constitutes growing up. According to Winnicott, the transitional object (usually a piece of fabric) is the child's 'first "not-me" possession', and thus the first stage in her or his development from absolute dependence on the mother as an object subjectively conceived to relative independence of (and relationship with) a whole range of objects objectively conceived. The transitional object is separate from the child, but not beyond control. It can be manipulated more or less at will, and invested with a whole range of feelings; it nurtures illusion. And yet, over time, meaning and value will drain out of this piece of fabric chosen at random, and thereafter subjected to arbitrary enhancements and indignities; disillusion is built into it. Occupying an intermediate 'area' or 'state' between inner and outer worlds, it becomes a 'resting-place', Winnicott says, a momentary hiatus in the war that need and desire wage on reality. Growing up, after all, requires both adequate illusion and adequate disillusionment.

Transitional objects tend to be messy. A wise parent, Winnicott observes, will allow the cherished piece of fabric to get 'dirty and even smelly', because washing it would disrupt the continuity of the infant's experience (the infant's necessary self-illusionment).[5] Indeed, the object's messiness – a guarantee, in effect, that the parent will not interfere – *is* its meaning and value, or as much of a meaning and value as it will ever acquire. The messes we continue to make in adolescence and (rather more sheepishly) in adult life are like transitional objects in that their meaning and value depends on other people's agreement not to clear them away. The untidy bedroom or office balance us between illusion and disillusionment: the objects we cram into them are made meaningful and valuable by the cramming, but not to the extent that they can't be carelessly dumped and strewn; we know that their meaning and value, preserved for a while by the arbitrary pattern into which they have fallen, and which we do not allow anyone else to disturb, will slowly drain away. This, too, is a resting-place, a hiatus.

Ramsay has spoken of the film's one moment of pure fantasy, when the mouse owned by James's friend Kenny (John Miller) flies to the moon, as a way to maintain 'an innocence, a breathing space in a relentless environment'.[6] The messes, too, are above all playful. They fulfil a similar function, in the Blakean dialectic of innocence and experience, as breathing space, resting place, or hiatus; and they fulfil it for the viewer as well as for James. They are *our* breathing space. Each scene of mess-making invites a haptic look. And yet each is integrated into narrative. Hiatus does not remain hiatus for very long. The messes gain their force in the film from the violence which retrospectively exposes them as absurd (as too much illusion), and is itself thereby exposed, in turn, as fatally lacking in absurdity (as too much disillusionment). This dialectic is the means by which the film understands James's death as the realisation of his life. To appreciate its scope and subtlety, we will need a theory of haptic narrative.

Mimesis

Marks's sensuous theory does make room, with a certain amount of reluctance, for narrative. She derives from Walter Benjamin and Theodor Adorno an understanding of mimesis as a 'form of representation based on a particular, material contact at a particular moment'. Mimesis, by this account, does not symbolize. It presumes a 'continuum between the actuality of the world and the production of signs about that world'.[7] To mime is to represent a thing by acting like it.

However, Marks's primary concern is with that which is in some way definitive or revelatory in mimesis: a particular contact at a particular moment. She draws, for example, on Roger Caillois's argument that mimicry is an 'incantation fixed at its culminating point', in order to describe how things which have touched leaves their traces irrevocably on each other.[8] She invokes to similar purpose Walter Benjamin's account of a language which, rather than functioning as a system, draws close enough to its object to make the sign ignite.

> The coherence of words or sentences is the bearer through which, like a flash, similarity appears. For its production by man – like its perception by him – is in many cases, and particularly the most important, limited to flashes. It flits past.[9]

An incantation fixed at its culminating point, an appearance in a flash: mimesis of that sort is not at issue in *Ratcatcher*.

For Aristotle, mimesis was the main characteristic of the poetry (epic or dramatic) which represents men and women in action. Marks does mention the most influential modern account of these representations of men and women in action, Erich Auerbach's *Mimesis*. According to Auerbach, she notes, 'mimesis requires a lively and responsive relationship between listener/reader and story/text, such that each time a story is retold it is sensuously remade in the body of the listener.' An account of story's sensuous remaking in the body of the listener might constitute the basis for a theory of haptic narrative. Marks, however, immediately backs away from the implications of this emphasis on the act of narration by remarking that cinema, as a 'more physical object', is likely to prove 'more convincingly mimetic' than literature.[10] The argument opposes the cinematic image as physical object explicitly to words, and implicitly to narrative in general, because the act of narration, in literature or in film, precludes objecthood. Does it also have to preclude physicality?

Auerbach has a lot to offer film theory: or at least Auerbach as taken up by Siegfried Kracauer in his *Theory of Film*, first published in 1960. It is strange that Kracauer, with his emphasis on cinema as the 'redemption of physical reality', has not himself been taken up by sensuous theory. Or perhaps not so strange, since the physical reality he had in mind was a reality apprehensible not by an incantation fixed at its culminating point, or by a sign's abrupt ignition, but in its endlessness, as a continuum.

> The concept 'flow of life', then, covers the stream of material situations and happenings with all that they intimate in terms of emotions, values, thoughts. The implication is that the flow of life is predominantly a material rather than a mental continuum, even though, by definition, it extends into the mental dimension. (It might tentatively be said that films favour life in the form of everyday life – an assumption which finds some support in the medium's primordial concern for actuality.)[11]

Kracauer's flow of life is a flow that can only be understood in and through narrative: in and through a particular kind of narrative, that which lets it flow, rather than fixing it, or burning it up. It was in seeking to define an apprehension of flow that Kracauer turned to Auerbach, or more precisely to Auerbach's account of the modern novel. Auerbach had celebrated James Joyce, Marcel Proust, and Virginia Woolf as writers who present 'minor happenings' either for their own sake or as points of departure for a 'penetration which opens up new perspectives into a milieu or a consciousness or the given historical setting' (*M* 547). Joyce, Proust, and Woolf, Kracauer explains, 'coincide in decomposing the smallest units of older types of the novel – those which cover a series of developments as they occur in chronological time' (*TF* 219). Such writers, Auerbach concludes, in a statement Kracauer quotes in full, 'hesitate to impose upon life, which is their subject, an order which it does not possess in itself' (*M* 548/*TF* 219). What was wrong with the theatre, Kracauer thought, was that it never hesitated to impose an order upon life. The units of which a play is composed 'represent a crude abbreviation of camera-life'. A theatrical narrative proceeds, as it were, 'by way of "long shots"' (*TF* 219). There are no close-ups in theatre. Eisenstein, Kracauer adds, abandoned stage for screen because he could find no equivalent to the close-up in theatrical practice (220).

Kracauer consistently found in Auerbach's emphasis on the modern novel's preoccupation with 'the elementary things which men in general have in common' (*M* 552), support for his own view that film's task is to 'explore this texture of everyday life, whose composition varies according to place, people, and time' (*TF* 304). It is a view by no means incompatible with sensuous theory. Indeed, Marks's emphasis on intercultural film could be said to develop Kracauer's emphasis on variation according to place, people, and time.

Did Kracauer develop a theory of (mimetic) narrative? Up to a point. In his view, the purpose of film as a medium and an art was to 'establish the continuum of physical existence' (*TF* 63). Endlessness could be narrated. It could be told in images which arise out of the flow of life without thereby being severed from it: images which themselves belong to the continuum of physical existence. Kracauer's favourite metaphor for material existence was that of the 'thicket'. For him, the world was always and everywhere densely packed with things to be seen, things which one sees by forcing a way through them. It is no surprise, then, that he should conceive of the narrative forms at film's disposal as 'routes of passage' through the continuum of material existence (64). The route of passage is precisely not, I think, a rite of passage. Many forms of narrative are modelled on the rite of passage: a once-and-for-all transformative occasion during which the candidate steps outside ordinary time and space into a liminal realm where old status and identity fade, and a new one emerges. Journeys, in fiction and film, are most often rites of passage. Kracauer's routes are the opposite of rites. They are adventures in familiarity.

Kracauer proposed five routes of passage through the continuum of material existence: the travelogue, or feature film involving travel; the minute inspection of 'causal interrelationships', as in E.W. Pabst's *Geheimnisse einer Seele* (1926), Orson Welles's *Citizen Kane* (1941), and Akira Kurosawa's *Rashômon* (1950), which all 'start from a *fait accompli* and from there wander back to shed light on its trail' (*TF* 66); immersion in 'the infinity of shapes that lie dormant in any given one' (66), as in Curt Oertel's

Michelangelo: Life of a Titan (1938); the unpacking through interior monologue of 'the innumerable experiences an individual is likely to undergo in a single crucial moment of his life' (66); and depictions of material phenomena such as waves or machine-parts which 'defy content in favour of rhythm' (68). The most promising of these routes from the point of view of sensuous theory would seem to be the third: films which, as Kracauer puts it, 'caress one single object long enough to make us imagine its unlimited aspects' (66). His primary example of a film which caresses is Robert Bresson's *Journal d'un curé de campagne* (1951). Here, the object caressed by our gaze is an ever-changing face. Kracauer's term for this object's narrative function is textural. The caresses, he says, 'thread the film' (66). Bresson has meant a great deal to Ramsay, and her film, like his, could be said to caress its young protagonist's face. But not consistently enough, I would argue, for those caresses to constitute its thread.[12]

What about the third of the five 'routes of passage'? *Rashômon*'s reversed narrative represents, Kracauer says, a 'cinematic effort to impress upon us the inexhaustibility of the causal continuum' (*TF* 66). It's hard to see how else one might understand Ramsay's understanding of James's death as a realization of his life. But how haptic, exactly, are the films Kracauer has in mind? When *Rashômon* or *Citizen Kane* 'wander back' from their originating *fait accompli*, they do so in order to expose differences of interpretation as to what actually happened, and why. Such exposure may in fact *sever* meaning from event, the act of mimesis from the mental and material continuum in which it arises. Whose version of events should we trust? *Ratcatcher*, by contrast, moves towards rather than away from its *fait accompli*. It opens up the causal continuum in order to ask how and why one (small) thing led to another. It opens up that continuum haptically, in narrative. Ramsay has always insisted that *Ratcatcher* does not amount to 'social realism'. 'I was trying to go into the psychology of the scenes, going into why we're shooting this way, why we're looking at it that way, trying to get under the skin of it a bit, inside the boy's head.'[13] Can Kracauer help us to grasp how Ramsay got under the skin of the story she tells?

Naturalism

It became axiomatic for Auerbach, and therefore for Kracauer, that the modern novel's concern with the 'elementary things which men in general have in common' crystallized above all in the attention it gave to chance event (*M* 552; *TF* 304). Randomness is the means by which daily or familiar life exceeds the categories we impose upon it. For Kracauer, film's 'susceptibility' to the street – 'a term designed to cover not only the street, particularly the city street, in the literal sense, but also its various extensions, such as railway stations, dance and assembly halls, bars, hotel lobbies, airports, etc.' – expresses its fundamental affinity with the haphazard, its antipathy to providence (62). Contingency's signature, written all over the street, is mess.

> Many objects remain unnoticed simply because it never occurs to us to look their way. Most people turn their backs on garbage cans, the dirt underfoot, the waste they leave behind. Films have no such inhibitions; on the contrary, what we ordinarily prefer to ignore proves attractive to them precisely because of this common neglect. (54)

Kracauer took pleasure in noting that Walter Ruttmann's *Berlin: Die Sinfonie der Großstadt* (1927) includes a 'wealth' of gutters and litter-strewn streets; while Alberto Cavalcanti, in *Rien que les heures* (1926), seems 'hardly less garbage-minded' (54). In such films, he added, the camera acts like a rag-picker.

> Since sights of refuse are particularly impressive after spectacles extolling the joy of living, film makers have repeatedly capitalized on the contrast between glamorous festivities and their dreary aftermath. You see a banquet on the screen and then, when everybody has gone, you are made to linger for a moment and stare at the crumpled tablecloth, the half-emptied glasses, and the unappetizing dishes. (54).

Ratcatcher must be one of the most garbage-minded films ever made. Ramsay manages to pack more litter into a single Glasgow housing-estate than Ruttmann ever did into the whole of Berlin. James's third and final mess could be reckoned the miniature aftermath of a festivity already gone sour before it's over (he has withdrawn from, or been left out of, the dancing).

The representation of mess in literature and the visual arts has a long and distinguished history.[14] Mess, I have said, is contingency's signature. Chance is potentially the matrix and occasion both of desire and of death. On the one hand, it has, as the Dadaist Hans Richter explained, a certain sensuous appeal, the 'erotic pleasure' of an 'unknown gift', of limitless possibility;[15] on the other, it may bring about, in an especially poignant way, the end not only of all possibility, but of all thinking about possibility. Chance presides over ultimate determination: over events in the face of which, when they come, we are helpless; over an effect whose cause we can barely conceive. We acknowledge it by euphoria and despair, by states of mind and body in which nothing any longer makes any sense. Illusion-sustaining mess, actual or represented, *good* mess, enables us to understand contingency as the matrix and occasion of an exemplary desire: a desire whose fulfilment has all the qualities of divine grace except divinity. Illusion-destroying mess, actual or represented, *bad* mess, enables us to understand contingency as the matrix and occasion of an exemplary death: not the death which happens as the outcome of an identifiable sequence of cause and effect, but the death which need not have happened at all, the death which is pure death. James's messes are illusion-sustaining. So, it could be argued, are the mounds of garbage filling the yards during the dustmen's strike, which serve as an impromptu adventure playground. 'I looked at some photographs from that time,' Ramsay explains, 'and they were quite surreal – kids pulling things from the rubbish, dressing up, finding old dolls, killing rats' (*R* viii). But Ryan Quinn's sodden corpse on the canal-bank destroys any number of illusions, including all those he himself might once have harboured.

In literature, illusion-destroying mess has been the preserve of Naturalism. *Ratcatcher* is a Naturalist film. The dustmens' strike has turned the housing-estate into a 'place of deterioration', as Ramsay puts it. James's destiny is 'written', she notes, in the harshness of his surroundings (*R* x). Zola himself could not have made it clearer that there is no hope for this young boy immured in dirt and disorder. The heuristic advantage of determinism (a far greater one than historians of either literature or film have been prepared to acknowledge) is that it opens up the chain of causes and effects to minute inspection. We know roughly *what* is going to happen, and can concentrate instead on the how and why. How is it, exactly, that one thing leads to another, and why? The relentless downward spiral of the standard Naturalist plot often incorporates plateaux, or points of arrest, during which the protagonist, momentarily buoyant, enjoys the illusion that it might all work out in the end; before this temporary support gives way, and the downward spiral resumes. Each mess James makes is a plateau, a breathing space, a moment caught between illusion restored and further disillusionment. The integration of these moments into narrative allows us to understand his death, when it comes, as the realization of his life.

But something more must surely be involved in that realization than mere disillusionment, which happens to us all, in varying measure. How can we be made to grasp a disillusionment so severe that it results in suicide? Naturalist fiction and film conceive that severity as a lapse into bad or illusion-destroying mess. Kracauer, again prompted by Auerbach, put considerable emphasis on the need to address, in film as in literature, the lower end of the continuum of human experience. The world viewed in the modern novel, he wrote, 'extends from sporadic spiritual notions all the way down to scattered material events' (*TF* 298). *All the way down*: film, like literature, must lower itself. 'We cannot hope to embrace reality unless we penetrate its lowest layers' (298). The camera embraces reality by rag-picking: by a look down at the gutter, at rubbish. To acknowledge mess is already to have been lowered. Lowering, thematized as mess, is an aesthetic act. This is Kracauer at his most Sartrean.

Naturalist fiction both declassifies and declasses, in ways that Bataille, as well as Sartre, has taught us to understand (above, pp. 47-8). There is as yet no theory of formless narrative. Bad mess is the formless incarnate. In Naturalist fiction, we might say, bad mess drives out good. Description tells the stories, up to their bitter end, that narrative as traditionally understood could no longer tell. Is that also the case in Naturalist film? A full answer would require some account of description, or description's equivalent, whatever that might be, in cinema. The short answer I will give here depends on further enquiry into the haptic, and its thematization as mess (good or bad). Sensuous theory, while by no means denigrating or disavowing the optical, tends to code the haptic as good in itself. It has not fully acknowledged the diversity of haptic experience. Naturalist film, however, must by any account be reckoned at the very least to skirt bad mess, and more than not to dive right in. Is it possible to speak, without sounding too much like Melanie Klein on an off-day, of a good haptic and a bad haptic? In the final part of this essay, I shall argue that *Ratcatcher* envisages haptic visuality as a way to render the loss of illusion, as well as its nurturing.

Levelling

The messes James makes, in *Ratcatcher*, are never integrated fully into narrative. They remain purposeless, in the larger scheme, or merely playful (merely innocent, we might say). But they also invite their own destruction. James sweeps the mound of salt off the table before anyone else can (as they surely will). Adults do not take kindly to conjunctions of pickled onion and cream bun. The messes have already begun to turn sour. The cereal James dribbles on his father's prone body shows up its intricately obscene tattooing with canal mud. The precarious balance these messes maintain between illusion and disillusionment will not last long. Their turning sour is itself a story of a kind, a story that narrative as traditionally understood can no longer tell. *Ratcatcher*, a Naturalist film, brings on the encounter with bad mess; brings it on, I shall argue, haptically.

Ratcatcher's main precursor in European art cinema is surely François Truffaut's *Les Quatre cent coups* (1959). Antoine Doinel (Jean-Pierre Léaud) is an altogether less melancholy child than James, and his truancies have a kind of wild ambition to them, a fierceness, as well as *élan*; they abound in fantasy. James drops petty spit on his sister Ellen as she passes underneath the kitchen window; Antoine and his friend Rémy (Patrick Auffay) turn the pages of books into pellets to be fired gleefully from their attic fortress at pedestrians in the street below. Antoine, however, is riding for a fall.

When his father (Albert Rémy) turns him in for stealing a typewriter, Antoine ends up in a cage in the police-station. For the first time in the film, the camera identifies with his point of view. A slow pan reveals the prisoners in a second cage, a notice on the wall ('Dératisation'), a policeman at a table. More striking is the lattice of wire-mesh pressed so close to the lens that it blurs. To occupy Antoine's point of view, at this moment of maximum humiliation, is to begin to see the world differently. When the wagon arrives to take all the prisoners to holding-cells for the night, Antoine is last in. Truffaut alternates shots of his face at the wagon's barred rear-window with shots from inside it, looking out through the bars at the brightly-lit streets and buildings beyond. The bars are a blur, and so too is Antoine's head turned to gaze out through them at a rapidly receding normality. When we next see him from outside the wagon, tears stream down his cheeks. The shot dissolves to an indeterminate pock-marked surface, which gradually resolves itself, as the camera tracks along it, into a wall. This is haptic visuality, with a vengeance. 'Haptic visuality sees the world as though it were touching it,' Marks observes: 'close, unknowable, appearing to exist on the surface of the image. Haptic images disturb the figure-ground relationship.'[16] In this case, the world haptic visuality fastens us to is all bad mess. The camera carries on past the end of the wall, to reveal a corridor, a gate, and a policeman silhouetted against the light. Optically rendered symbolism confirms the experience of confinement. Antoine is on his way into an institution. Tie, belt, braces. Empty your pockets. Sign here. The film's declassification of narrative – its lapse into the bad haptic – has already enacted his declassing long before the formalities of symbol and ceremony take place.

That lapse does not empty the film of narrative. Antoine escapes from the 'observation centre' to which he has been committed during a game of football. He sets off, as we soon find out, for a sight of the sea. After throwing off the rather half-hearted pursuit, he runs solidly along the verge of a road, past fields and buildings, across a stream. For a little over a minute, the camera keeps pace, tracking along the road slightly ahead of him. The only sound is the sound of his breathing. This shot is a form of companionship, and a form of acknowledgement. It acknowledges both what he now is, and what he might yet none the less become. The pace it keeps, for more than a minute, is illusion's last, endlessly productive gasp. Antoine has been brought low, all right. Levelling him, the film has levelled itself down to him. It has also levelled with him.

After the row about the football boots, James slams out of the house. We catch up with him running full tilt along the towpath. Ramsay places the camera at a lower angle than Truffaut. The camera keeps pace with James from low down on the far side of the canal, as he runs in parallel to his shadow in the water below him. Ramsay, unlike Truffaut, does not allow us to see the world he passes by. We hear the urgent rasp of his breathing, and a little circumambient sound (dogs bark). Then James stumbles, and falls to the ground. The camera stumbles with him, as it were. Ramsay cuts to a closer shot of him, still running, now in slow motion. We become aware of an intervening fringe of bushes and tall grass on the canal-bank, slightly out of focus, like the bars of Antoine's cage. Staccato barks make it difficult to hear James breathing. Narrative's stumble has brought on the haptic. But the haptic, in this instance, tells a story. The camera moves ahead of James, to stare at empty space. It loses him. It loses him in, or into, near-silence (the dogs have stopped barking). He's a goner.

Ramsay, too, has levelled down to, and with, her protagonist. What she has levelled down to and with, since this is a Naturalist film, is his death.

James spends the night with Margaret-Anne, remaining fully clothed throughout, fully innocent. 'James,' she asks, holding him to her, 'Dae ye love me?' 'Aye,' he answers. Ramsay cuts to Da and Ma swaying, in a tight embrace, as Frank and Nancy Sinatra duet on 'Something Stupid'. The 'something stupid' is, of course, saying 'I love you'. 'Something Stupid' is a song about how hard it is to 'make the meaning come true'. Da and Ma hold sway for well over a minute, as they struggle stupidly, and with absolute commitment, with honour, to make the meaning come true. Montage, or parallel editing, renders illusion's last gasp symbolically. Then the downward spiral resumes.

Next morning, James arrives home to find the army removing the mounds of rubbish. The adventure playground will soon be no more. One of the film's most profound insights is into the damage done to him by the cursory removal of what is in itself a foul and dangerous mess; and with it the last opportunity to create sustaining illusion even in the most hostile of environments, even out of nausea. James essays a more conventional redemption: a rite, rather than a route, of passage. He tries, in vain, to scoop Margaret-Anne's glasses from the canal, where her persecutors had flung them, with his connivance. Redemption is hard to come by. Not so disillusionment, which James now brings on by destroying Kenny's fantasy that his mouse has travelled to the moon. Kenny, in turn, reveals that he had witnessed James's failure to help Ryan Quinn out of the canal. James once again takes the bus out to the housing-estate which has all along nurtured his own primary illusion, of a new life away from the place of deterioration. But the houses have been locked against him. We watch from inside one of them as he wanders out into the wheat-field beyond. Ramsay cuts to a close-up of his face. Like Antoine Doinel before him, he is on the verge of tears. By the time he gets back, the streets have been cleared of rubbish.

The film's final (Naturalist) levelling down and levelling with is to follow James as he slips in his turn into the canal: an immersion in the haptic which figures the haptic as immersion. There is time only for one further burst of illusion as the members of a ghost family advance across the wheat-field, proudly bearing their household goods towards a new life. That we know this to be an illusion is a consequence of the work of levelling done in and through narrative. *Ratcatcher* does not abandon narrative for the haptic. Rather, it creates, with beautiful integrity, a haptic narrative: a dialectic of illusion and disillusionment articulated as the lapse from good mess into bad, an unbinding never wholly unbound.

Notes

1   *The Skin of the Film: Intercultural Cinema, Embodiment, and the Senses* (Durham, N.C.: Duke University Press, 2000): henceforth SF.

2   'Haptic Visuality: Touching with the Eyes', 3: http://www.framework.fi/ 2_2004/visitor/artikkelit.marks.html, consulted 28 March 2007.

3   Interview with Geoff Andrew, *Guardian Unlimited*, 28 October 2002, p. 3: http://film.guardian.co.uk/interview/interviewpages/0,6737,834228,00.html, consulted 16 March 2007.

4   'Men in the 90s', in *British Cinema of the 90s*, edited by Robert Murphy (London, British Film Institute, 2000), 156–66, p. 156.

5   *Playing and Reality* (London, Tavistock, 1971), 1–5.

6   Interview with Lizzie Francke, *Ratcatcher* (London, Faber and Faber, 1999), ix. Hencforth R.

7   'Haptic Visuality', 138–9.

8   Ibid., 141. Roger Caillois, 'Mimicry and Legendary Psychasthenia', translated by John Shepley, *October* 31, 1984, 17–32.

9   Walter Benjamin, 'On the Mimetic Faculty', in *Reflections*, translated by Edmund Jephcott (New York, Harcourt, 1978), 333–6.

10 'Haptic Visuality', 138. Erich Auerbach, Mimesis: *The Representation of Reality in Western Literature*, translated by Willard R. Trask (Princeton, Princeton University Press, 1968): henceforth M.

11 *Theory of Film: The Redemption of Physical Reality* (Princeton, Princeton University Press, 1997), 72: henceforth *TF*.

12 Another route of passage which sensuous theory has done a great deal to promote, but which has little bearing here, is that taken by the travelogue. See Giuliana Bruno, *Atlas of Emotion: Journeys in Art, Architecture, and Film* (New York, Verso, 2002), which briefly invokes Kracauer to establish cinema's affinity with the street as 'the site where transient impressions occur' (43).

13 Interview with Andy Bailey, *IndieWire*, 13 October 2000, p. 2: http://www.indiewire.com/people/int_Ramsay_Lynn_001013.html, consulted 13 April 2007.

14 David Trotter, *Cooking with Mud: The Idea of Mess in Nineteenth-Century Art and Fiction* (Oxford, Oxford University Press, 2000).

15 *Hans Richter*, edited by Cleve Gray (New York, Holt, Rinehart & Winston, 1971), 98.

16 'Haptic Visuality', 1.

Index